For Love of the Land

For Love of the Land

Angela Goode

ABC
BOOKS

To Mary, Hilary and Charlie

Published by ABC Books for the
AUSTRALIAN BROADCASTING CORPORATION
GPO Box 9994 Sydney NSW 2001

Copyright © Angela Goode 2000

First published March 2000

All rights reserved. No part of this publication may be reproduced, stored in a retrieval system or transmitted in any form or by any means, electronic, mechanical, photocopying, recording or otherwise, without prior written permission of the Australian Broadcasting Corporation.

National Library of Australia
Cataloguing-in-Publication entry
Goode, Angela
   For love of the land: the achievers and the innovators, the pioneers and the brave.
   ISBN 0 7333 0616 0
   1. Farmers–Australia. 2. Country life–Australia. 3 Australia–Rural conditions. I. Australian Broadcasting Corporation. II. Title
630 92294

Designed and typeset by Robert Taylor
Photography by Angela Goode
Set 11/13.5pt Caslon 540
Colour separations by Pageset, Victoria
Printed and bound by
Australian Print Group, Maryborough, Victoria

5 4 3 2 1

Acknowledgments

This has been a large project and I picked the brains and accepted support and assistance from many people. I am indebted to them and thank them. Some of those I particularly want to mention are:
Tony Roberts, Roberts Ltd, Tasmania; Perry Gunner, Adelaide; Ian Folder, Botanical Resources Australia, Hobart; Neil MacDonald, Keith; Kate and John Scott, Roma; Michael Aldersey, Naracoorte; Dr Wendy Craik, National Farmers' Federation; Jan Street, Armidale; Mick Peirce, Wardaman Aboriginal Corporation, Katherine; Michael Glasson, Elders, Alice Springs; Neville Chalmers, Wesfarmers Dalgety, Alice Springs; Ian and Bindy McClymont, Muttaburra; Jo Lovard, Darwin; Bob Griffin, Hamilton; Peter Groves, Colac; Robert Sykes, Bairnsdale; Stewart Percival, Eden Photographics; Alan Richardson in Perth; Sally Dakis and Belinda Varischetti in Hobart; Marius Cuming in Mount Gambier; Greg Hayes in Kununurra; Dennis Buckley in Darwin—all of ABC Radio.
And finally, Tim Curnow of Curtis Brown Pty Ltd.

Contents

Preface / viii
Map / x

Part I Leaving the Nest—South Australia
The Journey Begins / 2
Pushing the Limits—Tom Brinkworth / 3

Part II Sailing South—Tasmania
Top of the Tall Poppies—Jim Allen / 18
A Blooming Dynamo—Paul Roberts Thomson / 24
Milking a Rebellion—Robin Dornauf / 32
Out-stepping the Rest—Gerard McShane / 38
Logging on to Conservation—Tom and Cynthia Dunbabin / 51

Part III Raw Energy—Western Australia
Team Players—Lawry and Jenny Pitman / 58
Pioneers in the Land of Hope . . . and Glory—Mick Quinlivan / 65
Culture Shock—Peter and Kirsten Biven / 68
Burning Ambition—Mark and Jan Biven / 79
Going Against the Grain—Neil Wandel / 86

Part IV Roaming out of Roma—Queensland
'That Girl' with the Million Dollar Block—Bloss Hickson / 92
Remote but at Ease—Brett and Vanda Hick / 102
Fertile Oasis for Change—Richard and Judy Makim / 107
Inventing a Drought Therapy—John and Lindy McClymont / 114

Part V Taking the Heat— Kununurra and the Northern Territory
Nothing is Impossible—Wilhelm Bloecker / 122
Mocking Convention—Gordon and Rosemary Mock / 130
Seeding a Free Spirit—Spike Dessert / 136
The Buffalo Farm of Kakadu—David Lindner / 144

Part VI Centred Around Cattle—the Northern Territory
A Swag on the Ground—Jan Hayes / 158
Anguish of the Pastoralists—David and Penny Bayly / 167
The Dream of a Self-sufficient Man—Bill Harney / 177

Part VII To Paddocks East—New South Wales and Victoria
Sensitive, New-Age Glamour—Peter Glennie / 190
From Liability to Asset—Elisabeth Cuming / 196
A Life on the Track—Ron and Hilda Cherry / 203
In Harmony with the Earth—Tim Peel / 213
A Personal Battle Creates a Boom—Hedley and Irena Earl / 220

Part VIII Full Circle—South Australia
Fight Hard to Win—John Wamsley / 228
At Journey's End / 239

Preface

'There's a new soft generation out in the bush,' people would say to me. 'They do nothing but whinge and grizzle. The pioneering spirit has been bred out of them.'

Well, that got me thinking. Had all the wonderful distance-shrinking technologies like mobile phones, the internet and email turned bushies into wimps? Has ready-made electricity buzzed in on overhead cables made them soft and complacent? Where were all the self-reliant heroes who did it tough, and forged their own distinctive style far from the conformism of cities and crowds? Fast transport reaches into almost every backwater of this vast land; has it eroded away the fabled resilience, resourcefulness and independence of outback Australians?

The barbs about wimps and grizzlers worried me. Had we seen the last of the rural legends—those who conquer a hostile climate, and isolation, stoically and with dignity, to follow their dreams? I talked with Stuart Neal of ABC Books. My aim was to produce an essay on contemporary rural Australia. I wanted to talk to today's workers on the land, to find out where they were heading.

The National Library of Australia came in on the project when they heard what I was intending to do and helped with travel costs in return for recordings which were to go into their sound archives. I hadn't reckoned on being weighed down with technical necessities like audio quality and voice levels when I was out bush, kind of imagining I would be taking notes in the back of utes and the cockpits of cropdusters. The quieter and more sedate alternatives of sitting under a tree or in a homestead kitchen were nevertheless highly bearable, and the resulting digital tapes will provide rich pickings for researchers.

What a wonderful year and a half it was making this epic Australian farm tour. I have snooped over the fences of places from one end of the country to the other, checking out pastures, peering at stock and listening to a truly mighty bunch of high achievers on the land.

The first question everyone usually asks is, how did you choose them? I didn't. Well, not initially. I got people all over the place to suggest names to me of likely 'victims'. I said I wanted to talk to forward-looking people making their living from the land, who stood out from the rest because they were more fearless, more diversified, more experimental, or more individual. Perhaps they were the unconventional neighbours that the district laughed at, but ended up copying. Or they could have been the quiet survivors who held their line through droughts and price crashes and ruled triumphant in the end.

So from the names I gathered in the areas I was to visit, I made my choices. I attempted to somehow reflect the range of eclectic enterprises found in rural Australia, as well as a fair representation of the extraordinary people who run them—most of whom I fell a bit in love with.

The result of more than a year of almost constant trips out of my home district of Naracoorte in South Australia is an exploration into the souls of the people of the land. It is a journey too through a landscape that etches deep its influence and demands on the lives of its inhabitants. This odyssey has also changed me. The land cries out for young blood, for new science and for understanding. I now hear its cries more clearly.

To all those who so willingly recorded their stories and views on tape and were so generous with their time, my deep thanks.

And yes, scratch the red dust and you'll still find the stuff of legends.

Angela Goode

Map References

Part I
1. Kingston South-East, South Australia, Tom Brinkwo[rth]

Part II
2. Ulverstone, Tasmania, Jim Allen
3. Wynyard, Tasmania, Paul Roberts Thomson
4. Deloraine, Tasmania, Robin Dornauf
5. Melton Mowbray, Tasmania, Gerard McShane
6. Dunalley, Tasmania, Tom and Cynthia Dunbabin

Part III
7. Corrigin, Western Australia, Lawry and Jenny Pitma[n]
8. Esperance, Western Australia, Mick Quinlivan
9. Beaumont, Western Australia, Peter and Kirsten Biv[en]
9. Beaumont, Western Australia, Mark and Jan Biven
10. Gibson, Western Australia, Neil Wandell

Part IV
11. Mt Moffit National Park, Queensland, Bloss Hickso[n]
12. Lindfield Station, Queensland, Brett Hick
13. Arizona Station, Queensland, Richard Makim
14. Inverness Station, Queensland, John McClymont

Part V
15. Kununurra, Western Australia, Wilhelm Bloecker
16. Kununurra, Western Australia, Gordon and Rosema[ry]
17. Kununurra, Western Australia, Spike Dessert
18. Cooinda, Northern Territory, David Lindner

Part VI
19. Deep Well Station, Northern Territory, Jan Hayes
20. Stirling Sation, Northern Territory, David and Pen[ny]
21. Jalijbang Station, Northern Territory, Bill Harney

Part VII
22. Moree, New South Wales, Peter Glennie
23. Armidale, New South Wales, Ron and Hilda Cherry
24. Wagga Wagga, New South Wales, Tim Peel
25. Glenthompson, Victoria, Elisabeth Cuming
26 Geelong, Victoria, Hedley and Irena Earl

Part VIII
27. Mylor, South Australia, John Wamsley

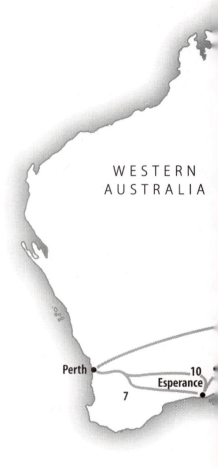

Road and air routes

WESTERN AUSTRALIA

Perth

Esperance 10

7

Part I

Leaving the Nest—South Australia

The Journey Begins

It was late spring in 1997 and I was sitting on the verandah in the sun on a day so still that bees working two metres away on a rose were annoyingly loud. The honey smell of blackwood blossom oozed across the lawn in heady wafts on the occasional breeze.

Crimson rosellas flirt and debate in the bay tree, then squabble in the spotted gum heavy with blossom and bees. In long grass along the roadside, red and white heifers ink-blotted with shade graze among gum saplings. A bachelor colony of kookaburras in the gnarled limbs of a red gum sound like bar boys cracking bawdy jokes and falling about at their cleverness. A far-off horn denotes the end of a shift at the meatworks and temporarily distracts the courting activity of a pair of swallows that had been ducking and weaving among the verandah posts catching insects. They mated unselfconsciously on the edge of the gutter before a mildly curious audience of young swallows.

This is my home, where I daily watch a pair of bush stone curlews nesting and sleeping among native grasses; where waterlilies are unfolding in the pond; where there is family, and dogs and horses; and where I like to be. Hay bales embroider the paddocks. New vineyards with porcupine posts spread like mutations. A lightness of mood pervades the district. The district is starting to smile again after so many dour years. I hesitate to leave.

Pushing the Limits— Tom Brinkworth

Some 16 years before, and newly married, we lived near Padthaway in the south-east of South Australia on a cattle station owned by a nuggety, determined bloke called Tom Brinkworth. He used to arrive at the homestead door for his monthly manager's meeting on the dot of 7.30am, normal start-work time—the significance being that he had left his home north of Adelaide at 3.00am and would put in an unflagging, solid day's physical and mental work. We left when Tom wound up his cattle stud. Since then, fascinated by this former pig farmer's roll through the south-east making rapid-fire purchases of numerous famous properties, we, and everyone else watched his progress trying to guess his next move.

Today, Tom Brinkworth is a part of the nation's landholding elite, owning about 100 000 hectares of prime grazing country with some 23 000 cows to be mated annually, a total of around 50 000 head, and up to 150 000 sheep cutting about 5000 bales of wool annually. According to Business Review Weekly's *1998 Rich 200 List*, he is worth $60 million.

Yet Tom was so unprepossessingly low key that an auctioneer at the booming Adelaide ram sales in the 1980s ignored his entering bid of something around $200 000. Someone sent out word that the short bloke in the shabby washer hat, work shorts and boots at the back by the door was in fact the legendary, but rarely sighted, Tom Brinkworth. He was successful in buying the ram.

Tom was to be my first victim. In recent years, for a man who claims he is shy and dislikes publicity, he had hardly been out of the news. He makes news for his firm stand on salinity and drains. He campaigns for more wetlands. He upsets his neighbours. He speaks his mind and shows no fear.

In the middle of 1997, Tom suffered a heart attack, had a bypass, then a serious stroke. He had to learn to talk, read and write again, and by early December this man of metal was ready to record his life story, the first time he had agreed to such an exposé.

For Love of the Land

Tom Brinkworth

Tom Brinkworth

Across the once swampy lands of the south-east, over low range country, through sand plains and mallee, the last hour of my trip was past and through land all owned by Tom and his wife Pat. Their house is inland from the coast near Kingston. The last time I saw it, it stood naked and new in a paddock. Fourteen years later, it is enclosed in a dense garden of native trees and shrubs, and alongside, Tom has his own self-contained office complex.

That's where I found him—in a room with huge red gum tables and benches, with numerous deer heads with mighty sets of antlers on them staring imperiously from the walls. Tom, now 60, wore a dense, wiry beard and was thinner than I remembered him. The characteristic gentle manner and shyness were still there. Pat, sadly, was away for the day.

We took up our positions at one of the massive tables in the echoing room. His is one of those classic stories, where a boy, the son of a livestock auctioneer, leaves school at 14, having only made it to Grade 6 and defies all the doubters and especially the teacher who said he would only be good for sweeping the streets.

Tom Brinkworth grew up in a house by the sea at Tumby Bay on South Australia's Eyre Peninsula. He had younger brothers Peter and Bill and a sister, Jill—the writer Jill Llewellyn. No-one ever realised he was dyslexic at the time. He was regarded as having no natural abilities, so he spent most of his school days doing two or three years in the same grade, being regarded as 'a bit of a dumdum'. He couldn't master reading or writing. Despite that, he said he never felt a failure.

'When I left school, I was never given money. I was given a hundred chooks.' His father had left the livestock firm and started a poultry farm. Needing extra help, he paid Tom's wages in chooks. By the end of the year, Tom had about £100 saved. 'I never spent anything. Never do. Still don't,' he says with the slight jut of the chin and soft chuckle that I remembered so well.

He built up layer numbers and sold fertilised eggs to the Y-Worry Hatchery in Adelaide. He was all of 15 at this stage. He had started with pigs even while he was at school. He would take a bucket and pick up lunch scraps from the kids. He would buy slips or weaners and grow them out to make a few bob. Then he bought a few cattle and had them agisted around the district at 2/6 a week.

'I was always keen on farming but never had any dough.' About 30 years later, Tom would have the largest piggery in the southern hemisphere, housing 90 000 pigs at any one time and over the years bred several million.

His family's farm was only five acres, so it was no doubt a relief when at 19, Tom bought his first block of land.

'It was another five acre farm. I had saved pretty well everything I had ever handled, I think. Dad went guarantor for the loan and I went on from there.'

Tom put up chook sheds, built the numbers up to several thousand. ' I just kept building it up until you couldn't fit any more on the block.' He smiled, remembering the one-boy operation where he mixed feed, collected eggs, packed, cleaned out the sheds. He hired his first employees in his early twenties and one still keeps in contact with him. The young Tom had started his empire, a term which by the way he rejects in favour of calling his present vast holdings 'just a farm'. He bought 20 acres at Gawler River for more poultry sheds and started serious pig farming then.

'Once we filled that 20 acres and you couldn't fit any more sheds on it, we bought another block at Wasleys next.' A place at Sheoak Log followed, dedicated entirely to pigs. 'By the time we sold it out, we were having a pig born every two minutes, 30 an hour. Multiply that by 24 hours, seven days a week,' he says in his quiet way of the enterprise that started simply because he liked pigs, but then found that they could be very lucrative if you picked your timing right and took a few risks.

Indeed, this was pioneering stuff because as Tom points out, 'at that time there was no real experience with other people producing large numbers—mass production.' Tom was borrowing heavily to expand and became a major buyer of barley from the Australian Barley Board, taking over 10 per cent of what the entire Japanese market took.

With 150 people employed and the business at its peak, Tom said it in a sense had become too big and faced the prospect of having to take over an abattoir to ensure throughput. With his main ambition in life to run sheep and cattle, which until then he couldn't afford to do, he took on a partner to help him run the business and form an alliance with Australian Bacon.

. . . 'he had worked for a bank and I thought with my education and background I really had no expertise in those matters and I was more interested in getting things done, bulldozing ahead.' This turned out to be a disastrous move. The gentleman concerned has since fled South Australia, leaving a trail of unhappy former business associates including Tom. 'He ended up getting a good many million . . . certainly a lot of dough out of it. In my lifetime I have employed a number of thousands of people, and in my entire life, I can only name two or three people at absolute maximum that I would call bad. Very few bad people.'

But he says the experience didn't alter him. 'No, I'm still just blind at trusting people.' And although he lost money, 'money is not what you do things for'.

Having lost enthusiasm for the pig business Tom says now that his distasteful experience with establishment businessmen was 'probably a bit of a blessing in one way'. The business ended when Adelaide Steamship took over Australian Bacon and collapsed in contentious circumstances. Tom began a new era as a sheep and cattle grazier in the south-east while still retaining his Sheoak Log and Gawler blocks.

In 1970, he bought the first of his south-east stations and started to move his operations. Once again he could contemplate doing the physical work that he enjoyed rather than the big administrative task of organising 150 piggery employees.

Tom Brinkworth is now the largest landholder in southern Australia and has put together over 40 stations of prime grazing country. Brinkworth land stretches for 150 kilometres parallel to the south-east coast. Out of the total amount of $6 million in levies to be contributed by all landholders in the south-east under the Dryland Salinity Board, Tom and Pat Brinkworth are required to come up with $1 million.

As well as those vast numbers of sheep and cattle, he still has pigs. 'Yeah, between ten and thirty.'

'Thousand?' I ask in all innocence, by now getting into the swing of big numbers.

Tom laughs. 'No, just pigs. In the backyard.'

Then there is the deer enterprise. This man can do nothing by halves. When the deer market fell in a hole about seven years earlier, Tom bought up big, fenced in about 100 square miles and estimates there are probably about 10 000 deer of eight different species breeding up. He explains that this is part of a wildlife enterprise that generates funds from international hunters flying in to bag themselves trophies like the heads that continued to stare from the walls around me.

'I recently did read in the US that the largest landholder there is the King Ranch and their best income now is from wildlife.' Hunting, Tom explains, not only satisfies primitive male urges, but it is necessary for conservation of species. 'Hunting is a great way to encourage diversity of species and preservation of wilderness areas where people can actually justify keeping wilderness areas at no net loss.'

Hunters are charged royalties for the animals they take. But it is early days yet for this enterprise because trophy animals need to be between seven and ten years of age to be able to produce those prized

For Love of the Land

sets of antlers. Interest is sufficient for Americans, Scots, Italians and Spaniards, however, to have made trips. For Americans Tom says, 'It is cheaper to come here than it is to go to the Rocky Mountains.' Charges range from the minimum of $400 for fallow deer to hog deer at $3500. Red deer are $1500, and Samba are $2000.

'We've got the largest herd of Samba deer in captivity in the world,' he says with pride. Kangaroos carry a charge of $1000.

Hunters take the severed heads home in crates to their favourite taxidermist. The carcasses are always used, Tom says, and income from hunters' fees helps towards fencing.

I ask Tom how he would describe himself. He says, 'As a lunatic', and laughs, but goes on to say he sees himself as a very ordinary sort of person. When I reminded him of the Adelaide Show ram sale story, Tom commented, 'That story probably shows that I rather enjoy being common. People tend, if you are bigger than average, to look at you as something different. In actual fact, all that you are is ordinary.'

He enjoys reading biographies of people such as Churchill and Roosevelt, 'something that's motivating', and has managed to educate himself on a huge range of topics through books. He quotes Churchill as having said 'The hardest work you can ever do is to think, and that's why so few people do it'. I ask this man who is himself a wide-ranging and free thinker how much leaving school early has contributed to his unconventional outlook.

'A lot, actually', but he goes on to say that motivation is one of the greatest assets a person can have. 'I was certainly told when I was very young that I could do nothing, had no hope of doing anything but sweep the streets. I think that probably motivated me to try and achieve a bit more than that at the time.' Tom continues to explain that he is also a fighter, is determined and a person who likes straight talk. Nor does he suffer fools. He is also a man who likes his own self . . . . 'and I like getting my own way too. Unfortunately.'

I ask who have been influential in his life and Tom says Pat has been a 'moderating' influence, but he has also had wonderful staff, financial experts and many other helpers. Tom married when he was 25, having met Pat, 19, when he was making his first property purchase. They built themselves houses with Tom, characteristically, doing much of the physical work.

Tom currently employs about 50 staff, but he says the character of people wanting to work on the land has changed. The farming organisations, he says, have proved to be 'a mob of whingers'. 'Once the great ambition of young people was to be a farmer and become involved in the land. Now if you go to the city and ask young people if they would like to go on the land, that would be last thing they'd be motivated for because all we ever say is that everything's crook, it's getting worse, look for government assistance left, right and centre, and people just can't get motivated.' He does accept that it has been a difficult period at the same time. 'No question about that.'

'My way has always been a minimum cost production system with maximum volume output, believing, and I still do particularly with land, the most economic thing with your land is not 100 per cent of maximum production of land, it is probably 70 per cent, because to get the extra 30 per cent is so expensive.

'Over time you can look for that extra per cent of production as economics change throughout the world. But the world is never likely to be short of food and fibre again. What we actually have is an oversupply of both and will have for a very long time to come. What we have now is a shortage of wilderness and environmental diversity of species and that is very serious.'

With the ups and downs with wool and beef, how do those downturns balance with a philoslophy of not pushing the land to its full limit, I ask.

He says sometimes you get more dollars by doing less, rather than more. Sometimes the inputs can outweigh the returns. 'We wouldn't dream of making a bale of hay, because I just do not think other than something like dairying, or you were making hay and selling it to someone who wants it more, you could possibly justify it.'

Tom is very much an opportunist, buying in when prices are low. 'Very much so, if the price isn't right, we will do everything we can not to sell. If we think there is any potential of an upturn at a later date, we'll buy in.'

He and Pat put on the largest on-property single-vendor weaner sales in Australia, but also sell a lot of cattle privately. 'We are currently sending out ten double-deck loads a week, [45–50 cows times 10 trucks each week]. Most years we have four or five sales, about 1500 head each. This year, we'll be down, more being sold privately. There's not a strong demand. The cattle market is relatively weak. Last year it was shocking. It is improving, and will continue to improve, I'm sure.' Tom believes the outlook for wool is much better than for beef, and consequently is increasing his proportion of sheep.

'I'd say we have passed the worst of the economic downturn which has been going on for 10 or 12 years in sheep and cattle. It's been a long haul.'

I talk about his land purchases, which he volunteers will continue at his normal rate of about two stations a year. 'We are quite happy if we buy out the neighbours. We would normally pay more than anyone else if it suits our locality.' He cites the reason for the continual shopping spree is lack of feed. 'It's not that you want power or anything like that. You always tend to be short of feed.

'I seem to have the silly philosophy that if the neighbour's is for sale, you should buy it. Under that philosophy of course, we end up with an island.' And he laughs merrily. Consequently, with such a rate of expansion, Tom is not entirely sure how many acres are under his control.

'Oh, I could go and look it up,' he says. 'It would be about 300 to 400 square miles.' And yet, Tom Brinkworth does not believe he is successful. He emphasises he is still poor and cash flow is a problem. He claims he has heavy borrowings and going right back to his piggery days has had a continuous stock mortgage with Elders until within the past fortnight when he swung his finances over to a bank.

Duck shooting is one of Tom's great pleasures. Having some fine swamps on his land, he found himself particularly popular in duck season. His duck shoots became huge affairs, with up to 600 people at a time, and all everyone needed was an invitation. Realising he needed to put something back into the wetlands, he started charging shooters, just $5 at first, but now it is $20 and for that they get one of Tom's famous campfire meals of venison or beef.

Tom is a firm believer that controlled hunting promotes the health of a species. If the guns don't cull wildlife, nature will, and in a far crueller way. Without culling by shooting, numbers build up in good seasons to unsustainable levels in lean periods. The weak, old and very young die from hunger. How much kinder it is, says Tom, to remove that overburden of numbers and use them for food, instead of waste them. 'Hunting might take out 5 per cent but it makes no difference to the population at the end of summer,' Tom says.

From that straight-forward desire to set aside duck-breeding areas, Tom now finds himself once again in the spotlight, but this time as an internationally significant conservationist. He is regarded with reverence by environmentalists as a hugely important wetlands benefactor, having restored the swamps and diverted channels. In 1991, he established Wetlands and Wildlife, an environmental and conservation-based company that has 12 000 hectares of former Brinkworth country under its control. Before drains were commenced 100 years ago, the renowned grazing country of the south-east was a series of boggy swamps.

Tom Brinkworth

Tom Brinkworth's Watervalley wetlands are currently being assessed for listing as Wetlands of International Importance under the Ramsar Convention. (Set up in 1971 by 18 countries including Australia, Ramsar seeks to redress a worldwide lack of conservation of wetlands.) They are home to 160 species of birds, many of them endangered or threatened, and also fish, frogs and tortoises. Various grants, particularly National Heritage Trust funding, have enabled university researchers to be involved in intense studies of wildlife and the ecology. Watervalley forms a link with South Australia's Coorong and Bool Lagoon, which are already listed under Ramsar. The Brinkworth system has been dubbed by some as South Australia's Kakadu.

'It is something that should be done on a world [and] on an Australian basis, which we are doing. We are running with it and claiming tax deductions on it.' Tom says tax deductibility for environmental organisations registered as companies is a simple way of increasing environmental areas at no net loss to the landholder. If the environment is to be improved for everybody, landholders should not be penalised.

A proposal for tax deductibility status of Wetlands and Wildlife was put to accountant Peat Marwick Hungerford (PMH). It stated that land locked up for conservation purposes should be able to be claimed as a tax deduction, that it be virtually run like a charity. PMH said the chances of succeeding with that proposal would be two or three per cent. Tom's response, 'Let's be the two or three per cent.'

After some hard lobbying, a change was indeed made to the rulings. Federal ministers Ros Kelly and John Dawkins devised a scheme to provide environmental organisations with tax benefits. 'So we set up a company to become that and it was passed and agreed to by Kelly and Dawkins and is there today and growing at the rate of ten to fifteen acres every day and potential to continue to grow at a greater rate.' Tom is chairman of directors of 50 shareholders. Each year, Tom issues invitations to a wide cross-section of the community to view progress. Politicians and business leaders are taken out bush, sleep in a swag, have a meal cooked on the fire and go fishing and hunting. As a lobbying approach, it has been clearly successful. 'I tend to think that what I do and the way we live is perfectly normal and everyone else goes down the same line,' says Tom.

Wetlands and Wildlife has also spread its influence to the rugged Flinders Rangers where the company has bought Warraweena, a 355 square kilometre station property. All sheep and cattle have been removed and yellow-footed rock wallabies are finding their way back.

Shooters are encouraged to go up, pay their $20 a day, and take out as many goats as they like. Tom is clearly enthused by his purchase of craggy mountain ridges and gullies and talks of the therapeutic values of such wilderness areas.

'People are as nutty as fruit cakes until they have been there for about three or four days. They carry on the same as they do around cities. But then they start to relax and get back some relationship with nature and the environment.'

Such special areas must be kept for society and Tom is grateful that the state government has agreed to waive all government costs and charges for environmental projects such as his. 'We don't have to pay stamp duty, rates and taxes and all those sorts of things that are ongoing, on environmental areas,' says Tom.

Now, with a man today so passionate about the benefits of retaining untouched areas, conserving wildlife, re-creating wetlands and wearing the bearded mantle of many a conservationist, it is important to note that this was not always so.

'No-one has cleared more land than I have, or our family, other than the AMP. We used to clear land at the rate of up to 25 000 acres a year,' Tom says with a defiant gleam.

Until state legislation banned clearing, I posed.

'Well that didn't slow us down much for a long period of time,' and he smiles.

Tell me about that Tom.

'Well, I believe in the carrot rather than the stick in everything I do.'

So you just kept clearing despite rules that came in and said you weren't allowed to?

'Oh yeah. But it doesn't work anyhow. Because it's just stupidity. No-one can keep a tree alive on your place unless you want to. You can kill it, you can burn it, you can just continue to graze it and it will inevitably die. It might not die this week, next week, but it will die.'

So is this rising interest in wildlife a latter-day conscience of Tom Brinkworth?

'No, just commonsense of where you should be. You have to look after your environment to get anything to work in the long haul. It's got to happen. If someone doesn't, you can continue down the same road, which is a very sad road for your children and their children.'

Salinity, which is poisoning land in his area is one of the prime motivators. And Tom in his free-thinking way which either infuriates or inspires, believes salinity and degradation are not hard to fix. He has simply set his mind to looking at the big picture and come up with a plan—which to the consternation of the government department overseeing the various salinity projects under way, he has implemented.

'Well you just learn as you go along, but be prepared to do it', is Tom's view on the drain system he is currently putting through his place which links into the government system. He can do it far more cheaply, he says, and more quickly. He brought into the state the biggest Komatsu excavator he could find—168 tonnes of it—and a bulldozer, and they are now munching through salt-affected areas at great speed creating seven-foot deep channels through which salt water flows instantaneously.

'Drains are very simple. Recently the government, in their normal wisdom, decided they wanted to put more fresh water straight out to sea, which to me was absolute lunacy. And we took them on and that's been rescinded and changed and the water will now go down its historic watercourse where in places it has been dry for 40 years. What we believe we'll ultimately end up with will, in not too long a time, get back to traditional wetlands systems where they historically were. Some net loss to local landholders but a great net gain to society as a whole, because you'll have a better environment.'

Tom, I challenge, surely you're not advocating that we bring back the swampy environment that we used to have through the whole south-east?

'We'll bring back some of it,' he says.

Salinity is not a problem, says this man with unconventional views. It is only an indication of a high water table. 'Salinity arises from that over a long period of time because we get about a pound of salt that comes on to the ground every year just from rain. About a kilo to the hectare. It comes on the drift off the sea. It only accumulates if you get your water table too close to the surface, then it starts to evaporate and swing to the top. But you can reverse all that and we've demonstrated that here. Adelaide University do a lot of work for us, and in areas four to six weeks after you lower that water table you start reversing the whole system . . . Normally four to six weeks after you start, the quality of the water will start to improve.'

As you would imagine, Tom Brinkworth's drains and his opposition to the state government's plans attracted much media interest. Tom, who says he would prefer to be a recluse, became an active fighter writing letters to the daily paper and rural media.

'Oh, well they tried to take us on', a statement indicating Tom's view that the individual's rights are paramount. 'I started digging. They were promoting putting an experimental drain in the south-east and further north which has now been constructed and I thought they were on the wrong track. And the costings were all out. So I decided that we would go ahead and do a section of 36 kilometres ourselves and find out how things did work . . . We did it in our own way. But the moment I started digging, they contacted us and said, look, you've got to stop today or we're going to take action against you. Then they faxed me the next day—we're going to take action against you. Then they wrote and said the same thing, and we just said in our normal manner, that's okay, we're going ahead with this. They attempted to stop us, using the law.' And this mild-mannered renegade laughs softly.

So, you took no notice at all of these threats?

'No.'

What did you prove?

'A great deal. The system works extremely well.'

Mind you, Tom exerted a fair bit of pressure to get his way. His drain was to cross a government road and go through a Telstra cable. He knew he couldn't get permission to cut the cable since it was for a non-approved project. So, in Brinkworth style, he let the water dam up and flood the road.

'The local council knew that the water was going to cross the road so then they ended up conceding that we could put a crossing in because they were going to be in real trouble if we didn't, or someone was.' Triumphant in victory, Tom rubbed salt into wounds and made a celebration of the event. 'So we ended up having a public opening of the occasion where we were going to cross the road. On that morning, the board gave us written permission to proceed with the project.

'Then I started to take out an injunction against them about diverting the water from crossing the Bakers Range, which I thought was wrong. They were going from Fairview National Park across Bakers Range down through Blackford into Lacepede Bay. That, to me, was crazy. It meant diverting the good water from the Bakers Range that comes our way into the wetlands system, and they were going to divert the damn stuff out to sea. So I started saying, if you go ahead, I'll take out an injunction against you for diverting water from the main watercourse. At the end they agreed.' The compromise was that the outlet to the sea would be closed once normal winter run-off from rainfall filled the channel. This water is diverted into the wetlands system.

Add to all these confrontations the fact that Tom intends not to pay the $1 million due in drainage levies. He hopes to trade off his work against what the government is charging. 'We obviously are not going to pay both. We are not going to do the work and pay the levy. We will do one or the other.'

Exhausted by tales of brinkmanship and achievements, we took a break. Tom served up lunch in his office kitchen for the two of us, and, as he normally does, two workmen. Stewed beef and onions with boiled spuds. Delicious.

When I returned a few days later we talked more about drains. Tom had taken me to see the huge 'toys' at work. They cut through into flat, salt-affected ground. Cloudy, green salt water almost immediately covered the bottom of the new channel.

Tom had surveyor's levels to check depth and fall of drain. He had worked out the dimensions himself. 'In that region we are putting in a drainage scheme which is part of a government scheme; but the government has been talking about building this scheme for eight years now . . . We are not prepared to wait indefinitely for them to do it. We have decided to do it ourselves and we started 12 months ago.'

Although he acknowledges vegetation clearance has been a major factor in salinity, he is not embarking on tree planting. 'Currently it is not economic for a landholder to preserve bush for himself generally other than if you think you can do it through lowering the water table, which is really not a practical way of doing it. It is much better to drain. It is much more important to preserve your environment situation and stop the degradation of species, and economics wins in the end.'

In other words, if it is cheaper to damage the land and more expensive to restore it, nothing will be done for the environment. He emphasises once again that there should be no net loss to landholders who want to preserve or improve the environment.

Another example of Tom at his provocative best was his famous stoush in relation to the wide comb dispute in 1982. Believing shearers had a right to use whatever gear they wanted and should be able to work when they liked, he employed a team that had worked during a strike over the issue and been attacked. He armed his own station managers with guns to give the shearers protection if it was required, because the strike was still in force. An Australian Workers' Union representative arrived. 'I contacted the local police and said that we anticipated problems. We anticipated one of our sheds to be burnt down for sure, so we had the chaps on the various places hose off the areas at night to keep it wet to try to minimise that.'

Police escorted the AWU representative onto the property. He was allowed to walk over the shearing shed and he was escorted into the shed and down the row of shearers. 'There was some confrontation, but

For Love of the Land

nothing violent at the time because the police were there, and he was escorted off the property and not allowed on again and the front gates were closed and we went on shearing . . . The threats were that there would be violence when they hit the roads coming out on the Friday night, so we changed the dates so the knock-off day was going to be on the Thursday.'

After all that drama everyone used wide combs without a problem. 'It was quite a colourful period of time when you look back on it today and over something that was absolutely pure stupidity.' Tom was so proud of the men who worked on through that strike that he rewarded each one with a small silver goblet inscribed 'For bravery in looking after their own civil rights throughout a strike', ' . . . or something along that line. I just thought it was a bit of a memento to keep for themselves for what they actually did over principles.'

UPDATE: Tom and Pat Brinkworth sent a shipment of 2100 pregnant beef heifers to Mexico in September. The agents say this was an Australian record. No-one before had ever sent so many cattle in a single order. The deal was worth about $1 million.

Part II

Sailing South—Tasmania

Top of the Tall Poppies—Jim Allen

It was autumn before I could again take to the road, this time to Tasmania, with my old mum for company. While ringing around to locate my interviewees, I spoke to a livewire called Ian Folder who runs Botanical Resources Australia, a company that refines and exports the herb pyrethrum as insecticide. As a former big company Sydneysider who now works with country people, he got my pen scribbling.

After the distrust and mania of Sydney business life, Ian was lyrical about how weighty deals were done in the country on just a handshake. 'But I'd forgotten how innovative the farming community was,' he enthused. 'There are more innovative ideas, and I have more success in dealing with locals than gathering learned experts around tables,' as was the way in Sydney . . . 'where some people around board tables couldn't run a corner store. People on the land can turn their hand to anything. They are doers,' he said.

Ian also said it was tough adjusting to having to think for himself and be responsible for his own decisions. He took a few lessons from those around him and changed his outlook. 'Farm people take problems in their stride,' he said.

The country is bleached and dry. From Naracoorte we head east through the swollen hills of Western Districts Victoria. Beyond the stately trees and grand buildings there is peeling paint and depression. Wool has knocked the spirit out of a people used to easier times and the finer things of life. Risky investments and billowing debts have picked off many old families.

Near Geelong, affluent city weekender farms with designer sheds, expansive plantings of trees, stylish ponies in front paddocks and Country Life homes, attested to the oft-repeated country mantra by farm people within striking distance of cities: 'The best crop you can grow is houses'.

Into Melbourne over the gravity-defying Westgate bandaid covering the boils of dockland slums, grey smoke and red rust sheds of industry. Our boat awaited us in a Suez Egyptian vista of palm trees. Tropical-style apartments had windows shuttered and blank to the view of queuing cars and container vessels and coffin-like buses full of mesmerised tourists being yelled at by gold-jewellery-clanking tour leaders with glossy dyed hair and big teeth. But *with the excitement of a couple of country simpletons released from chains, my mother and I followed signs and waving arms and eventually ended up on the boat for Devonport.*

It was not a smooth crossing. Kicking and plunging like a horse with a prickle in its saddle blanket, the boat thumped its way across Bass Strait, determined to toss me out of my top bunk. Gusting winds removed my left contact lens and flung it into the foamy waves below when I stepped out to admire the view.

Next morning, following the north coast we headed west to Ulverstone and into the hills above Gawler. A vista of Elvis Presley electric-blue sea kept pulling at our eyes. Big, round, red-soiled hills seemed to be half dragged into the water. A fringe of houses clinging to the edge of land were also in danger of being sucked under. This fertile, north-facing coast with its bone-white beaches and warm climate is the best stretch of soil in Tasmania, and some say in the nation. The land sells for about $3000 an acre, but a family here can live off 200 acres of well-managed, intensively worked country.

With the view at his feet stands Jim Allen, a man of old-world charm and the tight-fitting flesh of a man much younger than his 62 years. Jim was among the first to grow heroin poppies and pyrethrum in Tasmania, has been twice the winner of the top poppy crop and is a top onion grower. Although he had his grounding in the working-horse days, Jim is very much a man of today, using all the expertise available to engineer his successes. Jim's wife Dot had died just five months before and he was bravely soldiering on—serving us tea just as Dot would have wanted it done, in fine china cups with biscuits. He lives alone now on his magnificent 330 acres of sloping, red basalt land warmed by the sun and brushed by the soft air from the nearby coast.

Jim's lineage is etched deep in the soil of the area. His great-grandfather came from England as a ploughman under a bond which he had to work off. He took up land on the coast not far from Jim's place. The family's history is dear to Jim as he looks back on the changing times plotted meticulously in numerous farm diaries. He notes how his father could live off the proceeds of 80 acres of potatoes, all done with horses, and employ five people full-time, yet, 'there was just as much [profit] left over at the end of the day as there is now'. Then there were more farms, more people employed full-time on the land, methods of farming were slow and inefficient and production

Jim Allen

levels were modest. Today, with fewer farms and larger populations to feed and clothe, fewer people employed on the land working with extreme efficiency, fortunes should be made. It's not the case and Jim and I puzzle over the mathematics of where all the money from farming has gone.

Jim reckons he's worth about half a man these days and he employs one man full-time plus a little bit of casual labour at harvest. 'The amount of stuff we produce compared to then is just unbelievable.' In 1935, his father thought 10 tons of potatoes to the acre was exceptional. 'We are talking now of 18 to 20 tonnes as reasonable, and 30 tonnes as exceptional.'

Those increases have come with the added costs of irrigation, large amounts of fertiliser, pesticides, weedicides—none of which his father knew anything about. His workmen were expected to hoe out any weeds that appeared. 'My father would stop the horses if he saw raddish over on the hill and he'd go and get it.'

Jim decided at the age of 11 that he wanted to take over the farm. He left school just before fifteen. 'My first job when I left school was trapping rabbits. The place was overrun with rabbits and I had about 60 traps. The rabbit truck would come three times a week and the rabbits would just hang under a chaff bag which would keep the flies out. A fellow called Ron Edwards would come on the rabbit truck and he had an envelope with lovely new pound notes in it. Oh, I drooled over Tuesdays.' That was his income for the first couple of years.

In 1958, when Jim was 20 and not long before he got married, a serious shortage of potatoes Australia wide sent prices to wondrous levels. Despite his crop of potatoes having glassy end, a condition caused by uneven rainfall, the Sydney market paid more than £100 a ton, which resulted in the mighty sum of £2000 for his three acres of crop. That crop paid for half the building cost of Jim and Dot's brand-new house. 'Today, three acres of spuds wouldn't put the spout around the house,' Jim huffs.

We set up chairs and a table in the garden so I can drink in the sensational view while we talk. Hundreds of noisy parrots work in the gum blossoms behind the house.

Jim helped establish poppies as a glamour crop when they were introduced to Tasmania in 1964 by Steven King, an agricultural scientist from Britain, working for the Glaxo Group. King had put a pin in the map identifying the most ideal spot for poppies . . . just a tiny bit west of Jim's place.

'It's a very lucrative thing now for the coast,' says Jim, who adds that before poppies, everyone grew vegetables, making growers extremely vulnerable to the price whims of the big processors. Poppies give 'competition to the vegetable companies which have tended to be multinationals and have got us screwed down on price pretty well now. Every bit of competition you can get helps. Similarly with the pyrethrum industry.

'I've got a friend who was a field officer for Edgell's, he's retired now. He came up and wanted me to put another paddock in for spuds. I said, no, I'm putting poppies in there. And he said, you've got that pyrethrum, you're putting that in too. This bloody land's supposed to grow vegetables and food, not stuff to cure headaches and kill flies.'

When Steven King came looking for poppy land, the isolation of Tasmania and sparseness of population appealed to him. 'That may have been something to do with the drug problem associated with it,' says Jim. However, 'this industry here is very strictly policed. Each paddock is grown under separate licence. In fact I had, in this very paddock', Jim waves in front of us, 'an exchange student who'd come to look at poppies and unwittingly, while they were still green, I reached across the fence and snapped two heads off and broke them open to show her the seed and to explain a little bit what the industry was all about. A couple of weeks later there was an inspector knocking on the door to inform me there had been interference in my poppy crop.'

To motivate poppy growers to lift their production, the processors offer annual inducements and awards. Jim's processor, GlaxoWellcome Australia Ltd, presents the top grower with a gold watch and an engraved trophy.

'There are 450 poppy crops, but I've got one that'll give it a nudge.' Jim's quiet manner can't conceal the pride. 'I'd love to win it because that would be one in each decade. One in the 1970s, one in the '80s, and one in the '90s would top it off.'

Jim says he has a great sense of loyalty having been with Glaxo from the early days when Stephen King set up the crop and they became good friends over a beer. The opposition poppy processor, Tas Alkaloids, offers a car to the top grower—this year a BMW. Jim Allen has no thought of jumping ship. He is uncomfortable with the modern tendency to opportunism, even if he finds the thought of a BMW attractive.

Pyrethrum was introduced to Tasmania about 12 years ago, so Jim thought he would have a punt. 'The beauty of that crop is that once it's planted, it's established for five or six years. It's been quite good,' said with quiet satisfaction that his returns have been better than most. The crop doesn't need spraying, there is worldwide demand for it and production meets only about half of existing customer orders. The Tasmanian climate is perfectly suited to the crop. Indeed, Jim Allen has enjoyed his farming life in this pleasant slice of utopia.

He looks around behind us to the craggy mountains where he and his father used to take their cattle in summer. In winter, the peaks are covered in snow.

'I've travelled a bit, but there's nowhere in the world I'd rather be,' he says.

UPDATE: Jim wrote to let me know that he had indeed won the coveted Top Crop award, giving him the rare honour of taking the title once in each of the past three decades. He won $2000 worth of travel and a new watch. His crop achieved the highest return ever achieved: $6451 per hectare.

A Blooming Dynamo— Paul Roberts Thomson

This north coast of Tasmania is beautiful, seductive and warm. Stayed the night at Boat Harbour, a piece of the Riviera without the glitz. We ate fish cooked fresh from the sea and chips arranged like flowers in a bouquet of tissue paper eaten on the beach while the setting sun turned the sea the same colours as the boat sheds behind us—pink and blue.

It was a Sunday morning when we drove to the top of a plateau above Wynyard to meet Paul Roberts Thomson, who was inside doing the week's ironing in the kitchen. Bronwen, his wife, was away for the weekend seeing family. He is all coiled energy, whippy body, lean, dark and very charming. He'd be finished soon he said, so we went for a walk.

Table Cape is so named because it is flat and square and pokes out into the sea like a table. The land rises up sharply from the flats below. On top, the rich red dirt glows like freshly polished cedar. When the tulips bloom in spring, you would wonder if someone had gone crazy with the Liberty florals and draped a rather hectic cloth over the cedar. Even the glistening white lighthouse at the end of the paddock could be construed as an outsize salt shaker waiting for lunch.

I had come to hear Paul's story of how he turned an underperforming sheep, cattle and vegetable farm into a tulip-growing bonanza which now exports tulips back to Holland. When we returned to the rambling old weatherboard farmhouse, with its garden full of flowers, Paul was hanging up the last of the ironed shirts.

We plonked down in leather chairs with a wheezy spaniel at our feet. His asthmatic gasps have been preserved on the archival tapes for all time—but luckily, Paul, who speaks in a torrent of words that tumble and fall over each other, drowned most of the wheezes out.

Paul, aged 43, is part of a family of seven Roberts Thomson high achievers—three doctors, a teacher doing a PhD, a nurse/cattle breeder, and another graduate doing welfare work with the Salvos.

Paul Roberts Thomson

They were brought up under their father's philosophy of not being afraid to be different. That urging appears to have had a big impact on Paul, who says when he took over the farm he expressly set about finding something that no-one else was doing. 'Dad has this philosophy that if you do what everyone else does, you'll most likely only make a living, and it will most likely be pretty hard work.'

The history of the family's settlement of the area begins with Paul's grandfather who sounds a gloriously florid colonial character, a major with the British cavalry in India with a passion for missionary work. He bought the property Paul lives on in 1910 but knew nothing about farming, preferring to leave his wife and farm manager to get on with growing his stud sheep and running the place while he made frequent trips out of the country for missionary work. 'His wife and farm manager got on better when he was away,' says Paul without expanding. By 1936, when the old man retired, the 100 acre farm was only just surviving. There were ten children. Two of them, Paul's father and uncle, took over, with apologies from their father that the place wasn't capable of sustaining them. They had some good luck, though, with the outbreak of the war and by the time Paul's father returned from war service duties, his uncle had turned the business around by growing oats for horses and potatoes, and had enough money in the bank for Paul's father to buy a separate farm for cash. With the postwar wool boom another three farms were purchased, without a penny ever being borrowed. The family's stud Shropshire sheep which they had bred from the 1920s and the later-introduced Dorset Horns stood them in good stead. 'In the 1950s anything that had four legs and a bit of wool was worth a fortune—even a Dorset with steel-wool-like wool', and we both raise our eyebrows and roll our eyes at the contrast with today's tragic industry.

So, with 700 acres of good dirt, 400 of which was 'some of the most productive horticultural land in Australia', the two brothers were set up for lives of prosperity. In the 1950s they got into stud cattle—the new glamour breed of Poll Herefords and continued on successfully until 1981, when they divided the partnership and Paul took over the management of his father's share. His uncle's son continued with the other share.

So Paul in the 1980s, with a degree in agricultural science and Bronwen with arts and social work degrees, set to rethinking the direction of the business. Times were vastly different from the munificent wool and stud sheep days. They looked for something that would take them through to 2000. He predicted then that genetic engineering would have a big impact on stock breeding and reduce returns for breeders, so he looked to a future making use of the advantages they already had, their superb soil and a warm gentle climate. But not vegetable growing—'too much today work'. Under the former family partnership they already had a taste of growing up to 16 different things, among them sheep, cattle, pigs, potatoes, peas, poppies, hybrid brassica seed, snow peas, sugar snap peas, carrots, summer swedes and cauliflowers. 'Under the dreamy days of the 1980s, it sort of looked like something that one would avoid if one could,' said with another wry smile, because 'today' work now surrounds Paul's every waking hour.

Tulips were suggested by one of his former agriculture professors in the 1970s and he and Bronwen spent a few weeks looking into them in Europe on holiday . . . but it wasn't a serious idea, not until 1984. He had to be galvanised by necessity first.

After the family partnership dissolved, Paul for the first time in his life became acquainted with debt when he bought a bigger share and had to pay out his uncle and cousin. 'Then we actually settled down to the realities of everyday life. I think it is fair to say I didn't really know what tough times were. Life had always been pretty good.' The farm wasn't going brilliantly. Between 1981 and the early 1990s they paid no tax, 'which tells you the business wasn't going terribly well.

'It never occurred to me I was going to go broke, and we weren't going to either. The concept didn't interest me. But it was a good experience to go through, to actually have some tough times and feel a bit of pressure. It's probably a pretty handy sort of experience,' says this bloke who 'fell out of the cradle wanting to be a farmer'.

In 1984, in partnership with his sister and brother-in-law, they made the leap into forming Van Diemen Quality Bulbs and importing 1000 tulip bulbs from Holland. 'Of course we had myriad problems,' Paul says. 'We didn't know what we were doing. The Dutch didn't know what we were doing either.' This was because there had been an embargo until then on the export of bulbs from Holland. Flying blind, they did three years of trial work until 1987 and tried to multiply up the bulbs for bigger plots. With a jolt they realised they had already worked up a debt of $30 000. All they had achieved were enough bulbs to plant a plot the size of a living room.

'We either had to make it bigger or give up. So we decided the only thing to do was go to Europe and do a whole lot more study.' I tended to think that others might have given up at this point. But for six weeks, Paul and brother-in-law Brian did nothing but study bulb growing and 'got serious about it'. 'We sold the other farm and the cattle stud and with that we retired a bit of debt, but most of it just went straight back into the bulb business.'

At that time the embargo on export of bulbs from Holland was completely lifted, so Van Diemen Quality Bulbs brought in Australia's first-ever container load of flower bulbs. It was mostly filled with narines and just 30 000 tulips. They had reckoned on foolproof and healthy returns from the narines, but Paul believes now that they had a good sales job done on them by people who were trying to offload narines. Shortly after they bought at 55 cents, the price fell to 20 cents. A tempest ended the erstwhile narine business when the shadehouse blew down. Paul just happened to be on the ferry to Melbourne that rough night and people had indeed been thrown out of their bunks.

The tulips, however, went along nicely. Following their initial trial work, quarantine restrictions were waived so they could be grown in open paddocks like an intensive horticulture crop; and their first full container load of tulip bulbs duly arrived, 8 tonnes of them. They discovered the costs of growing tulips were huge, about $40 000 a hectare, but they didn't necessarily see this as a drawback.

'One of the reasons we are in tulips is that the barriers to entry are quite high. It is not easy to get into tulip growing.' His reasoning is that there will be few competitors to invade his markets. 'Having said that, you can't very easily get out of it. I've got a lot of capital infrastructure that is pretty useless for anything else. A lot of money, hundreds of thousands of dollars have been spent . . . we're in the game for the long term.'

The business is based on planting out bulbs, which after flowering double in number. These are then harvested, graded and the best sold to commercial flower growers who discard the bulbs after picking the blooms. Paul's second-grade bulbs, which are not good enough to sell into the bulb trade, are planted on his farm in plastic houses to produce tulip flowers that are air-freighted to every capital city in Australia two to three times a week. They also have an extensive mail order catalogue for domestic gardeners, now in its tenth year.

He exports 12 tonnes, or 400 000 individual tulip bulbs back to Holland so Dutch growers can grow top quality flowers in the northern autumn and also has set up a sharefarm operation in Holland to grow flowers to be auctioned at the Dutch flower market. He says the export side of the business has room to expand. It is early days yet. The import and export of bulbs by countries around the world is to ensure a year-round supply of blooms. 'Consumers now expect flowers out of season and think nothing of it.' It is far cheaper and easier for growers to discard the bulbs after they have bloomed and buy in new stock each year.

The work is unforgiving. 'If I make a mistake, then I have wrecked the following year's production. Because of the big dollars involved, getting it right really matters.' His dreaded 'today' work now lasts for 11 months of the year. Flowers are picked seven days a week. 'If you see an opportunity, you don't just knock it back because it didn't fit some utopian idea you had about the ideal enterprise, because life tends to be about compromises.'

The business this year will grow 18 hectares of tulips which should yield up to 300 tonnes of bulbs. He will also plant three hectares of dutch iris and one hectare of daffodils. He employs 11 full-time people and more at peak periods for a year-round average of 18 employees. His payroll is more than $500 000. He wouldn't discuss what the business makes, but I think it is fair to say it is healthy.

Paul says he is fostering markets in Taiwan and Hannoi for tulips. With a separate group of growers from his district, he has formed Table Cape Exclusive Produce and sent a first consignment of onions to Asia. He expects before long to make 50 per cent more than the contract price available locally. The group is also growing liliums on Paul's farm for a market in Holland, and other countries in the northern hemisphere are interested.

An hour on, and with words and ideas still bouncing energetically out of his fertile brain, Paul says he is a long distance thinker. 'I'm always trying to set something up for tomorrow.' The export forays are an insurance for when there is a glut in the Australian market. 'While I could make better money selling my flowers and bulbs in Australia, I am determined to get out into the international marketplace.' He likes to feel the 'heat', learn about costing, pricing and protocols.

If you think that is enough to keep this human dynamo occupied, sorry, there is still more. He also has stud poll dorset ewes and grows pasture, pyrethrum, poppies, peas, onions and barley 'to fill up the gaps' on the farm, but they form only 10 per cent of the total business. And then on top of that there is the tourism side of the business which Bronwen runs, in addition to the mail orders. Tours are during the height of tulip-flowering period from late September to mid-October.

Computing is also one of Paul's passions. He writes all his own programs for mail order and cash control and has set up a web page. He can cost any one enterprise totally through using his own programs but, interestingly, he says the biggest revolution on their farm was the fax machine.

In what is probably a relief to those involved in his business, Paul says he is moving away from just managing crops to take on a three-year appointment as a director of TAFE in Tasmania. He said he thought if he used his brain power to continue to expand the tulip business any more, 'then maybe I might keep building it at a pace that's not particularly comfortable for everyone,' he said, laughing in recognition that creative hyperactivity can have its drawbacks.

So we stopped and had lunch—a great big bowl of pasta with tomato sauce made by Paul, with proper parmesan, a bottle of wine and Paul still going strong about the business he loves.

As to whether his son, 14, or daughter, 18, would continue on with it . . . 'I believe that farming is too hard and requires too much commitment for anyone to be involved in it unless they really want it,' he asserts. 'It is not much short of criminal to try to get a child, son or daughter, into farming when really they should have been a doctor, a fitter and turner or a bus driver. It is just not right. How can one compare the value of an unhappy life against the ability to boast that you are a fourth generation farmer. The two are not comparable.

'For the past 12 months I have worked 56 hours a week. It's a big commitment.'

Then off we hiked, at a brisk pace naturally, talking all the way, to tour the sheds, see tulips blooming in plastic domes, women sorting flowers and the bulb room where trays of graded and sorted bulbs were ready to fill mail orders. Paul scooped up handfuls of bulbs, asking what colours we preferred and shoved them into brown paper bags, telling us to refrigerate them for planting in early spring and fast flowering.

As we drove away, what this man, of a family that has prized education and qualifications highly, had said about education kept going around my brain. 'Education is mainly about broadening your vision of the possible, rather than teaching you anything in particular', admitting that he himself had been an obnoxious know-all at 21 when he returned to the family farm after university.

'I think education is a major detriment to people making a lot of money. I'll never be very rich, I'm quite certain of that. I don't have the right mentality. The people who make a lot of money in life are often very, very focused and very determined and they can see life in very simple terms—most things are black or white; life is not complicated, it's easy.

'The more education you get, the more you can see the shades of grey. And really, if you want to do something like make money, shades of grey are a damn nuisance.

'I'm very much into shades of grey these days.'

UPDATE: Paul's co-operative group of growers, Table Cape Exclusive Produce, put 150 000 lilium bulbs into the Australian market this year. They aim to produce one million lilium bulbs next year.

Milking a Rebellion—Robin Dornauf

We pulled ourselves away from the north coast like ants from honey and arrived in the lush, rolling dairy country of Deloraine. We were within sight of the craggy Western Tiers and Cradle Mountain with snow dribbling from a few peaks.

From my research, Robin Dornauf appeared to be the largest private and individual dairy producer in Australia. He milks 1800 cows. Only consortiums or companies milk more. But there is more to this man than a vast cow herd.

At his historic stone house built on the high side of a road that climbs up from the Meander River and the main street, it was clear that the last thing this dairyman on the move wanted to do was sit down and talk. The phone was incessant. There was no small talk. We were down to business efficiently and quickly. Built like a boxer, Robin was unexpectedly very softly spoken and when I commented on that, having had to fiddle with the recording levels for a while, he replied, 'I have found that if you have something to say, people have to listen if you speak softly. It gets better results than shouting.'

So without shouting, Robin Dornauf, aged 35, has led a rebellion in the Tasmanian milk industry. He and 20 fellow renegades have diverted about 25 million litres of milk a year from the monopoly milk processor United Milk Tasmania (UMT), put it on the boat and shipped it across Bass Strait to Melbourne. Despite shipping costs and double handling, they were earning more and sending a tough message to UMT which they say has not been rewarding them adequately. The 25 million or more litres lost to UMT represents the work of 8000 cows and is roughly 8 per cent of the total production of Tasmania. UMT is consequently short of milk and the milk market in Tasmania is in disarray. It had never been done before, this challenging of the big player. It was a bit of a Robin Hood story, with some bushranger thrown in.

At the time we met, the milk hijack was nearing the end of its first

Robin Dornauf

season. Robin said things looked promising, trials and tribulations notwithstanding. They had secured contracts with major processors and manufacturers in Victoria. Robin said all this matter-of-factly, indicating that what they had done was fairly straightforward, simple to set up, and technically not difficult. All they were doing was carting the milk a bit further and putting an extra emphasis on quality. I suspect he's the sort of man who calls potholes in the road mere dimples. Robin might have thought the process simple, but obviously others didn't . . . no-one else had tried shipping milk before. Robin couldn't really work out why.

He went on to say that it was only 24 hours from collection of milk at the dairies to delivery in Melbourne. Although shipping historically hasn't had a great history of reliability, they have had no problem. Of Bass Strait: 'If we treat it like a highway, we're only 400 kilometres from Melbourne, and it's not an issue that it's water or land really.'

But what about the cost of getting the milk to Melbourne? Yes, it is dearer than road transport, he agreed, and they would like to get it down. Efficiencies need to be made on the wharf and the milk tankers need to be bigger, but the shipping costs aren't too bad 'once we've negotiated a good rate'. And the way he said it, indicated he would push hard.

Robin, the son of a former UMT director, Ian Dornauf, surely must be feeling the heat for the group's act of treason. But he is as cool and as composed as any master strategist should be. Robin said the processor was probably worried about how large his company would grow.

'There's been a very strange attitude, probably brought about because they thought it wouldn't happen, that it was only a bluff. But we were very certain right from the first moment we looked into the possibility, that it could and would happen.'

'When our first load of milk did go, all hell broke loose. It was surprising . . . the effort they went to to derail, to denigrate, whatever was in the armory to fire at us. If they had put the same effort into running their business, they might not have had a whole group of farmers wanting to achieve a better price.'

Robin says UMT told him that Tasmanian Quality Milk (TQM) should supply all its milk to them, or none. 'So that made it fairly easy for me.' He supplied none. Robin said because Tasmania was a small marketplace, companies frequently treated farmers with a cavalier attitude—a take it or leave it approach. 'Basically, we have the island mentality that you're limited to this as your market—you either deal with us or you don't.' Robin said already cattlemen were shipping livestock to Melbourne processors and that put a floor in the

Tasmanian price. He said all farmers should be getting paid the Melbourne price less the freight difference, and not less.

Victorian dairy farmers are getting 20 per cent more at the factory door than Tasmanian farmers get. Robin's men think that by sending their milk from their tightly located dairies with associated lower transport costs, they'll be 10 per cent up on Tasmanian prices. With efficiencies they could even achieve the same net returns as Victorian farmers.

Robin says his group has discovered that processors are very keen to deal with one entity, and not a whole range of individual farmers which they then have to supply with services and field officers. 'To be able to go to a processor and say we've got 25 million litres of milk, we'll deliver it to your door, are you interested? Yes, they are. They are very interested and we expect to get a better return, which will offset our extra cost of freight.'

An impediment to TQM increasing its volume further is the freight capacity in the ship. So Robin and his merry band are in the process of setting up their own plant to evaporate the milk, save space and lower freight costs. The processors don't mind if the milk is concentrated. 'Just on our current 25 to 30 million litres of production, we could save $1.2 million a year on freight.'

The dairy farmers in the group all approached Robin to be involved in the battle for better prices. 'They would be the type you'd want to go to war with because they are very solid.' For instance, they had a problem in spring, when the supply of milk is overabundant. A processor in Victoria reneged on the agreed price, but the group was united in its stand to not supply. They decided they would pour milk down the drain if they had to in order to achieve their goal. 'That makes us a very strong bunch,' said with quiet defiance in his voice.

The idea for the breakaway group was hatched by two New Zealanders who had been in Tasmania for only four years—Neil and Paul Amourgis. No doubt with the clarity of outsiders' eyes they could see a revolution was required. The three of them, Robin, Neil and Paul, work closely together, Robin having been co-opted because of his long family association with the area and rapport with farmers.

The timing of Robin's milk war has not been good for UMT, which recently spent $60 million on a new processing facility. 'The thing that they haven't done properly, in my view, is that they have built the plant but they haven't encouraged increased production, or their current production to stay around.' No doubt this increased capacity gave Robin leverage to push for better prices.

'They haven't had the competition from any other processor in

Tasmania. There are other milk processors but all of those are at their current capacity. They don't require any extra milk.

'That plant [UMT] now for seasonal reasons as well as others has closed down for five months. It's a $60 million plant closed down. It doesn't make a lot of sense, specially with us shipping our milk across to Victoria when it could be going through that plant.' The battlelines are drawn clearly.

So who is this bloke who is willing to challenge the power of the mighty processor?

Robin's father had been a credit manager with a stock and station agent when he decided to become a dairy farmer with 90 cows. Robin was one year old. After Robin and his brother matriculated, they both returned to the farm because they loved it. They all worked together until four years ago when Robin and his wife, Karen, decided to go out on their own. The partnership carve-up was in cows, but no land. They had bought a dairy farm and thought they would operate it with their own cows.

'For whatever reason, Karen and I decided that might be a bit comfortable and we decided at our ages, if we were going to have a bit of a go that it would be best done in the next ten years, so we looked at a whole range of things. We left a sharefarmer on our property. We ended up coming to an agreement to lease a large farm with an option to purchase at a fixed price in five years.' This was not a dairy farm, so they did something Robin admits was highly risky—borrowed money to build a dairy on someone else's farm. Having an option to purchase with only lease payments in the meantime helped them to lever themselves into a much bigger property than they could have done otherwise. 'It enabled us to put our limited capital into cows and things that actually produce money.' They started off with 600 cows but now have three separate dairies on the property to handle the 1800 cows.

When I commented on the size of his herd, Robin modestly said it was 'possibly one of larger herds' and then deflected further attention by commenting how herd sizes in general had increased. He remembers when he built the dairy that an 18 000 litre vat was the largest he had heard of at the time—'yet six months later I was ordering a 25 000 litre vat', and they are now commonplace. He says he is still highly leveraged and has to be careful and always hopes the seasons will be fair. In their 40–45 inch rainfall, irrigation is not essential but Robin does water a percentage of his farm. Lack of rain reduces production by between 10 and 15 per cent.

Robin employs a manager to oversee the dairy operation so he can give his time and energy to TQM. He employs about 14 people and says good labour is very difficult to find. He has three trainees and one apprentice. 'We would be better off employing a qualified man and paying him two or three times the amount in the short term, because of the bikes that are wrecked and the stupid mistakes that are done.' He goes on to say, however, that a good trainee is far preferable than an older person in the longer term. He says people don't mind the 4.00am starts and 6.30pm finish because they get time off between, have good facilities and are well rewarded. He says it takes just three hours to milk 1000 cows at the peak of the season using a 50 bale rotary dairy. 'The milking part is not exhausting.'

Robin says he is trying to produce maximum milk at the lowest cost. 'If we can lift the average of our 1800 cows by one per cent, we have created a lot of milk.' This, he says, makes more sense than lifting the top cow by 20 per cent. Because they are sending milk to Victoria, he says it is critical that his milk is better than average, so he trains his dairy operators to have a good feel for every cow's health. All the machinery and equipment is new and well maintained.

This man who moves like he is going somewhere fast then had to get down to the depot where his group's milk tankers transfer their loads into special shipping containers. I followed at a great pace, begged him to stand still for a few minutes while I tried to photograph him, then left him organising the next milk shipment to take to the seas in search of higher prices.

UPDATE: There has still been no improvement in local Tasmanian milk prices despite the sale of UMT to Bonlac, which promised a better deal to dairymen. The Dornauf herd has grown to a massive 2100 cows.

Out-stepping the Rest—
Gerard McShane

The past few days had been slightly surreal. We had been staying near the antique town of Bothwell in an uninhabited 150-year-old mansion belonging to a friend. Restless spirits kept tramping through the house at night, coughing through walls and knocking on doors. I don't think I am the type who is sucked in by ghost stories, but it certainly wasn't my mother walking in her sleep or standing on the other side of a thick sandstone wall with a consumptive cough. I got up and checked. She thought it was me with the cough. No-one was there. It wasn't frightening, but our senses were on edge. In the ancient village of Bothwell below, little had changed for a century apart from the arrival of Eftpos. As I walked across the footbridge beneath willows and elms to collect the morning paper from the 140-year-old general store, I trod the same path as the convicts and troops of 1832. Tourist interloper in the gentle rhythm of the town, I felt about as out of step with time as the ghosts in the house.

Next stop was the lower Midlands to see a man who delights in being out of step with everyone else—Tasmania's largest individual woolgrower and stud merino breeder, Gerard McShane. While his 1000 bales is small alongside large mainland operators, this was to be a story about more than just wool.

Gerard McShane, aged 50, with 21 000 acres of prime Tasmanian grazing country, is charming, confident and urbane. His mind whirls freely with creativity and freshness. He oozes optimism and energy, despite current low wool prices and a severe drought. He is technologically brave and bold.

So when he told me early in our talk that he had never learned to read or write, it is fair to say I was reasonably staggered. Gerard has thought his way to success using logic, by listening to experts, by using others to read and write for him. 'I was a dumb bum,' he says of his boarding-school experience.

Gerard McShane

We were sitting at a magnificent huon pine table about four metres long, with the sun streaming in through expansive windows. When this highly respected sheep breeder who sells genetics all over the world makes this confession, I feel enormous admiration, then confusion . . . Isn't education the key to success? I recall then what Paul Roberts Thomson had said, that education can make life needlessly complicated and hinder the path to riches. Ah, life has its intrigues.

Gerard lives at a property called Lovely Banks, in an elegant old stone home with columns along its front verandah, set back from the Midland Highway which dissects his vast landholdings. He normally runs about 35 000 sheep and 450 breeding cows but because of the current drought, 10 000 sheep, all calves and half the cows had been sold. 'So we are going backwards flat out,' says this bluff and open-faced man with a smile.

I wanted him to start at the beginning and tell me about his enterprise.

In 1984, he says he did something that everyone told him was foolish. He decided to be really radical and find out what the customers of his wool were actually looking for. After ringing mills all over the world he learnt 21 micron wool, good, dense and long was their preference. He couldn't source rams that would give him that in Tasmania so he took sheep classer Rob Russell on a hunt all round Australia. 'What I was after was a certain type of sheep with a low prickle factor.' He found what he wanted at a little stud in South Australia—Oriental Park. It is a daughter stud of the renowned Collinsville stud which is famous for its heavy-cutting wool. 'Bringing Collinsville sheep to Tasmania was crazy, according to everybody,' says Gerard with amusement. 'I know that. I am an idiot, have been for a long time. It doesn't worry me, it's what the clients want.'

The CSIRO discovered that wool of over 30 microns is what irritates the wearers of wool clothing, turning them off the fibre. If these thick fibres (the prickle factor) are kept to less than 5 per cent, then wool can be worn next to the skin quite comfortably. 'We are down to wools that have a prickle factor lower than point one. Some rams are zero.'

Because his country is heavy, hilly and usually damp, Gerard says it is hard to breed fault-free sheep. 'If we are breeding a fault it will show up quicker than anywhere else. So that's the good part of breeding sheep to send to the mainland because we sort out all the problems here.' For example, fleece rot and footrot.

He did discover footrot on the property in 1996, just one and a half months before his annual ram sale. He immediately called the sale off. 'To my surprise within a week to 10 days, every client had either written or phoned to say they could not buy those sheep anywhere else in Australia—we still want those sheep, no we don't want you to pick out a few for us, we want to buy them and you have got to put the auction back on again.

'Then I realised all the bullshit that goes on in the stud game was out the door, because my stud is client driven rather than owner driven. They tell me what they want, and if it fits into my program, I will give it to them.' He has been criticised for taking that approach.

Honesty is a quality he values highly. 'That's what's lacking in the sheep industry, I believe. I know this is not going to be liked by a lot of people around the countryside but I think the day is gone when they are relying on talking their way through the problem or hiding a problem. I would rather put it out in front of people and talk about it.

'It was probably the highlight in my experience in the stud game that I had clients who said the sale's got to go on. I had a seasonal record ram sales that year.'

Gerard's sizeable acreage has been amassed by purchases over the years of seven adjoining properties. 'We are very very lucky, but you've got to realise I put a lot of time into being lucky.'

And another of his favourite sayings which also powers his actions: 'If you don't make a jump, you're never going to land on your feet.'

It is a quality—this making your own luck—that he may well have inherited from his father. Brought up just out of Hobart and one of a big family, Gerard's father set off to make his own way when the family property could not support them all. He made his way up the east coast to Surfers Paradise and there he was noticed by an old farmer as a newcomer to the area. The old bloke said he was about to retire, 'He said he was too old to climb up and down the hills to get the bananas', so they got talking and Gerard's father, being inquisitive, asked all about banana growing. 'Over three beers he learnt all about growing bananas, and knew the bank was taking over the property the next morning. So he got out of bed very early, rode his pushbike up the hill to have a look, and thought, well I'm not busy, so he rode his bike to Southport and saw the bank manager at 10.00 when the bank opened.' He suggested that he run the place until the bank found a buyer. 'So he got the job, in around 1929 at the start of the Depression, and it wasn't long before he put to the bank that he should buy it at the price the bank was taking it over for.'

When he returned to Tasmania in 1932, he had £80 in his pocket, a

For Love of the Land

small fortune in those days, and was able to go farming on his own. He bought a series of small farms, built them up and sold them, eventually deciding to grow wool 'because when he looked around, those who were doing best and having most fun were woolgrowers'.

Gerard is one of five brothers and a sister. He was the only one to leave school early, the other boys went to agricultural college or jackarooing. All six wanted to go on the land. Their father said he couldn't possibly set them up.

'He had the foresight and perhaps faith in what we had, and he lent us the deeds of his property, which takes guts. From that, we used the deeds to buy another property. We used the deeds of that property to buy another property, and we kept growing. We had a partnership and majority rules. And that's the way it worked right through. We worked in a partnership from 1964 until 1982. Sheep had no names. We were there to make money. We knew at the end of it we wanted a property each, big enough to look after what we wanted to do. We were just woolgrowing, filling bales of wool. In the partnership, although brothers were starting to marry, wives had no say in it, and at a partnership meeting, you said exactly what you liked.'

Gerard's father is the source of much commonsense advice. 'He said if you don't learn from watching where mistakes are made, then give up.' And the interesting saying: 'Don't work hard and make money unless you know how to spend it.'

'I then as a youngster couldn't understand what he was getting at. I happened to be in Hobart one day and he said, see that old fellow there, I reckon he's got three million pounds. And he said, look at the miserable fellow. He's miserable because he doesn't know how to spend. And he said, if you're going to finish up like that, don't bother making money.'

He extended this adage to Gerard's boarding-school pocket money account. Gerard had managed to save a bit of money, 'and he flipped the lid, absolutely flipped the lid. He said, 'I am borrowing money at 7 per cent, you're getting 2.5 per cent, we're losing 4.5 per cent. Gee, we're not going too well are we? That was my first lesson about money. I've carried it ever since.'

Not many people know about Gerard McShane's inability to read and write, the reason he left school so early. 'It took me 20 years to actually own up to anyone that I didn't know how to read or write. I got cunning. I used people. It was something I have had to live with and at one stage I nearly went back to night school, but I have just battled along and I have a very understanding wife who does a lot for me, and I use people. If I want something written, I get the professionals to do it. They can do it better than I can anyway, even if I could read and write.'

Gerard says he can read a little now, but not very well. He won't do it in front of people. The trauma had been revealed. His confession had been made. 'That was a surprise to you, wasn't it?' he said smiling gently, as though afraid I might have thought less of him.

The Gerard McShane approach to farm expansion is also well defined. 'I've always believed that when farming is at the highest, it's really at the lowest and when farming is at the lowest, it's really at the highest.' I ask him to please explain this riddle.

'If everything's running high and the sheep are high, and the wool prices are high, and the cattle prices are high, the graph has got to go down. And so that's the way I look at things. When things are so low, there's one way for the graph to go—up. So that's why I say, when things are at their best, they are actually at their worst. I've always looked at it that way.'

So here, during a crippling drought and horrifyingly low wool prices, he's quite happy.

'I would be happy if I found another property that I could buy because the interest rates are so low. When things are booming, interest rates are too high for me to muck about with.'

Pessimism and despair are his friends. 'Turn all the negatives into positives and go for it.' Unconstrained by convention, this man with the free-wheeling spirit makes anything seem possible.

While I am quietly absorbing his thoughts, he comes out with another provocative statement. 'But one thing I will not change. I have 3381 days left in farming.'

You can't be serious, I say. You have plotted your retirement so precisely?

'Yes, you've got to retire.'

He has sons of 22 and 20, and a daughter who is nearly 17. He says the reason he puts a date on his retirement is that the men working for him retire at 60, and if that's good enough for them, it's good enough for him. 'But more than that, there's a lot of people out there who hang on to their properties too long and they start going backwards. The son never gets a chance, can never get any creation, and I don't want that to happen. My assets are the next generation. When I turned 50 and announced that I had 3647 days left, they said, good heavens, we haven't really got long to get going, have we? That was the best bit of news I had ever heard in my life.'

'When the time comes, whether they are up and running, it won't really matter to me, because somebody will run it, or it will be sold, or it will be leased. I don't have any hang-ups, and yet this property is one of the original grant properties.' Gerard has not yet decided where to direct his energy after sixty.

Then that leads into his thoughts about the next generation taking over the farms of their parents. Once of the reasons he believes rural industry is in a mess is because too few farmers are properly trained. 'That's where our farming industry right across Australia is falling down. The sons or daughters come home and they are expected to run the properties without all the training. This sounds funny coming from me, and I'm sorry about that. But that's the way I see it. They should be trained before they come home and run the properties.

'You have to be a master of so many different segments, not just looking after sheep, also the land, controlling the finances.' Plus juggling international needs and marketing. 'You can have the best product in the world, but you have to be able to tell people.'

Gerard McShane started his Stockman merino stud in 1984. 'But I knew I wouldn't sell a ram for ten years, until I got it right. And at nine years, they kept knocking on the door, and saying, look, you've got hundreds of these rams here, and I think I broke the rules and sold the first lot of rams after nine years.'

So after winning Campbelltown Show in Tasmania, he took them to the mainland. In his first year at the Melbourne Show, he got supreme champion for one of the rams. 'Others had been showing rams for years and never got a bloody ribbon and here we were. But it was because we knew what we wanted and we went after it.'

Showing is marketing. 'But when I can, I'll pull the pin and won't bother showing any more sheep because it really is costly . . . as anyone knows that's in the stud game.'

Being in Tasmania and yet marketing semen to South Africa, South America, Uruguay, Argentina, and the Falkland Islands is also predictably seen in a positive light. 'From Lovely Banks, you can get to any part of the world. I just say this is the centre.'

In 1989, Gerard bought a top Collinsville ram for a poll merino world record price of $280 000. 'I had never seen a ram as good as that in all the rams I had looked at . . . and I was more worried about that ram going out of Australia than anything.' He recouped about $170 000 from semen sales. 'It did worry me at the time that I had broken the poll merino world record by $100 000, but given the same circumstances again, I would do it again. It wouldn't worry me.'

Gerard McShane

Collinsville's principal Paddy Handbury has since ruled that semen cannot be on-sold. 'I shouldn't have got where I got, . . . I was buying somebody's genetics and genetics shouldn't be sold as easily as the way I got them. It was too easy.'

Gerard defends the practice of selling merino rams overseas. Sheep must continue to produce wool in other countries otherwise mills will close down. They have to have a good supply of wool.

'We are not producing enough wool,' says this man who keeps coming up with amazing statements. 'If you starve your client, which is the woollen mills . . . they've got to overpay for wool, then they're going to close their doors. And every woollen mill that closes its door, won't open again.'

I point out that producers say they can't survive with wool at its current low prices. He tells me that's why he argues for more training for farmers. People need to learn to buy when prices are low, and it is then possible to make money. It is also important to have off-farm investments like shares and to sell them when they are high in order to buy more land.

Gerard and Elizabeth have a daughter at boarding school and she is yet to decide her future. His sons came home when they left school and worked as jackaroos under his manager from 7.30am to 5.30pm for one year, and got treated fairly hard. They understood what they were training for when they eventually did tertiary agricultural studies.

We talk about diversification and Gerard mentions his sister-in-law, Clare McShane, who founded Casaveen jumpers, which now sell nationally through mail order, retailers and at major field days. 'She started knitting . . . because she had five boys under six and they were wearing jumpers out. It started from a very basic need and then all of a sudden people were saying, that's a nice jumper, will you knit one for me? I think she employs something like 65 people.' Naturally the wool is prickle free. 'That's why woolgrowers right around Australia have to start changing. We've got to start producing what the market wants. Gone are the days when you have to just produce wool, and lots of it. You have to produce the right wool.'

There's no great mystery to picking a sheep with prickle-free wool, says Gerard. It's just softer. 'You should nearly, as my sheep classer said, be able to class sheep in the dark, that's how he learnt . . . Your eyes shouldn't class the sheep. Just feel.'

He talks of his frustration with show societies that won't introduce measurements into their judging of wool, the way it is sold to the mills, and again pushes the education barrow for farmers. He fears too many farmers with old-fashioned ideas, once they have been pushed off their farms by their sons, end up on show societies and prevent the industry making advances.

He illustrates his point with a story about the Melbourne sheep show. He sent a ram on the boat with Gerard knowing exactly what micron he was all over in different parts of the fleece. The stewards put the ram into the strong wool section although his micron was 20.4—simply because the wool looked to be broader. 'I didn't mind because at the end of the day, he went on to be one of six supreme champions of Melbourne. But in the wrong section. And that's why the education side of farming has to be changed.'

Meanwhile, Gerard McShane is introducing leading-edge technology into an area that has been characterised by stagnant tradition. Shearing sheds on all the properties are being overhauled to eliminate catching pens to make shearing faster and easier; a system of races delivers sheep directly to the shearers. He uses fibreglass spiral chutes to dispatch shorn sheep from the shed to reduce injury. He eliminates contamination of wool by reducing handling of it by having it put in bins on trolleys that take it straight to the press. 'It's a business, not just a career here, and I had to do the job properly,' he says.

Newly introduced from Western Australia is a $25 000 radical advance in crutching. 'One man crutching will probably crutch about 500 ewes in a day. We are just putting a machine together now in which one man will crutch about 3500 sheep in a day. You still need a handpiece in your hand but you do not turn it off. You just press a button and another sheep is delivered in front of you, and there is not the waste of time in turning the machine off, standing up, walking around, opening the catching pen door, catching your sheep, tipping it over, dragging it out and then turning the machine on. All that is gone. All you do is crutch the sheep, press a button and another one is upside down right there with you and you just crutch it. So every seven and a half seconds, you are crutching another sheep.'

Gerard saw the machine at a wool expo 12 months ago and bought it straight away. It is the first one to be made by the manufacturer and bears the number 0001, which indicates the manufacturer thinks many thousands will be sold. At six times faster than the old ways, it is not necessarily only going to save money, it will assist with management of the sheep, enabling them to be cleaned up quickly if they are dirty or being moved from one paddock to another.

This is just the beginning, says Gerard. Eventually all his sheep will be shorn in cradles. 'So I am saying to you, if you know how to iron you will know how to shear a sheep in a few years' time. They are the changes.'

The cradle will turn the sheep. An operator will have only to push a handpiece in straight lines and stand in one spot. Gerard predicts he will have them operating in 12 months' time. One of his brothers has indeed already invented a cradle 'after a few hours in his workshop' and can shear 120 in a day.

'Down the track, I hope to be able to have it so that every sheep that comes into the shed will have its own micron stamped on it.' Wool classing would be superfluous.

Cell grazing is one of the newer grazing methods Gerard is using to look after paddocks and prevent soil erosion. It requires very large mobs of animals being moved into smallish paddocks for relatively short times, sometimes only a day. After having grasses and weeds eaten and flattened, the paddock is allowed to rest for up to 60 days, which enables grasses and clovers to grow back lushly and vigorously.

'We are starting to lose sheep tracks, we are starting to lose erosion. We are starting to find that the native plants come but all the good grasses are there.' Gerard experimented for five years, but is now embarking on a massive fencing program to divide large paddocks into smaller areas. Last year he put up 280 miles of electric fences.

'For 30 years I think I started to go the wrong way.' Making mistakes is inevitable . . . 'but if you don't make a mistake, you've never actually had a go'. He has found this grazing method saves on worm drenching because sheep are always moving to new pastures. Some three-year-old sheep have never been drenched, which makes huge time and cost savings. Every month all sheep have faecal worm egg counts done and are graphed and checked continuously.

Lovely Banks is a demonstration property under the Potter Foundation, which encourages best farming practices and revegetation. 'I had a policy I would like to plant a tree for every sheep I ran. I think I planted 23 000 trees by hand.'

I comment that Gerard seems to tackle everything he does with a fresh, innovative approach. Was it a help not to be too educated?

'I suppose I was lucky in the fact that it meant I had to use professionals. Because I don't read a lot, I don't have ideas before the professional comes in. I take the blinkers off completely. But I wouldn't say that that's the way you should go. I think I have just been lucky in the fact that firstly, I had a very basic man for a father who could see things ahead. Secondly, I was lucky, I had five other brothers who helped me, and I suppose I used them. I just worked the first ten years, I virtually never said anything, but I was watching what was going on. When the time came I just wanted to put [together] all those ideas that were kicking about, and use professionals.'

Gerard said having qualifications sometimes prevented people seeking advice because they felt they should know the answers. Gerard said all his brothers had done very well, however, and 'they seem to be more contented than me'.

Irrigation is another area where Gerard McShane's creative mind has again come to the fore. He had always wanted to irrigate land, but not at the expense of his sleep. Many systems need moving during the night.

'When I had bought one of the last properties, a property called Kelvingrove, everybody said, why did you buy that, it's a dry miserable place. I believe it's a jewel in the crown. Everyone said it hasn't got any water. In actual fact it's got *miles* of water because at the back of the property, not on the property, but just over, it's nearly all rocks. And so when it rains, the little creek that's there is a bit like a downpipe on a roof. It just fills up and there's oodles of water. And as soon as it stops raining, well, there's not much there. It's the same as a downpipe.' Gerard monitored the flows for three years and realised there were millions of litres of water going to waste. He hit on the then radical idea of using centre pivot irrigators, revolving circular sprinklers that cover huge areas. After building two enormous dams halfway up the hills that could catch the rain previously wasted, four years ago Gerard brought the first centre pivot irrigator into Tasmania.

'It could cover more than a kilometre from one end of paddock to the other and water 225 acres in 24 hours. But the good thing is, it's all by gravity.' He has since bought two smaller centre pivots to cover 100 and 20 acres respectively. 'It's just so easy. The secret is I'm watering grass, that's the opposite to what you're supposed to do. I'm watering grass because it doesn't cost me anything. [For] the little motor to drive the wheels, I've got a bill of about 1.5 litres of diesel an hour to irrigate a 220 acre block.' His irrigated pastures have been used to keep sheep alive in this current drought year. Gerard has just installed a third dam, equivalent in volume to an 11-and-a-half storey building holding 410 megalitres of rainwater, all from the same stream. Since Gerard's pioneering work there are now 37 centre pivots in Tasmania.

Gerard developed a system of electric fences which the irrigator can drive itself over. The wires go down under the wheels on a slide and come out the other side. He was accordingly able to divide the area under the big irrigator into 16 paddocks and doesn't have to open gates, he can just drive over the fences.

He tells a salutary story about his experiences in sourcing pipes to get water from the dams to the paddocks. His first quote from a supplier was $530 000, and Gerard immediately put his dream on hold. Two hours later, the supplier rang and said he could do the job for $310 000. Gerard found it exciting that $220 000 could be saved in two hours. So he rang another contact in irrigation and promised him $5000 in cash to see what he could get pipes for. 'He came back within eight days and said, all the pipe you need to do that job is $48 000. Look at how much money I saved for a $5000 investment. Unbelievable! It's just criminal.'

He comes back to his theme of farmers needing to use advice and be more professional. 'I really believe that farmers are becoming peasants. Most farmers have never had four weeks holiday. All my men, they all take four weeks holiday; they all get off the place. But most farmers don't get away. I hear farmers' wives saying they've never been away for 15 years. Well you can't get any worse than that, can you? That's crazy. We've got to get smarter. We're crazy to allow that to happen. I understand now why a lot of wives are leaving husbands, because who wants to take on a job and stuck on a property for 15 or 20 years just raising a family and working day in, day out, seven days a week.'

UPDATE: A phone call. Winter was at an end and there still hadn't been any significant rain. Gerard had just had a dust storm, but he wasn't perturbed. He had also run out of irrigation water. Then, quoting his famous line, 'when things are at their worst, business is at its best', he told me he had just bought three historic properties—Huntworth, Sand Hill and Brooklyn—adjoining his place. In all, 7000 acres of beautiful country and 9000 Polwarth ewes, $4 million, walk in, walk out. He was busy putting on 700 tonnes of super and pasturing ready for when the rains came. He said he had had to talk hard to his bank manager. He now had a total debt of $6.5 million.

Gerard was also very happy as he had just been accredited MN1, the highest level of test for freedom from Johne's disease. He was the first merino breeder in Tasmania to achieve this. Many resisted being tested, scared lest they find it.

A month later: a jubilant phone call—the super had gone on the new properties and the rains were falling. The new land was bursting with green.

Winter 1999: The shearing machine was not in operation as predicted. Instead, he was trialling Bio-Clip, shearing by injection, on

2000 wethers. It would be another few years before the machine was in use. They had not had enough wet days to spend time indoors experimenting and perfecting it. Ditto with the crutching machine. It was being used for the rams but needed refining before big numbers went through.

He still had $6 million of debt, but he was quite happy—it pays its way and enables ten full-time staff to be employed and 71 part-time. This year his farms turned off 1489 bales of wool. He had 2874 days to retirement.

Logging on to Conservation—Tom and Cynthia Dunbabin

South, and halfway to Port Arthur from Hobart on the Forestier peninsula, to meet two thoughtful farmers who are making the most of the diversified attributes of their large and stunning coastal property, Bangor, near the town of Dunalley.

We spent the night at an artist's B&B not far from Bangor; just minutes away it should have been. I forgot what I had been told about following the front drive for about 10 kilometres. I kept thinking I must have passed the place and that I was heading on a back road to outer Mongolia, so I turned back. Twice. Desperately late and flustered, I apologised lamely at the pathetically-easy-to-find house right on the road with a beautiful garden, views of the sea and curvaceous coastline.

Cynthia Dunbabin, dark, neat and charming and Tom Dunbabin, handsome, tall and equally charming, despite gritting their teeth with irritation, sat me down and calmly got on with the job of telling their story.

What these two are doing on their fifth-generation 6200 hectare property is a blending of what has always been done there agriculturally, plus farm and ecotourism as well as the conservationists' bane, forestry. This surprising mix is done so well that in 1996 Bangor won a national Landcare Nature Conservation award. As well as running sheep and cattle, the Dunbabins' land is also the home of bandicoots, bettongs, wallabies, wombats, echidnas and diverse bird life; its surrounding sea is home to seals, dolphins and whales.

As well as 1000 hectares of pasture there are 5200 hectares of bushland and forest. Since 1992, groups of tourists come in by bus for the day to experience the utter beauty of Bangor's 35 kilometres of coastline which varies from white sand beaches with clear still water to rugged cliffs and boiling seas. In one of Bangor's many bays, Abel Tasman and his ships anchored to search for fresh water and edible plants. It was December 1642 and they were the first Europeans to visit Tasmania.

Tom and Cynthia Dunbabin

Tom and Cynthia Dunbabin

Members of the Oyster Bay tribe of Aborigines, the Pydairrerme, were the original inhabitants of the Forestier peninsula, living on wildlife, shellfish and crayfish. Their middens and artefacts are found all the way along Bangor's sandy coast. Whalers also set up four southern right whale stations between 1830–42. In 1830, the property's land was cleared so cattle could be grazed to supply Port Arthur with meat until its closure in 1877. The Dunbabin family bought their first block of land on what was to become Bangor in 1890. It is one of relatively few large properties in the area standing firm against the encroaching suburban sprawl.

With this stunning history to draw on, sensational scenery all around them and commodity prices which couldn't provide enough of a living, it was inevitable that Bangor, 50 minutes from Hobart, would open its gates to a curious public. There was also an element of wanting to inform an increasingly ignorant population about farming and rural enterprises. 'We got tired of reading misinformation about what farmers were doing, what Landcare was about and what forestry was about. We thought one of the best ways was to show people,' said Cynthia, who holds a Bachelor of Science degree with majors in zoology and botany.

In the 1996–97 year, 50 groups toured the property. Then because Tom and Cynthia got so busy running tourism and the farm, they stopped promoting and tours slowed down. They put out a 32 page booklet giving a comprehensive insight into their property, printed brochures and sent out media releases, and the tours now continue at a steady rate. 'We want people to know that you can have an economically running farm, take care of the land and still have things that people enjoy when they come,' said Cynthia.

Tom tells how they mainly went into tourism to iron out some of the cycles of boom and bust that regularly occur in agriculture, and to which they were especially vulnerable when wool crashed in 1991, considering that sheep made up 70 per cent of their enterprise. Tom, who has a Bachelor of Agricultural Science degree, is involved in industry organisations such as the Tasmanian Farmers and Graziers Association, various conservation bodies, and was a member of the former International Wool Secretariat.

He explains that forestry has been one of the shining lights of the farm since 1972, when an export woodchip mill was built at Triabunna about 80 kilometres away. I wonder how on earth a Landcare property with such a sensitive ecosystem that supports precious species of flora and fauna justifies involvement in logging, an industry that attracts attention for its alleged lack of care for wildlife and plants. Tom tells me that Bangor has been used for forestry for over a century, but then forests were clear felled and practices were 'absolutely abysmal'. Tasmania has led the charge in terms of getting better practices in place. 'The changes have been amazing. Streams used to be considered good places to snig logs down. That was the industry standard. Nowadays there's a 40 metre buffer around streams where you can't even cut down a tree, let alone drive a machine.'

Cynthia said that the impact of logging native forest every 40 years was very small. Rehabilitation took ten years at the most. 'Twenty years later, you wouldn't know anyone had been there.' Cynthia continued to explain that companies no longer cut trees in wet weather and they always drag logs on the contour of hills. They leave bark, leaves and branches in the bush to rot down into nutrients. They avoid bird nesting areas and, consequently, a pair of wedge-tailed eagles, endangered in Tasmania, has been able to breed undisturbed and continuously in a protected part of the forest.

'We see it as using a resource before it dies in the forest,' Cynthia says of the enterprise. 'And most of our logging is selective logging, but selected according to what we want taken out of the bush, so not necessarily selecting the best timber to go away,' she said.

'The logging is tailored to the ecology of the forest, rather than just to the amount of wood that you can get out,' said Tom. This message soothed the anger of a very aggressive conservationist on one of the tours once he was shown where trees were being logged. 'He hadn't realised the logging companies could be so sensitive.'

'Without the income from the timber, we wouldn't be in the position we're in today,' Cynthia said. She explained that Bangor's system of all-weather roads which enable them to move stock without damaging sensitive bush, and drive trucks without leaving wheel ruts in winter, has been built by the timber companies. 'If we hadn't had that [timber] income, I don't know whether at this stage we would be continuing to fence off those riparian areas. And I don't think the public understand that. The message you get back is that you are just ripping off the forests and taking the money away, and that's not true. Without the economic sustainability, this place can't continue; something's got to give in the end. And the worst thing would be if we sold up all separate titles and we had shacks and humpies all over the place and more suburban sprawl.'

Tom and Cynthia see logging as simply part of the evolution of the property. In Tom's grandfather's day, they earned good money from possum and wallaby fur, which was used in the mills in England for spinning. They sold wattlebark for tanning hides and also fish. 'So he was into diversification too, and using a natural resource without having to rip any one area off,' Cynthia said.

All through the family's time at Bangor, Cynthia said it was evident that the land had been well looked after, even if in earlier years this was an unconscious intention because of lack of manpower, lack of technology, or because the family were concentrating on other priorities. Today's economic pressures made for a tougher balancing act. 'Just to set it in context, when Dad and his father were here, and Dad's brother, my uncle, they ran about 2000 sheep and they probably had 20 cows, and they earnt a living,' said Tom. 'Those three families [in the1950s and 1960s] lived off that. Now in the 1990s, we're talking about 6500 sheep, we're talking about 1200 prime lambs, we're talking about 150 cows and we're talking about a reasonably substantial forestry industry. We're still only talking about three families essentially that live here. So the same sort of human [load] requires many times more animals and much more productivity to support it. So that's the problem and that's the pressure that's always there.' Tourism, or another enterprise like horticulture, was essential to be added to the list.

In her clear, thoughtful voice, Cynthia said how food and fibre cost very little in relation to the income of people. 'Society demands that the land produce the basics of life at an ever cheaper rate . . . 'and I'm not sure that we can demand that the land do that and expect the people who are working the land to continue to do it too. I think society has got to realise that we have got to pay more for those goods to be able to put back into the land what we are taking off it, and I suspect that is the real gap between the people who have never been outside [cities], who don't actually understand what the land's got to do to produce what they're using.'

And so to their national and very significant win of the Landcare Nature Conservation award in 1996. Their entry in the award arose from their aim of promoting sustainable land use. They initially became involved in local primary producer Landcare awards. Writing applications and submissions helped them focus on exactly what it was they were achieving at Bangor. They had no thoughts of being successful when they entered the major award, they just wanted to spread their message. They were amazed when they won at state level. Before the national judging, film crews visited them but they say they thought nothing of it. They just continued working on the farm. All they had wanted was recognition that farmers were good conservationists. These two dedicated, passionate lovers of their land are determined to make a difference and leave an ecologically sound business for the next generation.

Full of regrets that I could not walk on those white sand beaches, wander through the bush finding orchids and the tracks of bettongs, or row a boat into the bay, I packed away my gear, whisked my mother out of the artist's studio where she was stocking up with pottery to make a northbound dash to Devonport. The seas were calm this time.

Part III

Raw Energy—Western Australia

Team Players—Lawry and Jenny Pitman

After a week at home to restock the freezer with lasagne and stews, I travelled west to cropping country and to visit Esperance's new land farms. This would be a huge contrast to the well-established, multi-generation Tasmanian farms. In Esperance I would be talking to the last of our pioneers— young, crazy optimists, short on money, high on raw energy and gambling on success. Their farms were virgin scrub as recently as 20 years ago.

I drove south-east from Perth by hired shopping trolley. Well, it felt like a shopping trolley, but was cheaper to fill. I left the rural fringe, passing through York with its main street of heritage buildings to Quairading and a tiny motel with a noisy air-conditioner and a telly with fuzzy pictures. I was entering hardworking cropping country. Silos looking like lunar landing modules dotted the paddocks. On the outskirts of each town were huge grain holding bins like oval-shaped 'meat pies' of seed but with the metal edges pushed up all round by little silver struts holding the generous amount of filling covered with a crust of green tarpaulin. That this is also salt country is reminded by constant ribbons of newly planted trees following every hollow and contour in little channels.

In the autumn morning light, the yellow stubbles are a loveliness of washed-out colour, a fragile balance of hues, briefly caught. In five minutes the picture has lost its delicacy, to be replaced by transparent blue sky, pure yellow paddocks, a dark green slash of scrub. Perfect tone balances. They could be a flag.

I broke the eight-hour drive to Esperance at Lawry and Jenny Pitman's place, in the Corrigin area. Their land was cleared and settled in about 1910, so it's long past new land status; but I was told not to miss out on seeing what the Pitmans were up to. On my approach, I saw young, vigorous tree plantations. But in the hollows, the white scourge lurks, looking as innocent as melting snow but with claws reaching out menacingly.

Lawry and Jenny Pitman

The paddocks around the house are dusty with stubbles lying flat after sheep have done their job of cleaning up seed and breaking down stalks. A house of brick, the colour of wheat, braces itself behind fortress walls against wind and drifted sand mounded up outside.

Jenny Pitman, instantly likeable and with a sport player's fit body, briskly greeted me, put a kettle on and got out hot muffins and mini-quiches. It is only 9.00am and I wasn't yet hungry, but homemade and inviting, they tasted good.

Lawry appeared, smiling, open-faced and built like a wharfie. An astute observation as it turned out. He later told me he had been a gymnast too. Ribbing and stirring in the best bush tradition, the three of us fell into easy talk like old friends.

Outside, their son Todd and a workman kept things ticking over. Sheep were being brought in and drafted for trucking, and machinery was being prepared for seeding as soon as the first rains fall.

Their property, Valema Farms, is being built into a radical new demonstration farm for sustainable land use. It is the focus of experiments, trials and demonstrations by an astonishing 33 different agencies, groups and sponsors. Organisations such as the CSIRO, Alcoa, Western Australia's Conservation and Land Management, Greening Australia, technology companies, fertiliser companies, the Grains Research and Development Corporation give their expertise, conduct their studies, collate their results and will make their findings known to the farming population at large. In effect, Lawry and Jenny have given their farm over to research, while still continuing to operate it profitably.

Through persistence, boundless energy and involvement in numerous conservation and farm industry bodies, Lawry has won sizeable grants to investigate methods of combating salinity, preventing soil deterioration, planting trees, attracting native birds and animals, controlling pests and weeds and achieving optimum crop yields. Lawry believes, since the demise of the Potter Farms project, theirs is currently the only privately owned demonstration farm in Australia which also incorporates total monitoring of inputs and outcomes. 'Someone has to do it,' he says of why they are willing to have their farm invaded by numerous researchers, curious farmers and the public. The inter-relation of water, chemicals, soil, animals and plants must be studied to avert further ecological destruction and to give farmers hope for their future.

'Everyone says this magic word sustainable, but nobody knows what it means,' Lawry said when we had sat down in comfortable big chairs to explore their lives, motivations and plans. 'We are putting it to the test.' He went on to say that he believed sustainable meant looking after the land so it went on into the future in sounder condition than in the present. Accordingly, everything—weeds, worms, birds, insects—will be measured. Satellite mapping using thermal imaging and Global Positioning Systems will be used to determine optimum fertiliser rates, yields, spray schedules and soil health.

A mighty team effort such as this couldn't be achieved by a shrinking violet. I suspected clues to its success had something to do with the rows of team sporting trophies in the room, marching along ledges, across mantelpieces, through display cabinets and on walls. As it turned out, Lawry, of football, golf, gymnastics and hockey prowess, had been so successful at involving his neighbours and local community in the project that many now see it as their own, believing they thought of it first. He takes that as a great compliment.

With National Heritage Trust funding of $150 000, a project co-ordinator with extensive experience in soil conservation has been appointed, along with a prominent farm consultant as his deputy. Their country, like that in much of the former mallee of southern Australia has rising water tables, salt-poisoned land killing trees and creating wastelands.

Lawry and Jenny Pitman are high-profile farming achievers who have won a national award as Australia's best wheat croppers, and a state award for their no-till methods of cropping, extensive tree planting and advances in soil technology. This determined bloke with the lovable nature and wholehearted approach to life must have had some sort of scientific background, I suggested.

None at all, he told me. After school in Perth, he went to the port of Wyndham way up north and worked on the wharves for seven months. Pocketing his savings, he indulged a dream and went to Africa, ostensibly to become a game park ranger. Instead, he found himself doing all sorts of other jobs, among them, driving an ambulance. He returned to help his father with harvest, then was about to leave for work on the Canadian–Alaskan pipeline when he met Jenny who was 20, ace hockey player and the local teacher. Lawry, then 23, got married and settled on the farm. 'I really have no qualifications. My big learning experience came from being secretary of the farm improvement group [at Corrigin], and all my development has come from marrying Jen.'

It's a wonder Jenny took him on. When she met him, Lawry didn't own a pair of shoes. His mother had died when Lawry was 19, leaving a four-year-old boy for his battling father to care for. The farm was run down and a bit of a mess. Housekeepers wouldn't stay in the job. They worked seven days a week, and Lawry had no money. 'She reckoned I had potential,' laughs Lawry. 'But most people knew that I didn't because I was just a long-haired git who regularly got drunk on the weekends. I couldn't even pay for her twenty-first. It was a sad situation. But things have changed a fair bit from those old days.'

'I guess when you are young, you can never imagine what your life's going to be like. We had no money and we had nowhere to live and we ended up in a caravan. If I had really thought about it, I would have known I would hate living in a caravan—and then we had our first son,' said Jenny. And then the old family home burnt down, the youngest brother was killed when he rode a motorbike into a branch and Lawry's poor, broken old dad gave up, moved to Perth and eventually remarried.

What was a dust bowl 18 years ago, created in his grandfather's and father's time through using the old-fashioned methods of ploughing and working back, is now highly profitable. It took a horrifying drought in 1980 to force them to revolutionise their methods using contours, direct drilling and stubble retention for humus. They planted 30 000 trees to lower the water table, provide shelter for stock and birds and reduce wind speed. Lawry has monitored his every change on the farm daily since 1978, which he says will be useful for the Valema Farms demonstration project. They bought out his father's original 5000 acre holding and increased it to 8000 acres, or 3000 hectares. They have a shed full of up-to-date machinery.

Just to prove the difference the new methods make they told me how the previous year had been well below their average rainfall, yet they harvested one of their best crops ever. 'The method that we used to put the crop in was what gave us the yield . . . the method of zero tillage, where we used points on the old scarifier that are the width of your little finger, so there was minimal disturbance. The loss of moisture is almost negligible.'

We had sat still for too long and needed a stretch. Noisy, bright blue, green, yellow and black twenty-eight parrots, as they are called in the west, Port Lincoln parrots in South Australia and elsewhere, were giving a tree near the back door a working over. They had recently destroyed Lawry and Jenny's pistacchio crop and weren't popular, even for bird lovers like the Pitmans. The pistacchio project will be lucrative one day they said, but parrot control needs attention.

Before Lawry got any grumpier with the parrots, I changed the subject and asked him to tell me about the wharves, topical since the

National Farmers' Federation attempts to overhaul the Melbourne docks. He obliged with relish. 'We were all crooks. We took as much money out of the system as we could, 28 years ago. The wharf would go on strike at the drop of a hat. It was one of the most radical unions, in Western Australia. I used to get fined for going too fast. When we used to steal the beer from the state ships, it was always easy to load the pallets up and put two pallets down the gap in the centre of the pallet load of beer. At midnight the train used to stop and all these wharfies would rush out of the bush and grab a couple of cartons of beer each, whack them under their arms and disappear back into the night. That was the done thing up there in those days, and there was a lot of other skulduggery that went on.

'If you wanted a ship to go slow, we used to have a six-man gang working two hours on and two hours off. If you wanted to work on the weekend and there were no more ships coming in, you just sent one guy to the toilet for a couple of hours in your shift, and as everyone knows in a six-man gang if there's one missing, you can't work. So everyone would sit down and break open a crate of ice-cream or something, and just say it was damaged and have ice-cream for a couple of hours.

'So the experience that I had up there as a wharfie with a farm worker's ethic, was really quite difficult. The ethic as a wharfie is you make the job last as long as possible so there is always a job there. If it lasts through to the weekend you get double time, double time and a half, triple time. It's very hard coming from a farm, where you know you can get a job finished in an hour, so why take three hours to do it? That was my ethic. I became the head forklift driver in Wyndham just because of my skills at being able to judge with machinery but also because of my work ethic. I got a lot of pride out of being able to do the job a bit faster each time as my skills grew. But that's not the ethic that they had, and it was quite repulsive. Even though I had a lot of fun with the wharfies, I couldn't really stand them.'

Lawry said he got right into the spirit of the Wyndham wharfies by raising his very own grievance to incite a strike. 'I'd been doing this go-slow on the ship and I'd done my third two-hour stint in the toilet and was really getting sick of it. It had that shiny toilet paper—you know, shiny one side and rough the other—and I didn't appreciate the end results of using that. So I got to [a] union meeting and said, okay, I refuse to do any work on the wharf until we get Sorbent toilet paper. Being persistent and wanting to make my mark on the port of Wyndham, I continued with it. Got it through the meeting eventually and it was decided they'd go on strike for two weeks if they didn't get Sorbent in the toilet at Wyndham. And I got it there, so I made my mark.' Not one of which he says he is greatly proud.

It was late afternoon, after much laughter and talk, that Lawry and I discovered we had a major passion in common—bush stone curlews. In their district only four of these ground-nesting birds with the high haunting cry remain. In my district, on our farm, just two birds from what was a large population, remain. Foxes, cats and dogs have ravaged nesting curlews in all southern states. I have put netting and electric fencing around our birds' nesting site and the coming spring will be their first opportunity to nest safely. Lawry initiated a community fox eradication project which won a state award and went on to achieve second place in the national Landcare awards.

I finished up by asking Lawry what it takes to be a farmer these days. You have to be relaxed he said, to put up with everything that can go wrong, with new regulations and the pressures of farming. You also need to be open-minded and optimistic. As to the future, while it would be wonderful if his two sons or daughter went on with the project and the farm, that was their decision.

'We look at our kids and our future, and we don't know what's going to happen. You can't really plan too far ahead for them, to know what they're going to do, or how they're going to turn out,' said Jenny.

'I suppose that is the whole art of being a good farmer, is your flexibility and being able to ride with whatever comes and whatever problems are thrown at you' said Lawry.

On the way to Corrigin I screeched the trolley to a stop when I saw a large sculpture of a kelpie sitting by the roadside, with nothing but paddocks all around. Behind the kelpie were rows of neat plots with inscriptions of heart-tearing poignancy. This was a cemetery where working dogs and best mates are buried. For half an hour I wandered between the graves, reading headstones and wishing that I had known of this special place when the books of working dogs' stories were being put together. Then on to Kulin for the night before a big drive next day.

UPDATE: Early this year, Todd, the eldest son of Lawry and Jenny, was killed in a car accident.

The Pitmans are finalists in Western Australia for the 1999 National Landcare awards.

Pioneers in the Land of Hope... and Glory—Mick Quinlivan

Over long, undulating kilometres I travelled the rest of the way towards the town of Esperance, located on the southern coast of Western Australia—a place of ravishing beauty. But first a bit of background.

Before the film star Americans came in 1956—Art Linkletter and others who are now largely forgotten—this was a quiet port town of 700 people and a holiday site for workers from four hours up the road at Kalgoorlie. The lure of two million acres of virgin scrub in good rainfall areas made valuable following trace element research of the time, saw the Western Australian Labor government wooed to hand the parcel over to US developer Allen Chase. The Esperance Land Development (ELD) company took over from Allen Chase in 1960 with serious American long-haul investors with which the new Western Australian Liberal government negotiated a development pact. Large, established pastoral families such as the McBrides and Kidmans, as well as powerful US corporate investors, were among those who took up early parcels of land. During the 1970s, however, wool, grain and beef prices fell, and so did interest in ELD land. Since ELD was committed to taking up 100 000 acres every year to meeting development contracts and selling off 50 000 acres to fund more work, the company decided to entice a new breed onto the blocks.

Full of enthusiasm but with little money, young hopefuls from all over Australia were lured west to try their luck in the land ballots and make their farming fortunes. They paid 10 per cent deposit for a block of land of some 3000 acres priced at about $25 000. If they grew a crop successfully, many could pay off ELD and have freehold title to their own farm in a year or two. This was to be the last release of land in temperate, higher rainfall areas, so it was seen as an opportunity not to be missed. It took guts and blind faith to foresee productive farms carved out of endless kilometres of squat mallee. Awash with the spirit of adventure, they toiled in the dust with makeshift machinery, far from neighbours or a shop. Many failed. Heaps survived. I had made the trip to speak to some of the survivors.

Mick Quinlivan

First, I dropped in for a chat with Mick Quinlivan, who joined ELD in 1965 and was the bloke these young hopefuls had to impress if they were to be allocated land. ELD is now called Esperance Rural Properties, and is owned by National Mutual.

These days Mick, aged 56, is responsible for 85 staff, 220 000 acres spread over 11 properties, 22 000 head of cattle, 220 000 sheep, 24 000 hectares of crops and a large cattle feedlot . . . and that's just his Esperance Rural Properties job. He has 17 000 acres of his own land, a sheep stud, 18 000 sheep, 8000 acres of crop and about 400 cows. I didn't ask what he did in his spare time.

In 1973, Mick became psychologist, finance assessor and counseller at his office for streams of young men with dusty battered vehicles after the long unsealed drive across the Nullarbor. Full of hope in this remote town meaning Hope, they needed to be people who could handle isolation and have some chance of earning enough money to pay for their land. Most had little hands-on agricultural experience. 'Esperance was all first generation farmers,' Mick said of the lads willing to roll the dice. None were sons of farmers.

'I thought the most important thing was a little bit of intelligence,' Mick says of how, at the age of 30, he had to make decisions about who would win and who would lose. One of the best tests of intelligence was, 'I would observe they would leave the chequebook at home when they came to town.' Favoured applicants usually had some sort of training, but above all they needed to have a bit of fire in the belly—and if they had a partner she had to be just as keen to succeed.

He recalls that some walked into his office 20 years ago and could hardly raise the deposit they needed. Today they are doing very well. Having had such a big part in helping these young people make their way in life, as well as being involved in opening up such a huge tract of country, gives Mick great satisfaction.

The productivity of those two million acres means Esperance with its beautiful beaches, mild climate and the buoyant spirit of a frontier town, has a population of 12 000 people and great facilities. It is the site of two coastal wind-power generating plants which contribute 16 per cent of the district's needs into the local diesel-generated supply.

Culture Shock—Kirsten and Peter Biven

Before leaving home I had spoken to numerous people involved with Esperance asking for names of likely subjects. I kept getting the same answer, 'You should speak to the Biven boys.' I said I had heard of them, but was there anyone else? 'Yeah, sure, there are plenty, but Peter and Mark Biven have done pretty well for themselves. They'd give you a good story. They're the ones.' I really didn't want to talk to these blokes. It's not that they were pathetic drunks or known criminals... it's just that they happened to be my brothers.

Anyway, after agonising for a few days I decided to go with the flow. Why not? Besides, I hadn't suggested them, others had. And I admit I was delighted at the prospect of putting their story into the archives.

On Karl Berg Road, 115 kilometres east of Esperance, smooth clay roads between remnant scrub of banksia, she-oak and mallee, I was looking for a track on the right. Paddocks of stubble and pasture, driveways of tall trees, proud signs at front gates alongside creative mailboxes and there it was, a wooden house on what is called a hill in this area.

Waiting with an assortment of bouncing, smiling dogs were Kirsten and Peter Biven, both still in their forties, yet with 23 years of pioneering behind them. Kirsten, at the age of 19, came to Australia in 1975 from Denmark in search of adventure and the 'lovely bloke' she had met while they were on agricultural exchange in Canada. She was accompanied by a friend who had also been greatly impressed by the handsome moleskin-clad, suntanned Australian farmers who for the second part of the exchange conveniently worked on Danish farms not too far from their homes.

Kirsten, from an aristocratic and beautiful Danish dairy farm near Aarhus, in Jutland, joined Peter on his 'Go West Young Man' mission to find his fortune. They travelled from Adelaide to Esperance in his dilapidated 1964 Holden station wagon a month after Kirsten's arrival in Australia. Her version of the trip across the Nullarbor to a place she had

Kirsten and Peter Biven

no hope of envisaging is glorious. She still speaks with the ringing clear voice of the Danes, somewhat like the sound of bone china being flicked by a fingernail. Yet, fine and as small as she is, she carries within her all the spirit and daring of her Viking past.

'It was a total culture shock. Pete and I didn't have plates or anything to look after ourselves. I just had my suitcase and my clothes. So we went out and bought blankets, cutlery and things we needed on the trip. On the way over I kept looking at the roadsigns and saying to Peter, this place, where is it? I mean there is a name here but there is no place. And he'd say, well, did you see that house back there? And I realised these places had a lot of names and not many houses, which I wasn't used to. The gravel road across was still there, full of big potholes. It was before the sealed road came in, and they obviously hadn't done much maintenance on it for a while because the potholes were huge. We took a long time getting over. The old car didn't do it very fast and we had to stop [at night]. I was too scared to sleep on the ground because before I left [Denmark], I had heard about Australia having an excess amount of snakes and scorpions. I thought it was littered with them all over the place, so I preferred to sleep in the car. By the time I got over here I was quite worried about what Esperance was like.

'We called into Gibson, where Peter's friends were. It was a little town about 25 kilometres out of Esperance, and all my worst fears came [true]. We pulled up where these three or four young bachelors had been living for quite a number of months. I don't think the dishes or the bathroom had been cleaned for the same number of time. I remember being asked if I wanted anything to eat and decided I wasn't hungry at all. And then they just looked at us and thought they'd better find us a place to sleep for the night. Over at the grain cleaning shed there was this old dusty room full with spiders. They chucked a few blankets in there and that was where we camped the night.' Kirsten laughs at the desperate memory of it.

'It was an awful sleep and I just wondered where I had ended up. First of all I was missing the beautiful green trees of Denmark and the luxuries of being able to have a shower and all these sorts of things we take for granted. The scrub down from Norseman and on the way over ... the small stunted trees, it has actually taken me years to enjoy the mallee. It looked pretty stunted and blunted for me.'

It was hardly surprising Kirsten should yearn for home. 'I can remember as a child thinking we lived far away because I had two kilometres to the school bus, and eight kilometres to school, and the city was over 20 kilometres away which was a bit of a hike. I thought I was used to not having people around me all the time.' The contrast with her new-found and extreme isolation is sobering for those of us who have never relocated. 'I was from a lovely old farmhouse, with barns and all that belongs to a Danish farmhouse. It had been burnt in 1800, then rebuilt, with three storeys, three living rooms, and a downstairs kitchen. It is a lovely old house.'

Being thrown blankets to sleep in a dreadful shed in Gibson was rather outside her realm of experience. 'Yes, I was wondering how I could get out of there quickest, but there didn't seem to be any sort of public transport nearby. So I thought I'd be in the spirit of it and see what happened next. It couldn't be worse.'

'After sleeping a night and a half in this awful place, I think I must have looked distressed enough that we went into town to see if we could find some nice accommodation,' says this girl who knew no-one except Peter and her Danish travelling friend who by now was far away. 'Luckily enough, we found a little flat next to the sea, and I was pacified by that at that stage. The beaches in Esperance just blew me away, they're fabulous.'

Peter, a Glenormiston Agricultural College graduate and a quiet, thinking man, says he came to Esperance for a challenge and to get away from South Australia, and grabbed the chance soon after arriving to get into a block of land with a business partner. 'You had only to pay $2000 to acquire these 3000 acre farms, of which a third was ploughed and ready for cropping or nearly ready, and two-thirds was bush. We put our first crop in in 1976. With lots of hard work it came off quite well.' He makes it sound easy. After putting down a deposit on the total cost of $22 000, he said the hardest task was raising money for fertiliser. 'We got a guarantee from another farmer for that. We borrowed a lot of machinery and tractors.'

With the block being so far out of town at the end of very rough roads, Peter and his partner lived in an old school bus they had bought. 'It was pretty dirty, full of mice and rats, and it wasn't particularly comfortable,' Peter recalls with a wince. Kirsten stayed in town and worked as a barmaid and cleaner to bring in funds for their living expenses. 'Luckily for us, the season was good and the crop came off really well. It was a fabulous crop.' And what's more, after the slump in wheat prices that had turned most people off developing blocks, grain prices rose.

'The year we went wheat farming, the price of wheat went from $60 to $100 [tonne]. We got about 800 tonne of wheat off that first year. We shared about $80 000.' Peter bought out his partner, leased the grain cleaning works where they had spent their first disastrous nights in the district and earned enough to employ contractors to clear the bush and do the blade ploughing.

Kirsten recalls her first encounter with the block which was to be her home. 'If Gibson had been a culture shock, this was a double culture shock. The first time Peter showed me the block which he was very thrilled about having bought, he threw the sand up and said, look at this. And I looked and I really couldn't see much else than small bushes compared to the other big bushes . . . and I thought, this is nice, what are we doing next?' For someone who seems to be able to take shocks in her stride Kirsten says she was amazed that the land actually produced a crop for the partners. 'Because they only had one tractor, they worked 12-hour shifts at a time each, so one took the night shift and one took the day shift.'

For $2000 in 1977 they bought an old house in the main street of Esperance. 'I think last time it sold it was $200 000,' Peter says, laughing at how things have changed in such a short time. With a base in town, Peter and Kirsten were then able to move out to their block to get stuck full-time into clearing, root raking, ploughing and seeding. Their weekday home there for seven years was a caravan. Peter is somewhat reluctant to call the move to their own farm, at that stage, exciting.

With no power or rainwater tank, conditions were far from luxurious. 'It's amazing what you can do with a 44 gallon drum of water for a week,' Kirsten says, smiling. 'You can have showers, you can even wash some clothes and have your tea and your coffee or whatever else.' Then she adds reflectively 'It was hard,' remembering the dust from the newly cleared land that covered everything, the heat and lack of shade and the muddy, cold winters.

Pete agrees. 'Really hard.' But they upgraded to a bigger van with an inbuilt shower. They built a machinery shed and at last could collect water in a 1000 gallon tank. 'In those early 1980 years, things didn't go particularly well for us financially,' Peter says. 'We had a lot of crop failures and things got pretty tough. And at times then, we nearly thought of giving it away. It was hard to borrow money. We didn't have much equity and bank managers weren't particularly interested in lending money to new land farmers. Slowly, but slowly, we managed to claw our way back, didn't we?'

'Yes, ever so slowly at times. There were lots of ups and downs. We never ever thought we were going to see electricity out here or even telephones,' says Kirsten. But ten years ago they were able to retire the diesel generator and they have had the phone on for 15 years now—a great relief. 'It was just hopeless without a telephone. For four or five years, we had to drive all the way to McMora, about 25 kilometres away over a really rough road to make a phone call, organise to get super and so on . . . It was absolutely terrible.'

I wondered what kept them battling on through the hardships.

'Peter always dreamt about having his own bit of dirt, and I must have been slightly ignorant, because I thought, well, the Australians, they know how to do it tough so I wasn't going to let the side down,' she says with a tinkly laugh. 'I wasn't going to go screaming home to Mum and Dad saying I can't cope. It was an adventure and in the beginning we were young and full of energy, that sort of thing.'

It was lucky they liked each other—when they moved out to their block there weren't many others around. But when others did come, the fun really started.

'We had a lot of bravado between each other,' says Kirsten, who with her outsider's eyes sharply observed the customs and habits of the strange inhabitants of her new country. 'We had huge laughs, we had parties on the road, everybody was in the same boat. It was all have-nots, there were not many haves at these places, so we were moral support for each other. We had a good adventure. It was adventure, many of the things we did in those days. Like the way we lit up the fires to burn the blocks. I mean, you couldn't do it that way now,' and they fall about laughing as they reminisce about life before regulations. They'd be out in shorts and thongs instead of proper fire overalls and boots—when getting the job done was all that mattered, before bureaucracy put its papers out and organised seminars about safety.

'And if it was a good fire we'd celebrate with a carton of beer afterwards, and we would sit in the middle of the road because there never came a car. If they should come, they were more than likely to join in—so it was slightly bushranger country'.

'Remember that big storm?' Peter asks Kirsten. 'We had lit up our back paddock called the Dog Leg, which is about five kilometres from the back of the farm, as usual without a permit or anything . . . We had had a lot of trouble burning this particular country because it had been burnt once before. It was pretty light scrub. We lit this thing and it was getting windier and windier. Then to the north-west I saw this enormous black cloud and I remember thinking gee, it's going to rain. It wasn't rain, it was a huge Cock-eye Bob storm and it was dust and the wind was about a good 150 kilometres an hour and it went right through this fire. We just managed to scramble for our lives to the truck. Kirsten had to leave her shoes down there because we were in such a hurry. We couldn't find our way, there was so much dust from all the new land right round the district. It was an enormous storm. The shed nearly blew away. Kirsten's sister was over from Denmark visiting us. She must have been shocked. It was just an enormous storm. Anyway, we went back the next day to see what happened to the fire and it'd burnt the entire paddock, even stuff we thought would never burn. Then we went and found Kirsten's shoes.'

'My Danish clogs—I still have them.' And, sure enough, there they were by the back door, tough survivors.

On the practicalities of living and keeping food cold, Kirsten said they ate lots of potatoes, onions and pumpkins, things that kept well. The generator was on for just a few hours a day to save money. 'It was very much a question of making do. Hot water came from a copper. I had to heat up water, and Peter erected a little shed with a little 20 litre drum and a shower rose underneath it. For half a bucket of water you can manage to get shampoo and conditioner in, if you are very careful.'

The famous copper, painted green and growing plants, now stands on the back verandah where we were sitting overlooking a garden, swimming pool and paddocks with Kirsten's and the children's horses. Each weekend in the caravan days, they would trek back to town to the house to wash clothes, have fun, do business and make phone calls.

'We had to make sure the bank manager didn't see the state of our car when we went in,' says Kirsten of any mid-week trips. 'It was the guarantee for one of our loans and if he had seen the car I think he would have withdrawn.' They had told him they had a later model than it actually was. 'I was under strict instructions to park it at the other end of the street before I walked into the bank.'

Peter said that although other new land areas were doing well, it had been very difficult to get loans. 'I don't think you were supposed to come to an area like this without any money whatsoever and try to start off with not even having a spanner to your name. It was almost impossible to do it.

'Until that first crop, a lot of people hadn't thought it was possible to grow that sort of crop out here,' he says. 'That sparked interest in the area . . . but nobody wanted to go that far out and there was nothing out here. So you have to have some ignorant people to go and do it first up!'

It wasn't easy, as a city-bred person with no financial backing from family, to get into farming. Esperance was the only place it could be done, Peter said, and there were plenty there who had managed to do the same, working as shearers or contractors, and having a bit of luck with the seasons.

'If that first crop hadn't come off we would have been in a lot of strife.' Twenty-three years down the track, they have bought other farms, have a total of 5500 acres and are financially stable.

In 1980, they went back to Denmark and got married. Kirsten said as a child she had read books about pioneers in Canada and America. 'Here I was, I had ended up becoming a pioneer in Australia so they were very much in awe of it all and quite sympathetic to it all,' says Kirsten of her family's reaction to her unconventional lifestyle. 'It never occurred to the Danes that water was not something that came out of a tap, that we have to actually collect it from the roof.' Then they built the cosy wooden log cabin on the hill with Danish reminders everywhere—blue and white family china, photographs, tapestries, Danish timber chairs.

At the block, the ten to twelve-hour days continued. 'If Peter was the boss, I was everything else,' Kirsten said. 'We worked together. I was as much on the tractor as Peter.' In summer, they went clover harvesting. It is particularly dusty and monotonously boring work, but very lucrative. 'I got so bored that I decided to take a book with me,' Kirsten confesses, 'but that didn't do much good, because you drive at about five kilometres an hour or less than that, trying to keep a straight line . . . I'd veer off line as soon as I got into a good bit.' The only work she got out of was fixing tractors and mending tyres.

Peter said no amount of agricultural college training could ever prepare anyone for the sort of work they were doing. Mostly it was a matter of feeling your way, asking people who'd tried different methods. There were always new problems to be faced, diseases in crops, mistakes that were made, the balancing act between indoor and outdoor jobs when babies started in 1981—and then a few droughts as well.

'I remember coming home from hospital with our son in 1983 and driving in the driveway,' Kirsten recalls. 'The shorn sheep had to be stood up against the weather. It was June and it was very adverse and the condition of the sheep was dismal. There hadn't been any rain and they were simply so skinny they were falling over. We spent all day going out and standing them up and that was depressing.'

Giving birth in the bush anywhere is fraught with uncertainty and often drama. The first of their three children was born in 1981, before they had a telephone and neighbours were far away. Kirsten tells the story with stoic amusement.

'If you're slightly ignorant and don't know what can go wrong, you don't worry quite to the same degree as you do otherwise.' When the day dawned, however, Peter was out in the paddock, she was at home with no car and no means of communication. When Peter did eventually return, they set off in haste to make the long, bumpy one-and-a-half-hour trip to town. 'It only got panicky when we ran out of fuel,' says Kirsten, laughing. 'The poor car had no fuel gauge, and Pete had been panicking about putting fuel in this car all the time, but obviously it must have slipped his mind. He thought he had filled it up the day before. On the way into town, I think it was 30 kilometres out of town or something like that, putt, putt, putt, and the car ran out of fuel. I had quite strong contractions at that stage and I can remember this lady, an elderly lady stopped, and she said, anything wrong? The classic thing Pete said was, my wife is having a baby. And I remember thinking to myself, I don't believe it, I just don't believe it. This lady didn't offer us a lift. She offered to take Pete in to get fuel to the car. So off they went to get fuel to the car,' she says with rising inflection, and I am amazed that Kirsten can laugh about it, but she does, and quite heartily. I for some reason had thoughts of Monty Python, and Mr Bean.

'So they got fuel to the car and we got in on time and everything went well, but . . . it was a bit clumsy,' and she is still laughing. Being left by the side of a lonely road in the middle of nowhere, far from parents, friends, in a strange country, with contractions coming fast . . . and she can laugh about it. What a woman.

Peter follows this with a Dad and Dave impersonation. 'In hindsight, we should have taken her in, I suppose, to the hospital and got the car later. But we didn't think of that.'

Kirsten said the biggest hurdle to face in having a child was not that she had no extended family to help her but that she could no longer help Peter outside. 'We had to adjust a lot to that because Pete was out there doing it all himself, and I often felt slightly guilty not being able to go out and help.'

As the years went on and a few more babies arrived in the district, playgroups began and women gave each other support. 'You became very understanding of other people, because you realised how hard the change to motherhood was in the country. It was a huge step.' The school for the expanding child numbers was 50 kilometres away by school bus.

The cycles keep turning: from frantic development, breeding, building a community, to looking longer term with the leisure time afforded by having huge machines and using modern methods. 'Farming practices are a lot better now with spraying of weeds and direct drilling of crops,' Peter says. 'You are much more assured of an income. Years ago you'd only budget for six bags an acre, now we budget for between ten and twelve.'

Tree planting and shelter had always been a high priority from the early clearing days, especially for Kirsten who was used to huge oaks and elms. Vast plantings of advanced trees now border their paddocks and the natural salt lakes.

'It was amazing how little information there was when we started to clear the land,' Kirsten says. 'I remember going to the Agriculture Department to try to work out how to clear the land in the best way to leave some shrub behind, how to do it best for windbreaks, how far between, how wide these windbreaks should be, what trees to plant, but there was virtually no information to be got about that. That led to a lot of overclearing. If we had known what we know today, we would have left a lot wider windbreaks.'

Peter tells of the salinity problems that became evident after several very wet years. Dry land salinity is now acknowledged as Australia's most serious environmental problem.

'All of a sudden we noticed salt crystals on the soil in lower areas where we used to crop. You could see the way we were going certainly wasn't sustainable. So we had a bit of a panic and went straight into tree planting and up till about 1994, we had planted tens of thousands of trees and shrubs and I think we are quite confident now we have turned the situation around. Where we had bare scalds we have now got rye grass and clover starting to come back on those areas where they had previously grown, before the water table came up. If you're going to take all this bush away that has been here for thousands of years keeping the water table in equilibrium, you're going to ask for trouble. You've got to counter that and not overclear. It was something the Department of Agriculture had seen happen around the rest of the areas of the state but had completely forgotten or were not aware or weren't interested in informing the farmers of Esperance. We made exactly the same mistakes as they made around the rest of the wheat belt.' Peter said he had been told by a senior department officer that he had no salt problem, even when it was obvious.

'I thought, if he didn't know anything it was best to attack it myself.' Peter planted saltbush and trees around the low-lying areas. His idea was to soak up the water in the low-lying areas and use high-yielding crops in the high areas—use the water at the bottom of the hill, and you'll have no trouble at the top of the hill. He says the theory seems to be working.

Peter pioneered the introduction of saltbush to control salinity into his area. He initially tried 200 plants around a salt lake, and within a year they were two metres high, had started to self-germinate and spread. The next year he tried a couple of thousand, but many died as they were planted too close to the salt scald. The following year, he put 5000 in and they were more successful but when he tried to order more, he was told he couldn't have them unless he took 30 000 plants.

'I didn't want 30 000, so I rang up everyone in the area who I thought had a salt problem and asked them if they would consider buying any, and everyone did. Since then, of the people who ordered them, most of them are still planting saltbush each year. So there are quite substantial plantings in the district.'

As well as there now being time to care for the land, its pioneers can also indulge themselves. Kirsten started studying art in 1984 on her weekly shopping days in town and is now completing a diploma at university externally. The pine walls of the house are hung with her works.

And so to the future . . . Peter says the heady excitement of the early days has now past. 'It has probably taken its toll on us, all the hard times, although there are good times now. You are only in this life for a short time, and I think there are other things to do and see. I would say that within three or four years we will probably be gone from here.' They would lease the farm to their son or daughters if they wanted it. 'I would never take on something like this again, I can tell you,' he says quietly.

'There comes a stage when you have been through this, that the thought of another downturn would see me running for cover,' Kirsten says. 'The thought of going through hardship again, because you are under no illusions about it any more, has put me off.'

'Those hard times are always in the back of your head,' Peter says. 'You certainly don't want to make a bad decision and end back there and have to struggle. It's been good to pay back all your debts and loans and virtually worry about how much tax you have to pay each year now.

'Certainly Kirsten or I don't see ourselves living out here for any more than 25 years. I think that will do.'

Burning Ambition— Mark and Jan Biven

Mark Biven's story is similar to his brother's in broad terms, but it is illustrative in demonstrating the fierce and almost desperate drive these pioneers possessed. No careers counsellor, financial adviser, bank manager or any of the other experts such as those to pass judgment over our futures would ever have looked at this young city-reared man without money, without agricultural experience and without outside support of wife or family and said, 'Son, go for it.' For a start, Mark had not shown a great deal of interest in settling in one place. He had been on the move almost constantly after finishing four years of agriculture college training—working on fishing boats, at a merino stud in Tasmania, then travelling the world for 18 months where he, among other things, had worked on an oil rig in the North Sea. Mark said he had been searching for a future. The letter that changed his life reached him in England in 1976. Peter told him there was land for $9 an acre in Western Australia.

'I kept reading this letter and I must have read it about four times because I couldn't really believe it. After my four years at Roseworthy, we were always told, you will never get on the land because it's impossible. So this dream and this letter and I thought, hell, I've got to get over there.' He rushed back to Adelaide, bought a ute and a week later, at the age of 24, was on the road to get himself a farm. He arrived in December to find Peter had already put his name on a block they were to share and was offering him work harvesting his first crop. He was stoked.

'And then I saw the machine I was meant to drive. It didn't have any cabin or anything like that. It just had a seat. I didn't even get an umbrella! I did that for two months. Nowadays, I think our harvest takes three weeks.' He lived in the mouse-infested school bus, worked all day, had a 44 gallon drum of water and one of petrol, was chucked a bit of food—and loved it. 'I couldn't get over the sunsets. It must have been coming out of Europe, being always so cloudy. The tranquillity and vastness were very inspiring.'

Like Peter, Mark bought some second-hand machinery, did it up

For Love of the Land

Mark and Jan Biven

and went sharefarming and contracting. He also bought himself some fencing plant and was in high demand stringing up wires throughout the district. Fooling around one day playing games with the post rammer, he lost a few fingers when it thumped down on the post, and another time, rolled his beloved ute and wrote it off, but by now, infected with new land fever, he had found his goal.

In 1978, Peter passed over the lease on the block 10 kilometres from his that they initially were going to share. Mark was under way—but this block, unlike a lot of the new land up until then was not partially cleared. There were 3000 acres of bushes and trees growing in soil that was yet to be explored. It took a massive leap of faith to see wheatfields, pony paddocks, a house with smoke coming out of the chimney in the middle of a mallee wilderness. With the sort of co-operation commonplace among the early settlers, and borrowed machinery, Mark managed to chain, burn and clear 60 acres to produce seed wheat for future crops. He lived alone in a caravan like plenty of other single blokes and remembers them being great days. At the end of the day, these single blokes, freed of conventions such as dressing for dinner, or even washing because there wasn't water to spare, would gather like a bunch of half-wild savages for a few beers and a meal of unspeakable bachelor food supplemented by one of the ownerless sheep that conveniently wandered the roads.

I had visited Mark about that time and spent a few days in the caravan. It was a totally free and wild life with just one motivation—work towards the goal of a farm. Esperance, being so far east of Perth, is in a time zone all its own. The summer sun would rise at 3.00am and so would we. Mark was bagging seed from that initial 60 acres and we would work until we were hungry at about 7.00am, have a huge breakfast of sausages, eggs, bacon and tonnes of bread, then get back into the work. Peripheral things such as dirt, heat, fresh vegetables and clean clothes were ignored. It was an uncomplicated, goal-driven existence where friends and community were the treasured supports for diffusing stress, loneliness, giving advice and for providing high-spirited entertainment.

'You would never drive down the road in those days and pass a car. You would pull up and stop because you always knew who it was. You would sit there for hours, chatting away. It has changed a lot since then.'

You can imagine the talk . . . disasters, the good burns like the one when Mark and his helpers lit up four sides of 2000 acres of chained country. The heat from that fire became so intense that it drew to the centre and looked from afar like the atom bomb rising over Hiroshima.

The sound of debris falling out of the sky was like a roaring jet.

They'd no doubt laugh about the time a friend killed one of those road sheep and thought he would store it in Mark's fridge, presumably because he didn't have one. Unfortunately, he didn't check the gas. 'So when I got back to the caravan to show my future bride, my pride and joy this expanse of land, we opened the door, and this green slime juice, with an unbelievable stinking stench, slipped out the caravan door from the fridge full of meat, turned off for two weeks.' This was Jan Biven's first encounter with the block. A city girl, she was having a few problems even identifying the mass of bush as a farm . . . then having to deal with a fridge of rotten meat. You can only marvel at the powers of persuasion of a man on a mission! Mind you, it took him a few years to talk Jan into giving up a life of exotic overseas travel, midwifery, and the comforts of cities. She was in no hurry to live in the middle of nowhere, as she once described the future farm, now called Paningunya, on Beaumont Road.

In the meantime, Mark made trips back to Adelaide to bring back the necessities of life. One trip back over the Nullarbor in the ute with Peter, they had Mark's huge brass bed and a desk loaded on the back. They thought they had tied it on pretty well but when they hit a wind squall at Balladonia, the brass bed and dozens of boxes of cereal given as survival rations from their other brother who worked for Kelloggs, took flight. 'I had had enough. I was in tears and Peter was trying to console me, and he was laughing. I saw my brass bed going end over end down the highway, bits flying off everywhere. And cornflakes and rice bubbles everywhere.' Later, that would have been another story to raise a loud laugh around the caravan table.

In 1979, Mark had his first success—a big wheat crop of 900 acres. 'At the end of that summer, I think I had over $100 000 in the bank, and I thought, gee, that was easy. I couldn't believe it.

'I was very grateful to all the business people I had got to know in town because I didn't really have much money [until harvest] to buy fertiliser. Everything was "on the drip"—my blade ploughing was on credit, the fuel was on credit, fertiliser was on credit. You had to go and say to these people, please I am having a go, can you lend me some money. And they did, and that was great.

'I was very green, very naive on a lot of things, but I coped. Everyone was supportive. You were trying to create your own dream and we were pretty focused. Once you got into it, you weren't going to give it up quickly.' Nevertheless, plenty did give up and he saw a huge turnover of people.

Mark and Jan Biven

It is a bit trite to say that it took a special sort of female to take on the life, especially if she was out of the city. Mark met Jan, a nurse, at a wedding in Adelaide, suggested she have a holiday in Esperance, and wangled a job in Esperance for her. But after six months of nursing, driving tractors, collecting spare machinery parts and being part of the pioneer life, she decided that life in a rural frontier wasn't totally appealing. She disappeared overseas for another sixteen months of fun, and returned to marry her 'ambitious pioneer' in 1982. By then, the farm was up and away.

Jan, with a fulsome sense of humour and sharp appreciation of the ridiculous, attacked farming with gusto. She drove tractors, was a shed hand, became a qualified owner-classer of wool, and a tree planter. They entertained with dinner parties in a new big caravan where people sat on oil drums and eskies while Jan produced homemade bread from the oven—and every single bloke in the district would magically turn up if there was a roast on.

Jan's first impressions of Mark's dream farm were not quite in accordance with his. 'The only other farms I really had ever visited were picturesque with little rivers and big red gums, and when he said he had this farm, I though that's what it would be. I didn't think it was going to be a big flat paddock with nothing in it . . . At that time I didn't realise land was still being cleared in Australia, so it was quite surprising to know that could still be done.'

What these women had to put up with . . . if it was in the city, you'd have these blokes for every sin on the books! Jan writes in a memoir published in an account of the times *(Faith, Hope and Reality: Esperance 1895–1995)*:

> Being a greenhorn I got all the rotten jobs, like fire harrowing in an open tractor until I was completely black. Chaining was a particularly awful job, with dust and sticks swirling around an open cab. One day I could hardly see what I was doing, my eyes were full of dust and grit and I was obviously doing all the wrong things, judging by the frantic hand signals Mark was giving me from his personal tractor, the air-conditioned International with stereo. He marched across to tell me, yet again, what he wanted me to do. To this day I'm not sure what snapped inside him but, looking at me scraping dust and debris from my ears and nostrils, he took pity and told me to go and drive his tractor. It was a lovely thought but, of course, I believed that 'stupid me' couldn't possibly drive this revered, high-tech, expensive and complicated machine. It was at this

point he finally had to tell me the truth—that in fact it was pretty easy, once you worked out which way to put the cassettes in and how to turn on the air-conditioning. I was so furious with him and myself for being so gullible, but as I sat and watched him get dirty, I started to enjoy it. It was quite amazing that within a month we had a second air-conditioned tractor, one to call my very own.

By 1984, with clover harvesting and some good cropping years, they had established themselves well. These days Paningunya isn't far from the stereotype Jan once imagined. There is a stately front drive lined with trees. There are well-planned laneways, fine sheds housing huge pieces of state-of-the art machinery, a lovely brick house and well-established and beautiful garden. They have three great children, and no debt.

So life moves to the next phase and it seems the cycle has moved fast. Now children from the district have moved off to boarding schools in Perth, the school bus to the local school where once there were 32 children from the district on board, is emptying out. The community hall built through the efforts of Mark and Jan and a team of other enthusiasts and the help of a $100 000 grant is not as busy as it used to be when there was playgroup, tennis coaching, community celebrations, meetings and church with a visiting minister.

Mark and Jan's focus is now on Landcare and using progressive soil-friendly cropping methods of no-till and global positioning satellites for fertiliser and sprays. They are also enthusiastic about planting saltbush to combat the rapidly rising water table but are frustrated that not all landholders support Landcare. Mark regrets he didn't leave more remnant vegetation, but he is justifiably proud of a huge swamp he has fenced off with magnificent untouched scrub and tall trees.

Mark is also involved in SE Premium Wheat Growers, a group that supports breeding, marketing and trials of new wheat varieties. This group recently was funded by the Australian Wheat Board to follow the district's wheat into the marketplaces of Singapore, Vietnam and Egypt. The trip gave them an understanding of the mighty differences in cultures that the AWB has to contend with in selling wheat. For instance, the wheat shipped from Australia to Vietnam in bulk carriers is transferred to barges, then scraped up by hand and bagged by hundreds of people, and sewn up, as we used to here about 50 years ago. Then it is stacked and used bag by bag when they want to mill it. In the Middle East, they saw first-hand the difficulties of placing the

9 million tonnes exported each year through a maze of necessary payments to various operators.

Mark and Jan say they'll be leaving the farm in good nick for the next person, whether that is family or others, and that they will continue travelling in their post-farm years.

Going Against the Grain— Neil Wandel

After a few days enjoying the spoils of success and even noting among the pioneers the signs of serious midlife crisis in the form of small, old sports cars which rendered the scenic coastline to a blur, I went to meet a man who gets his kicks from stepping off the edge . . . agriculturally.

Neil Wandel is a solid chunk of a man, aged 47, and slightly stooped from 18 years of shearing. It was Sunday morning and he was taking his one day off a week. Unassuming and conservative to look at, you would not pick Neil for the opportunistic diversifier that he is, with a distaste for no-risk, predictable farming behaviour. As a lateral thinker, he is the sort of bloke who goes his own way despite cries of 'idiot' all round him. He is another who left school at fifteen.

From humble beginnings, Neil started shearing from the age of 16 and worked on the family's mixed farm not far from Clare, in South Australia. At 28, with his wife Mary, a young child and another on the way, he realised that 2000 acres would never support him, his two brothers and their families, plus their retired father, so they took off for the west in 1979. 'I wanted to make a mark'—and he has. His place now has a turnover in excess of $3 million a year.

It didn't happen without pain and heartache. They bought a cropping and sheep place of 3000 acres north of Esperance with little money of their own but 50 per cent vendor finance from a man who is still a friend and partner in mining, another of Neil's enterprises. With good years, fearless borrowing, luck and days starting every day of the week at 5.00am, Neil and Mary expanded their holding to its present 18 000 acres, plus 2500 acres of leased land.

The wool price crash in 1991 nearly sent them broke, and on top of that they had to shoot 3000 good sheep because of the ensuing wool glut . . . a job that he, like everyone, found heartbreaking and a tragic waste of good meat. The drama of seeing wool income plummet from

Neil Wandel

$580 000 to $200 000 in one year made Neil more than double his cropping enterprise. At peak times now, Neil has ten men on the payroll. Costs are huge, with chemicals and fertiliser alone amounting to about $600 000 annually—the way it needs to be for modern cropping to prevent soil erosion and degeneration.

He realised diversification was the way to ride out the lows. He sows 15 000–16 000 acres of crops—wheat, peas and faba beans—each year and has to have machinery worth $1.4 million to do the work, but to get full value from them he works his machines hard, around the clock.

'Farmers never say there is any profit in it . . . but . . . our operation is reasonably profitable,' he says. Despite success, Neil retains a gentle humility, the result of knowing that prices can fall without warning and seasons turn nasty. He speaks quietly, without boast, in a slight lisp.

Four years ago during a drought he started a cattle feedlot, more or less as an opportunistic accident. He had bought 350 cattle to graze his wheat crops, which he thought were about to die. Then an inch of rain saw the crops revive, pastures grow and the cattle return him an unexpectedly healthy profit. He now puts about 1500 cattle through each year for Woolworths that are fed on pasture stubbles, grain screenings, legume trash and hay—all of which he grows in what is a satisfying self-contained system. He reckons he could have lived on the profit from the feedlot alone last year. But there is nothing complacent about Neil Wandel.

He organised a contract with a piggery for a 1000 tonnes of grain a year. So when the grain receival bin is closed on the weekends, his machinery can still be kept working to send supplies to the piggery instead. With a need for even more weekend outlets and storage, Neil invested in a revolutionary Canadian method of grain storage he read about in one of the many journals he constantly sharpens his knowledge with. Huge plastic 'sausage bags', the only ones in Western Australia—2 metres tall, 3 metres wide and 70 metres long—have grain blown into them with a huge force fan. Looking like big fat white slugs in his laneways, the bags can store 2000 tonnes of grain at a far cheaper price than metal farm silos.

'There's so much pressure on at harvest time that you make a lot of decisions based purely on storage, such as what do you do with it, store it in the open?' One harvest he had three headers working in a paddock. The grain was wet, it was early in the season and 'everyone had their adrenaline going'. He was faced with 300 tonnes of wet barley that couldn't be sold, so although it was wet, they put it in the sausage bags. Because there is no air in them, the grain didn't go mouldy and it was currently being fed to the cattle in the feedlot. It would have been too expensive to dry it.

Because of his access to storage space, Neil is also able to be a grain buyer and trader. 'At harvest time, farmers make a lot of bad decisions. They grow good crops, put a lot of resources into it, but rush it into the bin. If it is rejected they don't know what to do with it.' Neil buys around 14 000 tonnes of off-type grain a year and either uses it in his feedlot or sells it when the market lifts, keeping it stored in the bags until then.

What I like about people who go about their business without fanfare is that they make everyone else in the district sit up and watch. For instance, Neil leased a huge shed down on the wharf of Esperance when shipping was quiet. He got it for peanuts—$120 a week. He had his grain dumped there by road trains after harvest, for drying, blending or cleaning. It was a masterstroke. Neil has so much grain to be reaped that he takes it off at 14 per cent moisture content instead of the 12.5 per cent that it needs to be when it is delivered to the grain bin or silo. The harvesters can work around the clock, not having to worry whether the grain is too dry or too wet. Neil just blends it or dries it in huge blowers to get it to the right average moisture content, saving massive amounts of paddock time. After two years, every farmer in the district tried to emulate him and the port authority put the price up on the wharf to $450 a week.

He has since bought a huge disused shed and erected it nearby. He runs a commercial canola and legume cleaning works there, as well as still doing his own blending and drying.

'I make a lot of decisions on gut feeling. You just know when the timing is right,' and he says that has nothing to do with education, just practical experience, which is assisted by a lot of thinking and reading. 'I have made a lot of gut feeling decisions that have been very profitable.'

He was also the first person to put gypsum on Esperance country—it was something the Wandel family had routinely done on the heavy soils of Clare—and now he owns two gypsum mines in partnership with the man who gave them the start with vendor finance. One at Scadden has yielded 150 000 tonnes. Formed by crystals blowing off the salt lakes in the district, gypsum, which is 30 per cent sulphate and 44 per cent calcium, interacts with clay particles in heavy soils and stops them setting hard as well as giving them a fertility boost. Some people in waterlogged country found they doubled their returns. He has pegged another big deposit east of Esperance as well.

For Love of the Land

'A lot of people think I am mad,' Neil says of the many innovations he has brought to the district. What he says he loves about the area is that people are tolerant of different ideas. 'They might think you're mad, but they won't knock you.'

On salinity control, he has also gone against the flow. He has planted many trees but is not convinced that doing so is economical, so he has put in drains, a controversial approach in his area. 'But it is the only thing we've done where we've reclaimed land.' Scrub, grasses and broom bush are now regenerating back to the edge of the naturally saline watercourse.

Neil got his start when his father lent him $30 000 to buy his first few hundred acres. Prices went up and the farm was paid off in three years. He'll help his two sons when they are in their early twenties, putting them on 5000 acres each to let them make their own mistakes. 'You can't farm with nothing today, you need a start,' he says.

He says he simply can't comprehend gloom about the future of agriculture. 'I find it hard to understand where people are coming from with that mentality, because I think it is an exciting time in farming. There are so many things happening, there's enormous potential out there.'

Part IV

Roaming out of Roma— Queensland

'That Girl' with the Million Dollar Block—Bloss Hickson

In May, invited to Roma in south-west Queensland to make a speech to the merino breeders at a noisy show dinner, I escaped for the day to go bush and talk to someone who is a bit of a legend up that way but who also has had to cope with plenty of lip-curling envy.

Bloss Hickson has cooked hamburgers in a roadhouse, is an accomplished artist, and in 1987, won a ballot for a million dollar cattle station, to the alarm of the sceptics. Bloss, aged 41, a conservationist, keen on Asian philosophy and Aboriginal coexistence, is the antithesis of the outback redneck. It is a credit to her quiet charm and gentle persistence that she and her cattle station have made their mark in what is commonly regarded as Man's country. When a mere Girl steps in and wins the coveted prize, few were likely to cheer. For Bloss Hickson, it was a dream come true. Already skilled at fencing and cattle work from a background on her parents' cattle station, Bloss set about building housing for herself and staff—with her own hands, putting up cattle yards and caring for pastures and trees. She won the respect of her peers, and now, after ten years of getting the station on its feet, has just started five years sabbatical to pursue other passions—art, cooking, the Australian bush and the promotion of good, clean Australian beef from her own cattle.

I met Bloss in Mount Moffit National Park, three and a half bumpy hours north of Roma. If the drive up hadn't been so beautiful I might have worried about the grinding rocks and soggy sand of the track that climbed up through tall trees to open plains and finally to the park. There I found the campsite where women in the shade of a big stretch of canvas were clearing up after a conference with the traditional owners of the area. A few delegates lingered around a dying campfire, black skins and white, laughing and talking over mugs of coffee and pieces of cake.

Bloss Hickson

Knowing some of the things Bloss had done and that she had lived outdoors in the harsh Queensland climate, I didn't imagine I would be confronting a pretty, femininely dressed woman with blonde wisps of hair escaping from under an eccentric sort of black straw hat. My expectations were probably guided by the stringy-bodied, leather-faced outback ringers who come out of the sticks for occasions such as the Roma Show, with jeans hanging low on hips, checked shirts and huge hats for shade and height. I thought a woman cattle station operator and house builder would have to be a bit battered at least.

Bloss, real name Margaret, Hickson is softly spoken and doesn't look a bit weatherbeaten. We sat down by a bubbling stream on a slab of rock overlooking a pool, and near a tall gum, whose shade unfortunately kept creeping away from us as the hours went by, so we kept shuffling along the rock.

I will let Bloss loose to tell you her story with few interruptions from me, except to say that she spent her early childhood in Bathurst where her father was a vet and mother a slow-learners' teacher, but both were off the land and had a hankering to go back. In 1964, her father did something about this longing. He flew around Australia and decided on the Gulf country of northern Queensland as the place to settle.

'The next summer, oblivious to the wet season, we packed up the station wagon and headed north to take a closer look' said Bloss. They found Melinda, about 100 miles north of Cloncurry on the road to Normanton, and bought it. 'We just thought it was wonderful, us kids, just one big playground. 'We built lots of cubbyhouses, we just loved it, absolutely loved it. It really shaped my life. It was in the days when we had a dirt road, we had no electricity, we had a little generator that went off at night-time. I was eight when we moved up there . . . it was total isolation. My mother taught us. [She] was a wonderful teacher . . . and she loved learning, so I guess she inspired that in us. She also did a lot of extracurricular things—she painted, which is where my interest in painting started. And my father worked us hard. We were always fencing. He always had plans for the property and we were his workforce, basically. We weren't always an enthusiastic workforce, but nonetheless, we got to be able to do everything. I guess I accumulated so many skills on the land because I had three brothers and my father didn't see much difference in us.' Her brothers are Pete, Bood and Roo, who were aged ten, six and four respectively when they arrived at Melinda.

'School would be out by lunch and then it would be into work. But it was great. It was a fabulous lifestyle. We didn't have television, so we used to play a lot of cards and bridge. We used to read a lot.

'The hardest work was the cattle work. We mustered the entire property twice a year. First in March after the Wet, then again in September. In our early days it was all a bit of a circus. The paddocks were huge, the cattle were semi-feral and the workforce was totally inexperienced. Mustering meant galloping through dense gidgee scrub chasing old cows far smarter than ourselves, constant busters and long days in hot dusty cattle yards, drafting, dipping and branding hundreds of calves. It was relentless for weeks until the last animal had found its way back to the paddocks.' Bloss said Melinda had a pretty ordinary herd of Shorthorn cows, so her father changed over to Droughtmasters and Charbray which suited the Cloncurry environment.

Boarding schools in New South Wales eventually took away the station workforce. Bloss was sent to Frensham, in Mittagong. 'I didn't really adapt to Frensham terribly well. I was a bit feral, unlike the rest of the girls at Frensham, but I spent six years there. I didn't have anything in common with them. The talk in a girls' school is always boys, clothes, social events, all these things which I just had no comprehension about whatsoever. It was hard. I wasn't particularly sporty either.' She wasn't too interested in learning the social graces either; in fact she says the whole experience made her quite introverted. 'I have never been able to handle authority very well, so I would just sort of retreat and go and do my own thing a lot of the time. Being from the bush and being totally in love with the bush, I found it quite artificial and pretentious.

'One year Mum came down with the two boys . . . in the white ute and the muffler had gone. You could hear them coming for about 20 miles . . . Everyone else had rolled up in their Mercs and BMWs. They made a grand entrance.

'I did quite well at school academically and was accepted into physiotherapy. But all I wanted to do was go cooking up in the Kimberleys—that was my life ambition . . . When I finally got kicked out of physiotherapy [for failing a subject twice] that's exactly where I went, headed up to the Northern Territory and got a job between Katherine and Kunnunurra cooking on a beef cattle station, which was fabulous. I loved it.' and her voice goes all warm and dreamy with reminiscence. She was cooking for the single men and would make lunches for all the men, including the Aborigines. 'The property had about 60 people living on it, about 40 of them were employed, the rest were just families, and of the 40 I guess about 20 of them would have been Aboriginal and there would have been about 10 single men as well as the governess and a few extras, like Miggsy, my offsider. She was an Aboriginal girl.'

The shade had travelled so we moved ourselves a few metres along the rock to escape the harsh midday sun, had a bit of a stretch and refilled our water bottles. Bloss said she had always felt comfortable with the men on stations. 'I've always been one of the boys,' she says. However, turning 40 last year brought a reassessment, a massive change. 'I told my father I was turning into a full-time girl, that was it. When I was young, my father always used to comment, to be a g-i-i-i-r-l—and he could really curl his lip up and say it in the most revolting fashion. It was the worst thing to be called in the world. I mean, to be a girl was just the pits, so I guess I had a personality problem from the beginning,' and she laughs. 'And whenever my father would get cranky with me, he'd turn round and say to me, you're acting like a bloody girl. So when I turned 40 I turned to him and said, Dad, I'm turning into a full-time girl, no more fencing for me thanks.

'I've grown up with men. I can talk to them about anything. I have the same interests. It doesn't matter whether it's anything on the property or anything in the environment. I build things, I've done everything with the boys, always will, even if I try to disguise myself in dresses and stockings. But I don't want to be one of the boys any more.'

After a year at the station, she returned to Melinda because her parents and eldest brother Peter had started up the famous Burke and Wills Roadhouse just north of the property. Pete was the bowser boy and manager, Bloss, at 20, was the 'short-order cook', doing hamburgers, toasted sandwiches, pies and chips. Just a couple of dongas, a kitchen, a dining room, a big cement slab for a courtyard and vines over the top for shade, it was 200 kilometres from everywhere, very basic but a lot of fun. The roadhouse was at the crossroads to Julia Creek, Cloncurry, Burketown and Normanton. 'We became the local social spot. Lots of people who had been very isolated suddenly came—a lot of locals, as well as tourists and fisherman. It was a great year, full of funny incidents. One day these two guys drove in backwards—they had come from Normanton. They had lost all their forward gears. Their necks were so cricked. They almost walked into the roadhouse backwards, their necks had got so rigid turning around all the time, that they reversed up to the counter.' The car was put on a truck to Mount Isa. The roadhouse later caught fire and was sold.

Bloss changed direction and studied silversmithing at art school in Brisbane and set to work renovating a house that her mother had bought. She taught herself carpentry so she could remove walls, put in extra windows and replace flooring. 'I got a job at the Hamilton Hotel as a barmaid and it was where all the builders used to drink, so whenever I had a problem I'd take it to the pub and they'd all give me the answers. I always asked if I could come and have a job on their building sites because I was very keen to learn, but they'd never take me on, unfortunately.'

After two years of art school, Bloss went back to Melinda, worked with her parents for a year, had a silver exhibition in Cloncurry and earned enough money to go overseas. 'I did well out of my silverwork,' says this multi-talented bushie, who because of her interest in Aztec silver, went to Mexico in 1985 and ended up doing design work for a group of Guatemalan weavers so they could sell their products in America. She went on to Europe and then returned home wanting to spend her life as an artist. Two weeks later, her mother suddenly died. Bloss spent a year at home helping her father, then got a job in Sydney as a cook in an Italian restaurant and became interested in the Chinese philosophy of Daoism, which encourages its followers to be humble and meek and not to idolise money.

'I've never been driven by money at all, much to my father's disappointment.' The extraordinary irony is that at this stage in her life, she won the 13 000 acre cattle property in a Queensland government land ballot. 'Everyone who I knew in Queensland was in this ballot.' Bloss had just turned thirty. 'I could not believe it. Me, with my strict Daoist principles about not wanting any material possessions, had just ended up with a million dollar property. It was a bizarre day that one, the day I became a millionaire.'

The Arcadia Valley is about 200 kilometres north of Roma, west of Rockhampton, and near Carnarvon Gorge. Bloss immediately flew to Emerald and drove to the block with her father. It was a cold, bleak day in August. Brigalow regrowth was everywhere and her first impression was bad. Next day, they went exploring and discovered she had a beautiful gem to polish and develop all on her own. The place she calls Huntly, not far from the small town of Rolleston, is in a fertile valley with the Expedition Mountain Ranges on one side and the Fantail Ranges eight kilometres away on the other. A lake lies at the foot of one of the ranges. 'It's classified as some of the best cattle-fattening country in Queensland,' says Bloss. 'So Dad, who was in the middle of a raging drought, was just so excited.' He promptly dispatched great numbers of cattle to Huntly.

'The conditions of winning the ballot were that I had to live there,' says Bloss. 'I had to have it fully stocked within three years and develop it so it was a viable grazing property.' So she set about putting in cattle yards and fencing, and building herself a house with a view with some help from her brother Roo.

'I bought a book on how to build a house. We scratched our heads a lot . . . and then we just did it. We cut some ironbark posts and put them in the ground. Dad kept giving his advice—build it square and simple. I had all these grand ideas, but we kept it square and simple. I had a stone floor. I collected all the stones from around the building.' All the while she was living in a tent. Nothing to it, she says. She laid the stone floor, put in posts, and built a frame according to diagrams in the book. 'You learn by doing it, and the first house is certainly not the best house I've built,' she says. The outside is clad in cypress pine weatherboards bought from mills at nearby Injune. A friend taught her mud-brick making, so she lined the walls with mud smoothed over wire mesh. 'After that I did all the walls like that, in all the houses . . . it's been wonderful insulation,' which she finished off with linseed oil and turps. So that was the first house. She built a second one for employees, as well as carports, 50 metres from the first. Then she built herself a separate bedroom, studio and bathroom. A friend made stained glass windows and there's a big bloodwood main beam down the centre. Bloss welded up her own bed out of swirling metal shapes she found in an antique shop. The house, sited on a ridge in the middle of the property, has 360° degree views.

'When I first got to Huntly, I decided that if I was going to get anything done I would have to do it myself, because I could wait forever for the appropriately skilled person to come along and do it. So I learnt to do most things. I welded, I could fence, I could build houses. It became almost an obsession that I was going to conquer this. I was going to do this all myself.

'When I first drew the block it was always "that bloody girl who took our block", and the attitude initially was, ah well, seven years will see her out and that will be the end of her. But in actual fact, I think they have all taken their hats off to me. I think I have even started quite a few trends—metal fencing, metal yards. Everyone's pulling down their old wooden ones and putting up metal.

'It's always very hard to do anything by yourself, but we were also struggling along because beef prices haven't been fantastic in the past ten years—struggling along economically to develop Huntly. I tend to be on my own an awful lot of the time. Summers, I was always on my own in the summer, because nobody ever came to visit me in the summer, it was too hot. Winter times were fabulous, I had lots of visitors.'

Help came from students, especially French exchangees, because of a link established by her father 20 years before. She said she initially employed only women because she had only the one sleeping and living area, but women were limited in strength, experience and knowledge, and it was hard to pick the right ones. True, there aren't too many like Bloss Hickson around.

'Everyone's always amazed at what I do. There is nothing I can't do if I want to do it. It's just been a matter of determination . . . I just don't get put off. Attitude is everything. If you are positive, things flow. I hate people who keep saying, we can't do this, we can't do that—because for me it never exists. You can do anything. You can make things happen. It's been easy, life's easy.'

When she was trying to claim from the government the rights to harvest timber on Huntly, she built a two-storey tree house, then held a summit up there, attended by ministerial advisers. The tree house pivots between four trees at the foothills of the mountains, is 20 feet by 20 feet, and has lovely views over the lakes. When the trees sway, everything moves with them. Bloss has even put a rainwater tank up there and surrounded each level with a metal rail of sculptural patterns.

The brigalow country—rich because of the nitrogen-fixing properties of the brigalow, a leguminous acacia—extends from the Darling Downs up to Charters Towers. It was once thought to be rubbishy country but now having been broken up through the ballots, is a huge economic resource for Queensland—home to large cattle herds, cereal crops and, recently, cotton.

I was feeling dizzy, either by the feats of this demure and gentle person, or from the sun beating down on my pale southern skin, so we again chased the shade. There was still more to discover about Bloss, although her story so far was spectacular enough.

Soon after getting Huntly, Bloss formed the Rolleston Landcare group to understand the ecology of brigalow and how to control some of the invasive weeds on Huntly. She also started the local newspaper, the *Rolleston Rag*, which continues still, but under another's guidance.

When a dam which would flood Rolleston to provide water for the cotton industry was announced two years ago by the Department of Natural Resources, Bloss took up the fight to stop it. The dam issue divided the community but fortuitously, according to Bloss, it also prompted the return of the Aboriginal custodians to the area when they were asked to evaluate sacred sites.

'They had all been removed from the area in the 1940s and taken to Woorabinda Mission, so there have been no Aborigines in the Rolleston district for years, which is very sad because it is full of cultural heritage. The Carnarvon Gorge is full of Aboriginal sites, paintings, initiation sites and here up at Mount Moffit, which is actually the headwaters of Carnarvon Gorge, it is even more so. It is like a shrine after shrine up here.'

Last year, after ten years of being her own boss and enjoying having Huntly to herself, Bloss found herself with company. Her father had retired from Melinda, the family had bought him out; and Bood decided to move in with Bloss. 'Suddenly I had a brother who had very strong ideas and so I decided to have a break for five years . . . It took me a long time to come to the decision but I have not regretted it since.

'My ultimate goal is to make Huntly a very sustainable and viable property,' Bloss says, and Bood shares these goals. So for five years Bloss is indulging her other interests. She'll support ways of getting traditional owners to once again be involved in their land, especially in connection with management of cultural sites in national parks which was the theme of the Mount Moffit camp. 'It is crucial for them to re-establish their culture . . . and regain some respect in our society.'

On the very day I was with her, news came through that the plan to flood Rolleston had been stopped due in part to the involvement of the area's original inhabitants.

Bood and Bloss have joined a small group called Rural Landholders for Coexistence, which is suggesting options for pastoralists on how they can coexist with the Aboriginal race. 'If Aborigines can get a forestry lease over Huntly, then I'll happily coexist with them,' says Bloss, explaining that traditional owners may in the future be able to have access to timber to generate income. Many want to get back to the land, especially for their children's sake. Nothing is going to change for pastoralists. They still have all the rights they have ever had over the grass and the functioning of that business as a grazing business.'

Still the projects unfold. The next and very new one is the direct marketing of their home-grown beef. Bood, Bloss, their brother Peter and another friend with business experience had successfully launched their own company, Bush Beef Pty Ltd, at a Paddington restaurant only the week before. Their aim is to prepare and vacuum-pack beef for direct selling to Sydney people.

Accompanying the launch of their beef products was *Our Cows and the Art of Cooking Them*, a lively, jaunty recipe book written and illustrated by Bloss, full of the sort of bush meals she has cooked for years and handy tips to ensure the best results. Bush Beef aims to sell direct on a large scale to city consumers in an effort to make production of beef more profitable. As they explain in the Foreword of the book: 'Food prices have been depressed globally by political and market forces for decades. In our bid to feed the world cheaply we are degrading our agricultural resource base. The price primary producers receive for our produce has rarely covered the cost to the environment . . . By marketing directly to the consumer, the money saved on middlemen will be spent instead on adding value to our service to you and the pursuit of sustainable land use.'

Bloss, as we packed up to walk back to the now deserted campsite, told me she was also continuing to paint. At an exhibition in Brisbane at the end of last year, she had sold 20 out of 30 works and was shortly going to do the rounds of the galleries in Sydney for another exhibition.

Under the trees was a green, old-style Toyota Landcruiser troop-carrier. This is home for Bloss Hickson at present. It is all she needs, she says, to continue her love affair with the Australian bush. She's got freedom, she's mobile, she's got her paints—and if she needs shade, she rigs up a canopy out the back.

Remote but at Ease— Brett and Vanda Hick

The Roma Show had nothing in common with the worn-out events down south teetering on extinction. After two lively days of parties, dressing up, competitions, displays, crowded bars, cattle, sheep, horses, working dogs, machinery and even Ashtons Circus, I caught a lift with my wool-buying son-in-law to Longreach, 700 kilometres north-west of Roma. This is big distance country and we travelled at night. Shearing was just beginning around Longreach and he planned to be in the area for two and a half days. I took my largely pregnant Queensland daughter with me for company and to share the driving. We had 1500 kilometres to travel in that time if I was to visit the three stations on my list.

It took six hours to reach Julia Creek, pushing north-west to ever warmer, open plains country with longer stretches between gateways. A fast lunch, then 40 kilometres out to Lindfield, which is part of the Hick family's empire of 234 200 hectares, carrying 15 000 head of cattle and 20 000 sheep depending on the season. I had come to meet Brett and Vanda Hick, both in their mid-thirties, who have spent their lives far from the facilities most people take for granted.

The dirt out here is red and the trees are stunted and prickly. The country is flat. At the homestead surrounded by a fence enclosing shrubs and trees, dogs wagged their tails and Brett Hick, slight of build with a smile as warm as the Queensland sun, came out to greet us. The country might be tough, but the people out here are gentle. We had tea and cake in the kitchen and were watched around the door by youngest daughter Vanessa, who was giving up her afternoon sleep so she could check out the visitors.

The Hick family came to the Julia Creek area in 1951 because land was cheap, the equivalent of a dollar an acre—mainly because few wanted to live so far from anywhere. Before the bitumen it took Brett's father five days to travel between Winton and Julia Creek; it

Brett and Vanda Hick and daughter Vanessa

had taken us four hours. It is still a 19-hour drive to Brisbane—a place where Brett has been just three times in his life. They shop at Mount Isa, four hours away.

This isolation with its heat, no schools, distant medical care and shops, high freight costs, cantankerous seasons and unpredictable rainfall, makes it difficult to get people there to work, even though there are jobs. Few women want to teach children at home for the primary school years and then wave them goodbye at 11 or 12 when they go to boarding school. For children to play with a friend, it can be a serious trip. On the day we were there Rennae, aged seven, was at the home of her closest, in distance, friend—140 kilometres away. Allan, aged nine, had left the day before by bus on school camp 800 kilometres away with around 35 other isolated children. Some of the children had to travel 1200 kilometres.

At the same time, Brett says there is no better place for young people to grow up. 'It gives them time, makes them develop mentally, they learn how to make themselves useful, they learn how to work, learn how to look after themselves, find their way around through life a bit.' He says city kids at a loose end would benefit greatly from the jackaroo life for a couple of years.

He can't see people in any numbers ever coming again to remote regions such as theirs, however—even if he and Vanda love the country and the life, even if the phones do break down and power blackouts are frequent.

Employers have learned through stringent necessity to do things with less people. Thirty years ago, the place he runs had more than 20 men and four different families. He has to cope with three men these days because of prices being down and costs up. Saying he doesn't see a bright future for primary industry, he didn't blame people for not venturing out into the bush. He did say, however, he got between 20 and 80 applicants to advertised jobs—'But half of them don't even know where Julia Creek is.' And although he has got excellent staff now, he does have bad runs. 'About five years ago, I had 12 people from August to December and there was virtually no-one worth feeding. There were drug addicts, there were wife bashers, people out of rehabilitation homes.'

While the decline in the population in these isolated areas is because of smaller workforce, there are fewer owners too. Brett says once around 10 000 acres would be enough but to support a family now you need 70 000 acres of Julia Creek-type country. Such disenchantment with harsh and remote regions by a softer population made me wonder in private if there ever will be a future race of solid, uncomplaining, no-nonsense people like Vanda and Brett.

You wouldn't find many young women spending an eight month 'honeymoon' living in swags with no power, no shower, just an old wood stove, looking after cattle on agistment simply because some stupid drought happened to hit just as she got married. That's indeed how Brett and Vanda continued to spend the next two years after that introduction to marriage, while they travelled between agistment properties spread over 1500 kilometres trying to keep their 5000 cattle alive for the time when they would be able to buy more land at the right price.

I had realised from photographs and trophies on the walls that horses play a big part in their lives, both for work and leisure. Brett's clear eyes light up when I ask him how important horses are to him. In his dry and low-key way he says, 'I find horses very enjoyable. They are completely different to people. People can be smiling at you and telling you that you are a good person, at the same time as they are pinching something out of your pocket. Whereas a horse, he never ever lies to you. They are very honest. If he's going to kick you, he'll always tell you first.'

At Thorntonia, north-east of Mount Isa and some nine hours' drive from Lindfield, 70 work horses are kept for mustering on its rough, wild and stony slopes. They have to be quiet and sensible because few employees can ride well these days. There used to be 6000 brumbies, but they have managed to cull them to 2000.

A lot of work on Lindfield is done by motorbike, but if the floods come again there could be 25 kilometres of continuous water and then horses come into their own. With a horse, Brett feels at one with the world, where he is king . . . and indeed he has proved that he is. He won the Cloncurry Stockman's Challenge in 1993, one of the prestige events in Australia. It was on a young horse he had bred, broken in and educated.

When he was 20, Brett worked in New South Wales for a bit of extra experience and it was there that he bought a 22-year-old brood mare with one eye for $1800. 'It was a lot of money for me, but she was proven bloodlines and she had a colt foal, six weeks old at foot.' That colt is now a 14-year-old stallion that is the sire of most of Brett's campdraft horses and many of the workhorses at Thorntonia.

Campdrafting, Australia's own sport, is something the Hick family get to about six times a year. His children, even Vanessa, aged four, all compete. For their holidays a fortnight away, they were excited about travelling 1900 kilometres to Darwin with a couple of horses to attend the Pearl of the North, the richest campdraft in Australia. The children feel so at home in the saddle, the older two recently helped move five separate mobs of cattle, a total of 3000, to Julia Creek, taking three days each trip.

We were outside in a flash when I suggested we see the horses. The stallion was saddled and Brett did spins and skidding halts sitting light and relaxed in the saddle, a large hat on his head. The setting sun made the shadows stretch to the horizon and the paddocks were washed in golden red, the same colour as the stallion's coat. You want for little more when you are at ease with the world.

Fertile Oasis for Change— Richard and Judy Makim

Pity any leisure-loving tourists who might have been at the motel that night. Everyone seemed to be up at 5.30am revving to get to work on the roads or the Julia Creek to Mount Isa section of the railway. It suited us. We were heading towards Normanton on the Gulf of Carpentaria at 6.00am, travelling through beautiful savannah country in clear morning light. Wedge-tailed eagles rose heavily from the overnight harvest of road kill. Kites and hawks flicked and dived through the air. Plains turkeys, or bustards, scattered into tall grass. Though much larger, they are similar in appearance and habits to stone curlews and sadly, as ground-nesting birds, they are also in decline. Up here, north of the dingo fence, they have dingoes as well as foxes to fear. The good numbers in the area possibly were drawn by plentiful water and grass in this excellent season. I woke up from my daydreams, realised we had sailed past my turn-off, checked the map and written instructions, stopped a car heading south, probably the only one for hours, and got back on track. I had never been so far north and the country was quite different from what I expected—lush grasses, wide plains, flowing creeks densely treed—some red dirt, a rough track in places, but mostly smooth. We came across fat, well-bred cattle, a few more gates and the country changed to having almost dense tree cover. It wasn't long before we found the turn-off to Arizona, the station owned by Richard and Judy Makim, 160 kilometres north of Julia Creek and only a few hours short of the Gulf. Now, if I had expected a harsh, dry landscape—after all, the place is called Arizona—I was in for a shock.

A green lawn, shaded by big trees, was surrounded by pink and white bougainvilleas, looking like pillar roses, growing on poles and cascading over an archway. Through this we walked to be greeted warmly by a smiling Judy Makim and the music of Handel floating through the open door of a large, beautiful homestead with verandahs as wide and shady as a Queenslander's hat, mud-brick walls and a

For Love of the Land

Richard and Judy Makim

white roof. Sculpture, artefacts and paintings, floor rugs, leather chairs and dark wood decorated a huge open-space room whose windows looked out on the semi-tropical greenery all round. The space needs to be generous, there are seven Makim children, a constant stream of resident workers and bundles of visiting friends. The place has the feel of an African hunting lodge and I felt like sitting and drinking cups of tea instead of working.

Richard Makim came in from outside. He is one of the powerhouse thinkers in the Queensland beef cattle industry, bursting with energy and novel ideas, and I had come to hear what he had to say about life in this distant area. Richard, a few months short of 50, was snowy-haired, pink-faced, fit-bodied and of youthful looks. He had on a striped shirt, cheeky red and white kerchief around his neck and a pair of white trousers. We talked of Coonawarra reds, how his region can learn from Africa, the books that have influenced him—but, above all, of his interest in cattle and beef, an industry that has had its share of woes in recent years. He speaks fast and purposefully, hurdling from one fertile concept to another.

We set ourselves up on a corner of the verandah where we would catch a breeze filtering through the sprinklers watering ferns in the garden next to us. Although it was still only nine o'clock, it was already warm, and this was their winter, the dry season.

As you will have gathered, this was no outback shanty—the house had more in common with what you find on the rural fringes of major cities. Richard's cattle-breeding philosophy is also unusual for the north. Not content to go with the accepted tropical flow of running Brahman, Droughtmaster and Santa Gertrudis cattle, this man with the questing, restless mind is experimenting with new breeds and unconventional crossings in his herd of 9000 cattle. In the mid-1980s Richard Makim joined forces with the CSIRO to bring in two African breeds—the Tuli and Boran. In all, he uses six breeds from three continents to blend as an artist mixes paints to create the definitive animal for the harsh tropical canvas of the north.

To the black British breed of Angus he puts the African Tuli—tenderness and flavour mixed with heat and tick tolerance and the ability to walk long distances. To the Italian Piedmontese he puts an Indian Brahman—white-coated, low fat, high muscle with the tropics-tolerant muscly humpback. To the African Boran he puts the Charolais—linking heat-tolerant early maturity with well-muscled, later-maturing French white-coats. He blends and stirs the genetic pot, aiming where possible for lighter coloured cattle to withstand the harsh sun, striving to improve the succulence and eating quality of northern beef, experimenting to breed animals with enough fat cover to withstand long truck rides to the abattoirs without bruising and stress. He is the beef alchemist, mixing and blending, crossing and recrossing his pool of international hybrids, keeping in mind the need for fertile, good-milking mothers that will raise a calf each year, and that are able to cope with droughts and floods. For his pioneering work, Richard was awarded in 1995 the Beef Improvement Association's Howard Yelland Award, bestowed on beef producers who have made a significant contribution to the beef industry.

Richard Makim knows this country well. He moved with his parents to the station next door in 1960 at the age of twelve. His sister, at age 21, had won it in a land ballot just like Bloss Hickson had. She then married a neighbour, so the Makim parents who were both off the land bought her out. Richard got to know Arizona from having mustered cattle for its owners; and he had a good idea of how many cattle were on it. At the end of the four-year cattle price slump in 1978, Richard and Judy with little money and a lot of courage, made an offer on Arizona. Timing and knowledge are everything . . . they were able to finance the purchase because there were more cattle on the place than the owners thought, and then the price of cattle rose. They built the mud-brick dream home ten years later, with motel-type units for children's accommodation, a schoolhouse, storeroom, station kitchen, staff quarters, coldroom, meatroom and an enormous netted-in vegetable garden to keep out birds and animals. Close to being self-sufficient, they milk a cow and brew their own beer.

Arizona has open downs country of Flinders and Mitchell grass as well as subtropical forest country of tea-tree, wattle, spear grass, sand ridges and ant hills. The house is near the creek where the two land types meet.

There is much wrong with the rural industry that rural people themselves should take charge of, Richard Makim says. After spending three years as a councillor on the Queensland Cattleman's Union, he believes change in the beef industry needs to come from individuals rather than agripoliticians. Rural producers need to be better lateral thinkers. They should also think holistically about the effects of their operations on the environment and on other industries. They need to work more co-operatively, and consider for instance sharefarming in such things as aquaculture if they have access to water. They should encourage urban people into rural areas to reverse the decline in population that causes schools and health facilities to close, and police and banks to be removed. In essence, he believes we should be sharing our land with people who have the time and skills that the owners haven't got.

I wondered, in view of Brett Hick's comments, how he expected city people to leave their comforts. 'The bush is no longer so hostile, communications have improved and many problems can be overcome,' Richard says. He points out that putting large amounts of money into cities is not necessarily the answer. Trying to provide clean water for large populations is increasingly difficult when so much of the water catchment is affected by pollution. He points out that urban people are brought to rural areas by mining companies. The implication is that if the agricultural enterprise is large and profitable, the workforce will travel.

He is passionate about the need for city people to know more about rural Australia, saying that conservationists regularly visit and make him angry when they say his country shouldn't be used for grazing. They don't understand that the open plains country never had trees—it was originally the bed of the inland sea. They get so much misinformation he believes, but as someone who is deeply committed to Landcare, he does his best to educate them. He points out wrily that the city human herd has done a dreadful job on its paddocks—put concrete and tar all over them.

Richard is keen on the US concept of Mythbusters, an organisation of spokespeople who can be called on to counteract propaganda put out by those with a political axe to grind. He says the issue of chlorofluorozine in cotton seed which showed up in beef in Japan is a case in point. 'The news that the stuff was harmless was late in being told,' he says. He believes rural women are the ones with the knowledge of issues and the ability to take them on in public. He was disappointed that funding for a Mythbusters organisation has so far not been supported by leaders in the meat industry; however, they are investigating the scheme's merits.

One of the Makim sons, Dominic, aged 24, has returned to Arizona after completing a commerce course at university. He also spent time in America where he had experience in grading and judging meat, the necessary skills for establishing meat quality standards which are at present being introduced to Australia. Dominic is also using his commerce skills to design a new approach to marketing Arizona beef. 'I have told him to find an extra enterprise that will support him, either in value adding or better marketing,' Richard says. 'People on the land are notoriously poor marketers. We virtually chuck our things

For Love of the Land

away, or give them to a wool board or a beef board or an abattoir. I think for the first part of the century it wasn't necessary to do it any other way. Everyone loved us and took our products and paid us fairly for them.' Costs and returns keep diminishing despite greater farm efficiencies like increased meat yield, increased calving percentages, better growth rates, better use of pastures, so the only way to go is to sell the products for more.

This approach was behind the formation of Horizon Holdings, of which Richard is a director. The company comprises 30 cattle producers and a group of business people, and makes beef jerky, a dried beef product, for both domestic and export markets. They turn off three tonnes a month, two tonnes of which goes to Asia. They worked on the theory that exporting fresh meat was not an option since refrigerators still aren't in many Asian homes.

Beef hasn't enjoyed great returns for most of the time they have been at Arizona and to fund fencing programs to protect the environment, pay for helicopters, and generally run the 67 000 hectare station which employs between four and six people all year, they have been heavily geared debt-wise. 'It's been pretty tough I suppose, but adversity never hurts anybody,' Richard says. 'I think adversity makes people sharpen up and learn to do things much better.'

Richard said beef producers should be doing more with the by-products of their carcasses. At present, abattoirs keep the hides, heads, legs and intestines and cattle producers haven't worried about them. They should instead keep control of them, form co-operatives and value-add. 'We are not only generous, but we're ignorant about what the stuff's worth and what its uses might be and how it might be value-added.'

He cites the example of a fellow he knows who is making 'lots and lots of money out of pigs' ears that he is using for dogs' snacks. He just went out to find something they were throwing away off an animal that he could buy very very cheaply—and he can't keep up to the demand.'

Richard is currently forming a co-operative to negotiate with an abattoir to kill on the growers' terms where they keep the by-products for marketing independently. 'There are probably 400 000 head of cattle in that co-operative. We'd probably kill 100 000 head of cattle a year.'

Richard Makim's individual views extend to what most people see as problems. Feral pigs, for instance. 'I don't like to talk about any of my feral things as a problem. I think they are a resource. We just haven't learnt to use them yet,' he said. He has discovered that the Germans like them, however, and over an eight-day period last year, 300 boars were shot and exported at $1.50 a kilogram, which is about double what he is getting for beef. Kangaroo skins from the big bucks are also being harvested, although not the meat since they are too far away from a chiller.

Although Richard Makim is bringing to his station modern management techniques of the temperate south, such as resting the country for long spells between short, heavy grazing periods, he says there are many differences. His paddock stocking rates have to take into account the big load of kangaroos, grasshoppers and feral pigs that also graze there. Arizona also can get anything between 90 inches of rain and as little as 6 inches, although in theory they reliably get 18 to 20 inches a year between November and March. During the 1960s they spent three months cut off from supplies. Most stations consequently ensure they keep big stores of fuel and food just in case; but better roads and vehicles, plus ready access to helicopters, probably mean the days of being trapped are over.

Lunch was ready in the station kitchen so we broke to have cold mutton and salad from the garden. A breeze blew through the gauze verandahs, and the fans rotated above, but I still found it warm. We had a six-hour drive ahead of us and a bundle of mail to post in Julia Creek for Judy, who had been working on getting circulars ready for a forthcoming community event.

With regrets that there wasn't time to explore the station further afield, we headed two and a half hours south again, turned left for Hughenden, another two and a half hours, then turned right for Muttaburra. By now it was getting dark. The track was rough, narrow, had numerous washaways and a mighty hump in the middle that made a ghastly scraping noise on the bottom of the car. I tried to put the wheels higher into the middle of the track but that put us into the rough on the side. It was a slow, tiring trip with our eyeballs bulging from watching for kangaroos. The last thing we needed was to thump one and be on that lonely track until someone came past the next day. It was with great relief that we pulled into the gateway of some friends, had a glass of wine, something to eat and found a bed.

Inventing a Drought Therapy—John and Lindy McClymont

We left our friends' airy Queenslander sitting high on its stilts catching breezes like a kite. Around us the country was flat, but the short cut we took through a neighbour's place led to low round breasts of hills and another nasty humpy road with deep wheel ruts made by tall four-wheel drives with no respect for small, squat, hire cars. Fearing that at any minute we would be suspended on the hump with four poor little wheels flailing in the air, we took to the side again risking an early birth and broken bra straps.

An hour later we turned through the front gate of Inverness, the property of John and Lindy McClymont, woolgrowers—another word up here for masochist. They had also endured seven years of drought. But I hadn't come here to be depressed, not after that road. I was told John was a novel sort of character with his own special way of coping with hardship—that he was no misery guts. I could immediately see that was true as we pulled up at the house on a slight hill a long way in from the gate. We were surrounded with dogs and people and chatter. This bloke with film star good looks, wearing a loose shirt, shorts, a pair of workboots, gorgeous smile, loose-limbed and relaxed, swept up my things and I obediently followed.

We had a welcoming cup of tea and biscuits, and then John said, 'Would you like to come and see my shed?' which I thought might be Queensland for 'Come up and see my etchings'. Everyone was saying things like, 'We'll never see you again', and 'We'll come looking in an hour', and laughing a lot, so I did ask sensible Lindy if it was safe to go with him. 'You must see his shed, it's where he spends most of his time,' she said. So I gathered up my recording equipment and camera and stumbled after his departing form.

Out the back door, across a wide yard, past old buildings, through an alley, we went into a dark, private, unmistakably Man-type space. You see, John McClymont is an inventor, one of many in the great

John McClymont

Aussie tradition of bush resourcefulness who make their own machinery and tools, but he goes a bit beyond that. We had been sitting in the house on his homemade handsome and comfortable chairs of bent and welded steel frames and laced-on cattle hide. The house was air-conditioned with a system he had invented and built. By the shed was a giant homemade cement mixer that looked as if it could be used in a human cannonball act. It mixes half a cubic metre of concrete at a time and was built so he could make his own concrete troughs from a mould his father created, pour cement floors and make fence posts. I looked out over the paddocks but after the seven bad years, they were empty—nothing in the paddock, no money being made.

Seven bad years and wool prices are so low that for the past two years John and Lindy, despite frugal living, have made less than it costs to run the place. Out in this country there are no alternatives to sheep. In reasonable seasons on their 100 000 acres they could shear 28 000 sheep. Last year they were down to 10 000 sheep. They needed 17 000 to break even. This year, with extra borrowings to service, 24 000 sheep are the break-even point. 'Hopefully we'll be up to that number shearing this year if we get a run of good lambings,' he says in that wonderful way of the optimist and gambler—mainly based on the fact that after seven bad years, they are due for a few good ones. He needs the banks to keep faith with them despite the swelling of their debt level to 13 per cent of his asset value, tiny by most standards but worrying when there appear to be no bright lights on for wool.

Not that this larrikin with the disarming grin and twinkle in his eye looked the slightest bit worried. He strode over to a complicated metal thing he made and calls a Rat which is dragged behind a vehicle and used for fighting bushfires. I couldn't really understand how it worked and the wind was blowing so furiously across the open plains that I couldn't absorb his words before they were blown away elsewhere. Then we looked at his concrete post 'factory'; something I could understand. He has devised a system of making very professional-looking posts and the first batch are now ready for being plugged into the paddocks. All he had done was make a big flat tray with dividers and poured concrete in and inserted bits of polythene for the wire holes in the finished posts—but he assured me it had taken a lot of trial and error to get the reinforcing right. His homemade posts will save a small fortune.

Making an award-winning sheep-jetting machine for applying anti-lice chemical had also been a good saver. As had the portable crutching cradle, which was so successful they made and sold them to local contractors enabling a small team to process 2500 sheep a day. The contractors particularly like it because they can charge less per sheep for crutching and therefore get more work, and still make very good money per day.

John was set on his do-it-yourself path by his father. 'He gave us a go when we came home from school,' said John in a voice as gravelly as a road across a gibber desert. 'And once you start, you can't stop because you get a lot of satisfaction out of doing your own work, in your leisure time. When I first came home, I tried to make a wool press.'

'It's good if you build something. You look around, you see what you've done. It's most important. It doesn't matter how old you are, you can go out each day and say, well, I helped build that. It makes your day feel a lot better right at the start.'

We draw up a wool pack to sit among the creative chaos of the dark cavern-like shed. He tells me that he decided when he left school not to go to university, but follow his father on to the land. It was in the middle of the first wool recession in the early 1970s. 'I thought there was more of a challenge out here on the land. Our parents had given us a good basic grounding in everything . . . and given us a share in the property when we left school.' He and his two brothers got a quarter share in the land and stock. 'When I came home, we made a loss for the first three years, but that makes you keen to get a bit of a go on. I wasn't home long, then I got drafted into the army for 14 months as a national serviceman.' He enjoyed the experience although he says it was a bit like going back to school, but there were a lot of western Queensland fellows called up together. He went into officer training and became a second lieutenant. 'So when I came home there was a bit more drive in me, I suppose.' There was a little wool boom in 1972 and he saved money as hard as he could, cutting costs through do-it-yourself inventions.

'You pick up a few dollars here and there, and it builds up over the years and you get ahead, and that's what we did.' They split up the family partnership with each brother running around 18 000 sheep. By the end of the 1989 and 1990 wool boom, John with one brother had bought more land and was going well. 'We were going as hard as we could go. We were young and that's the time when you've got to get going . . . Once you hit the "old farmer" group where I am now, you tend to ease off a little bit . . . but there's nothing like a good drought and low prices to get you going again,' says this poor run-down old geriatric who is all of forty-seven.

By the time the floor price was removed in early 1991, and poised to buy more land, John was able to use the accrued money to tide them over through the drought with the government's Income Equalisation Deposit scheme; but now that money has all gone.

The timing of the bad years starting right on the floor price crash couldn't have been worse. In 1991 there were big rains, but the grass was low on nutrients and the wool clip was down by 20 per cent. Then it didn't rain from 1992 until 1997, so there was no feed and sheep numbers fell. He was worried that his superb covering of Mitchell grass would suffer, that tussocks would die, but feels confident that with a good rain soon, the Mitchell grass could come up 'like lawn seed'.

John says he respects the aims of Landcare, he and was off to a field day in the coming week. For a bit of light-hearted entertainment, a challenge has been issued to a few of them to make toilets for the day. John's creation was still under wraps but I did note that it consisted of a weldmesh frame which would have hessian wrapped around it, but the actual throne was to be something surprising.

He told me that tree planting was not done on the open downs country, which was once part of the inland sea. Their main interest was the control of weeds and the protection of existing vegetation, such as gidgee and whitewood. On the rises there once were ancient forests where there is still petrified wood and agates; all around his area, the bones of dinosaurs have been found, the most famous of which is the Muttaburrasaurus.

Speaking of dinosaurs, did he still have faith in sheep I asked, somewhat cheekily. Yes, he said. He has great faith in the wool industry and is at present looking into setting up a company to do the early stages of wool processing, so woolgrowers in the area can add value to their product. Before they get under way, they want to establish a market in China.

Along the same lines, a group of 13 investors set up a tannery in Hughenden to process kangaroo hides, but that particular venture was not successful because kangaroo skins rose in price and people stopped buying them. He did show me, however, an exciting new line that a master tanner from Slovenia who works at the tannery has developed, and samples of which have been sent to fashion houses in Paris. It is kangaroo skin, made into a suede so fine that it feels like silk, and is so light and beautiful it could be used for an evening gown. They also are able to tan cattle hides so producers can add 'phenomenal value' by selling them into their own markets.

We left that interesting shed crammed with secret men's things that could be welded and built. The therapy of keeping busy is an important survival tool, I mused.

People could be forgiven for sitting around feeling depressed in this drought-ridden region where profit is a far-distant memory. It was good, instead, to hear of off-farm investment, value-adding and such words as, 'Tough times are not necessarily a bad thing'. John McClymont does regret the loss of race meetings and the demise of stockhorses, gone because of the need to survive and do things more efficiently. He feels also that people need to work more closely together. Although they are all under the same pressures, he says they are not united. 'You know how your neighbour's going, but if you join together, you could achieve more and perhaps get through the tough times better,' he says. We farewelled him, wishing like mad it would rain long and hard very soon. I still think he should do a screen test.

Part V

Taking the Heat—Kununurra and the Northern Territory

Nothing is Impossible—
Wilhelm Bloecker

Before leaving, I refilled the freezer, bashed the garden into shape and earned mother-points at pony club competitions. Kisses all round as I left for Darwin and Kununurra, where I was spending time with some of those involved in the renaissance of the Ord scheme after it was written off as a fizzer in 1980. It took people with real guts to move into a place so flat with despondency, isolated and hot. Afterwards I was going to a farm growing feral animals, in the heart of the Kakadu World Heritage area.

There's a glorious shock when the heat of the tropics hits as the doors of the airport eject each plane load, especially when one is clad for southern winter. I acclimatised by having a walk on the beach and then watched the city turn bright pink in the setting sun with my cousin, Jo, and a bottle of champagne. This was the life! By the time I got to Kununurra, I was right into the spirit of the tropics, laid back and slowing down. I duly wound the clock back an hour and a half; then found that everyone seemed to operate on central time anyway. And indeed why not, the border was only about 40 kilometres away. So at Western Australian time of 5.00am, everyone acts as if it is 6.30am, crashing around, talking loudly and having a wild old time. There was no point in hanging onto my pillow in bewilderment as two chaps enjoyed a loud conversation outside my window. I joined them with my cup of tea and watched kingfishers flashing over Lake Kununurra, and a mother wallaby with a joey hop by before being dispatched at speed by a stray dog.

My ten o'clock appointment was half a day away, so I wandered around the town lusting over Argyle diamonds, inspecting tourist shops and drinking coffee. By car, I scooted around streets with bougainvillea on fences and tropical palms. It was a delicious contrast with the cold of the south—but I did pause to hope we were getting some decent rain. What surprised me, though, was that there were so many of us outsiders. There seemed to be a northern tank army of senior citizens. Such are the joys of hitting out for the adventure trail to see some of this huge land. But why did they all look so uncharmed? I tried to chat to several couples wrestling with enormous pantechnicons hung with aerials, spare wheels, fishing rods, all the toys of people at play, about

Wilhelm Bloecker

how their travels were going, and all I got to my admittedly rather daft inquiry were sour, weary grunts. This travelling around Australia thing must be hell, I thought, living in a box on wheels cooped up with some old codger you've been married to for 40 years and with the only excitement being the changing scenery... and that can be unchanging for hundreds of kilometres.

In the main street with a traffic jam of old-timers' buses, the lack of enthusiasm and smiles made me think these poor old things had been sent packing by their ghastly offspring, who even while Gran and Grandpa were wrestling with the map to find their way out of town, were busy carving up the family loot. And here they were so far from home. Whichever way you look at it, Kununurra is a long way from nearly everywhere, especially Germany.

I was indeed meeting someone who had come from Germany and become a legend in Kununurra—Wilhelm Bloecker. In 1982, Wilhelm left behind a large and prosperous family farm, complete with beautiful farmhouse, big barns, fine crops, animals and large, comfortable EEC subsidies. What Wilhelm and his wife Gabi came to was a place with the bottom fallen out of it. Kununurra had collapsed, the dream had shattered. The expensive Ord experiment was in tatters. Cotton was a failure, plans for a sugar mill were about to fall through, and when they did, the banks withdrew support for sugar growers. Pests and disease, the heat, everything pointed to the final curtain for Kununurra.

The Bloeckers' property is 15 kilometres out of the town. To get there you drive through grey, dry-looking scrub and orange, weathered, craggy, flaky hills rising up all around, then suddenly there are flat, bright-green ordered fields of sugar and melons surrounded by irrigation channels. Everything is lush and neat, tied up with ribbons of water, silver and shining. Just past the new sugar mill I turned into a farm humming with efficiency. Most people had been either picking or packing since 5.00am. Wilhelm Bloecker drove up and unfolded himself out of a vehicle. I could see that here was a person who never could be described as unenthusiastic or lacking focus.

So inspired by Kununurra is he still that one of his most famous sayings is, 'We eat potential for breakfast'. He sees the place as so full of opportunity, where so many different crops can be grown that he is jumping out of his skin, keen to have a go at them all. Tall, lean and lanky, Wilhelm has deep-set, grey hazel eyes, a cropped goatee beard and lines either from laughter or squinting in the sun. Probably both.

For Love of the Land

Wilhelm Bloecker

Wilhelm Bloecker

Wilhelm and Gabi Bloecker gloried in the deep rich chocolate soil of the Ord valley where unlimited irrigation water was already laid on, where the sun shone brightly—and blessed relief, there were no EEC subsidies. They waited a year to get land because people kept hanging on, hoping things would turn around. With the failure of the mill, the price of land crashed from $900 a hectare to just $500, people sold up and walked out, broken and dispirited. Land was at rock bottom prices. 'Nobody knew what to do, that's why it was so cheap. It was a high risk at that time,' says Wilhelm in his light, clear voice, softly accented.

The Bloeckers had $200 000 from the sale of a dairy in Victoria that Wilhelm had bought some years before and had a friend manage; they aimed to buy their irrigation block and get it under production without borrowing an extra cent. Using second-hand machinery bought from defunct farms, they cropped just a third in the first year. It was all they could afford to do. Their soya bean crop planted in the wet season got them off to a good start, then followed sunflowers and pioneering rockmelon crops, planted by Wilhelm and three other brave farmers, which put melons into southern shops for the first time ever in the winter of 1983. They bought more land over the years and the farm is now 800 hectares. As well, they sharefarm an additional 650 hectares. And they still haven't ever borrowed a cent, even though the price of land went to $2000 a hectare.

We have a look through the voluminous sheds stacked with boxes and conveyor belts for grading produce. Huge coolrooms along one side of the shed roar every time someone opens a door. Wilhelm leads me back to his small office contained within one of the big sheds. An elderly fan circulates air and he takes up his position on a squeaky tilting chair and shows me to another. This is a no frills office—it is simply a place where decisions are made, phone calls are taken and where a door opens frequently with numerous staff inquiries fielded in either German or English.

When he had his first contact with Kununurra on a flying visit looking at land in 1980, Wilhelm saw its rich soil and irrigation and believed there was nothing better in the whole world. No farmers from the first or second generation were left, however. Most of the land in Kununurra was on its third or fourth owner, and it had been opened up only for 25 years. So at the age of 35, and looking for a challenge, he put a cousin in charge of the crops and pigs on the family farm. 'I had too much energy just to stay there and keep plodding along,' he says. Not that Wilhelm was ever your average plodder. In addition to having a Masters degree in agriculture, he had been a star sportsman who played 15 years of soccer at the highest level of the German amateur league and was asked to go professional at twenty-one. As an athlete, out of the northern German population of 15 million, he was among the top five. As a boxer, he was number two in the nation. He also competed as a decathlete, pentathlete and clay bird shooter. He was too busy to get married until he was 35, to Gabi, who happened to be a farm apprentice on Wilhelm's farm. She later went on to obtain a PhD in animal husbandry, Germany's youngest person ever, at 25, to hold a doctorate in agriculture. I was sad not to meet Gabi. She had gone to Germany for a family celebration.

Not long after they got their farm, the government in 1984 left Kununurra to make its own way, withdrawing subsidies and assistance to farmers. 'And that's when it really started, when the good farmers who had knowledge, who had enough money to start and give it a go, came in here,' Wilhelm says, warming to one of his favourite subjects. 'And from then on Kununurra just went on upwards.'

Wilhelm has no kind words for the system of subsidies which are a way of life in Europe. 'And that was another reason why I got here, and why I still like to be here, because we are not subsidised, we are competing on the world market. And we can compete . . . Free enterprise will pick up straight away if it is let alone. [Assistance] just works for you in the moment but in the long run, it will hurt you. If you are not good enough now, you will be even worse off later.'

The Bloeckers started exporting their melons into Hong Kong and Singapore about ten years ago. Demand, even through the Asian economic slowdown, has continued to be greater than they can supply and generally, for better prices than domestically.

I ask Wilhelm to describe his early days at Kununurra. 'When I first came here I saw the enormous amount of land because land is always very limited in Germany, and the abundance of water and obviously the sun on top of it. So I basically thought it must be right. But at that time I didn't know how to make it right, I have to be honest about that.' They had to learn how to fertilise crops, how to grow crops they had never seen before, work out which varieties grew at what time of the year. 'You have to learn quickly otherwise you're broke before you realise it.' But they were willing to work hard. How hard? I asked. 'Working 80 hours a week non-stop, and we've done that for years . . . We start in March and we finish in roughly early December without break.' There are no weekends and no days off. These days, however, they try to take a six-week break during the wet season, but never did in the early days. 'If you want to be successful, you have to like what you are doing, otherwise you waste your life,' he says.

'We still get up at 4.30 and we still work until it is dark. Then you go home and then you go through the mail.' He said as outsiders with a different culture from the easygoing Australians around them, it was not easy fitting in, but they were too busy concentrating on the farm to worry much. 'You have to do your own thing. It's not that you don't care about other people. If you want to be successful, if you want to do a good job, you are that much occupied. And still now, I don't know anything about the gossip in the town.'

They knew the basics of cropping, though—correct soil preparation, good watering, vigilance for insect damage, correct spraying—skills from the highly intensive farming system in Germany which have translated into a reputation for crops of the highest quality obtained through close examination of his plants and acute powers of observation. 'A lot of people come here without a decent farming background. In Germany if you want to be a farmer, first of all you do an apprenticeship, then you go to college, and the base you start from is so much better than if you start off here in Australia.' He says Germany's attitude that farmers be properly qualified began about 30 years ago, but a similar recognition is only now starting in Australia.

I wondered what he and Gabi had found difficult—perhaps the heat and humidity? 'Basically the way I see it, 85 per cent of weather is attitude and maybe 15 per cent is what you have to get used to. And if you see it like that, climate is not normally a problem.' More difficult in the early days was transport of produce to Perth almost 3500 kilometres away, 500 kilometres of which was then unsealed. 'We hardly could get transport, people forget about that. Now there is no problem whatsoever.'

Wilhelm and Gabi, with a workforce of around 40, many of them backpackers travelling through, grow in total 450 hectares of horticultural crops which include watermelons (5000 tonnes), rockmelons, pumpkins, honeydew melons and butternut pumpkin. In addition there are 400 hectares of sugar and a trial plot of new, genetically engineered cotton varieties. They also have chickpeas, sunflowers and maize.

Gabi is responsible for all marketing, normally spending three hours every morning on the telephone talking to agents to find out what the market is doing so she can set the right price for their goods. 'People totally underestimate still how much money can be made with transport and with marketing, by doing the homework and knowing exactly what is going on,' he says. 'At the moment we are getting one and two dollars per carton more than all our competitors. And that is a hell of a lot of money if you are talking a fair few cartons.' And he is—they sell each year in excess of 150 000 cartons of rockmelons alone.

Gabi still loads all the trucks. Wilhelm said in the early days of Kununurra, Gabi struggled against entrenched attitudes. 'Sometimes she was nearly crying because of the ignorance of the Australian men. They didn't accept women. She wasn't used to that from Germany any more. It is getting better, but I think Kununurra is a very good example. Of the five biggest growers, the women do the marketing. Gabi put a wedge into that and the others are following now. Now the agents are used to it, but in the beginning it was very, very hard.'

In the early years, their four children were always out in the paddocks with them, babies put in packing boxes to keep them out of the way of the forklift when Gabi loaded trucks. Their oldest child is now 13, the youngest six, and eventually their two sons will go to Germany to do farm apprenticeships and study, as well as training in Australia. The family always speaks German at home, unless there are visitors. 'It's such a waste if you don't do that, such a waste, because now they have already two languages and they learn another one at school.' He hopes their children come into the business. 'We don't want to force them, but we want to make it clear they have a good future up here. That is very contrary to a lot of other farming areas, where the parents have no reason to convince the kids to stay at home.'

Wilhelm's passion for his area extends beyond his farm gate. As chairman of the Kimberleys Sustainable Rural Development Group, he says they are concerned about problems of salinity, chemical run-off and soil degradation, erosion, the water table and that irrigation water is not wasted. 'We are the youngest and we want to tackle these problems before we have them and that's why we are started already now. We have got monitoring bores everywhere in the valley. We know that the water table is rising. We want now to map the underground to know where we can pump and where we can put in sub-surface drainage and things like that.'

The future for Australia lies in the north, according to Wilhelm Bloecker. Kununurra will grow. 'It's a very good place, and not only for farming, everything. I could start five other businesses and they would work here in town. There is so much untapped potential still here. And I think we should have a lot more immigrants . . . people with skills, that's what we need.' And the businesses he would start? Machinery manufacture and repairs, catering and party services, a lot more for tourists, such as environmental tours.

Which brings us back to his famous saying about eating potential for breakfast and his enthusiasm for a place that was written off just 14 years before. 'There is that much in this area you can do that is nearly unbelievable. It is mind boggling. If I couldn't grow any of the crops I am growing now, I still could make a living with other crops instead of what I am doing. Where do you have that? There are very few areas in Australia where you have such a diversity of crops, where you have got such a potential for other crops . . . A lot of tree crops haven't been tried here. Mangoes are slowly coming now. You can grow citrus, you can grow rambutans, you can grow nearly everything. There is just that much here that hasn't been done and can be done.' If he was forbidden to ever grow his present crops again, Wilhelm said he would grow mangoes, pink grapefruit for export and bananas.

On my way back to town, I was all for selling up and heading north to make the big fortune. An hour later, I wasn't quite so sure. Not many have the stamina, the foresight, the courage and determination that it takes. I'm not even good at growing vegetables down south, and I always forget to spray the fruit trees on time. And Kununurra is a long way from almost everywhere.

Mocking Convention—Gordon and Rosemary Mock

Some who did have courage to do something that most people at the time thought very odd, were Rosemary and Gordon Mock, former South Australians. I spoke to them on a hot Kimberley afternoon.

A midlife crisis can be blamed on a lot of things. But it doesn't usually make people leave a nice, comfortable affluent existence to live in a shed open to insects and tropical rain, and to establish a business that everyone says won't work. Gordon and Rosemary Mock were perfectly sensible wheat, wool, seeds and spice growers from Bordertown. They had also learned the benefits of value-adding through ownership of a seed-cleaning business. They had no dairy background, except for Gordon's six months when he was young and single in New Zealand, where he met Rosemary. They had a lovely house, their three children had a room each, a good library, music and ballet lessons. But when Gordon turned 40, they packed up and headed to Kununurra to start a dairy farm—surely a lunatic move by foolhardy beginners pushing into pioneering territory. Their dairy with its Indian Sahiwal/Australian Friesian cows battling heat, ticks and tropical grasses is Australia's most remote.

Their radical objective was to provide fresh milk to the Kimberley district and value-add to compensate for the extra costs of the north and the lower yield of tropical cows. They now also grow sugar cane, bottle their own underground spring water and reconstitute Riverland orange juice to put into cartons, make apple juice and a fruit drink called Kimblerley Crush, as well as have a farm shop for tourists. Along the way somehow, the Mocks also found themselves owning and running the town bakery for a few years; and then the local newspaper, the *Kimberley Echo*, when they stepped in to help out a friend financially who then suddenly died . . . which catapulted them into more accelerated learning.

Gordon and Rosemary Mock

We were sitting by a rock pool in the leafy garden of their house on poles. Carpentaria palms and bohinia trees protected us from the beating sun. Across the lawn, two little hand-reared black piglets came dancing by every now and again. A fountain made refreshing, trickling noises and birds called through the surrounding scrub.

The peace of the garden was deceptive. It was the middle of the tourist season and busy for the farm with hay carting on. Besides, the milk separator did a bearing that morning, they had treated the herd with selenium tablets, and vets were there doing routine health-testing of the herd. Milking started in an hour. The shop was swarming with people and the girls were struggling to keep up the flow of milkshakes.

Rosemary, wide-faced, generous and open, happily pulled herself away when I arrived. I had marvelled how she greeted every customer with genuine and fresh enthusiasm and served them quickly with a $2.50 milkshake before preparing for the next wave of hot and sometimes surly travellers.

When they settled in the district in 1985 with a truckload of farm machinery and the dog, and a carload of children and the cat, Kununurra was in the doldrums. Gordon had been there after he left school and had reckoned the Ord River area had the most potential of anywhere, but was too hot. After the horrendous Ash Wednesday fires in South Australia of 1983, Gordon and Rosemary felt they needed a change and since Ord land was cheap, went up and bought some.

'When we came here, the only milk that was available in town was usually about two months old. It had been frozen all that time. It was very expensive and it was low quality,' says Gordon, dry-voiced and slow speaking. 'We were looking for a business where we could value-add, where we could take it through to the consumer.' He was dusty from the hay and seemed a bit wary. So they milk the cows, grade and process the milk into various flavours in their own factory on the farm and distribute it to shops as Kimberley Milk, without intervention from middlemen.

Rosemary runs the farm shop from March to October, which also stocks tourist trinkets and books. It started off as a roadside stall selling bananas and dispensing water to thirsty travellers before the dairy got under way. The stream of cars down the dusty road to park under shady bohinias, African mahogany trees and frangipanis is constant. Children pat a calf tied up on the lawn and play on swings. The press of people at milking time to see cows milked is almost frantic and recharging camera flashlights sing like crickets.

'There was a fair bit of cynicism,' says Gordon of his farmer friends and family down south who thought he had finally tipped over the edge. 'There had been plans for two previous dairies. People had gone through all the paperwork and given it up. The north of Australia is full of broken, shattered dreams, so people had thought, well, here goes another one that probably won't come off. But we've proved them wrong,' said with a happy smirk from a kind face with untamed eyebrows and slightly crooked gaze that is slowly dropping its guard. He reminded me of a wary and wise old dog, circling and testing before allowing its tail to wag. I was to find out later that this guardedness becomes a necessity when all your friends are only passing through, a fact of life in remote regions. 'After a while you just kind of don't have close friends,' says Rosemary, explaining that they learn to put up a barrier to stop themselves being hurt when friends inevitably move on.

I ask Gordon to tell me how much of his bold move into dairying in the tropics had been a midlife symptom. 'I guess it was a conscious step . . . But it was also, well I describe it as a moment of madness, because it didn't really make a lot of sense, what we were doing. It wasn't a well-laid out and planned business plan or anything like that. It was "let's do it". I didn't do it for the dollars. I did it for the challenge and the fun.'

They admit they didn't have much idea what they were doing, and with three children in a primitive shed, foreign soil, pastures and irrigation methods, and strange rain seasons, they had plenty of drama getting the business going. Add to that, there were few people who knew anything about running tropical dairies that they could call on . . . plus they had to avoid soil previously used for cotton and sprayed with DDT.

'I think I had an advantage by not having milked cows before,' says Gordon. 'I didn't have preconceived ideas, because everything's different . . . It's a matter of doing a lot of guesswork yourself and trialling things and keeping a completely open mind.' The open mind had them feeding cows on rockmelons as well as more conventional cotton seed, chickpeas and sweetcorn.

It also had them finding shed life fun despite being very basic. 'There was no running water and we had to go down to the river for our bath,' says Rosemary. 'We used to cart water from the river for our drinking. We had a long drop loo out the back with a magnificent view of the mountains and the crops growing around us.' The walls of the loo were a concrete culvert tipped on its side.

'When the rainy season started, we had to shift furniture from one side [of the shed] to the other depending on which direction the rain was coming from,' says Rosemary laughing heartily. Compounding the frontier experience was a good covering of mould over all their possessions and furniture when they returned after a five-month trip down south for harvest and seeding on the Bordertown property. There's nothing like running two farms a continent apart . . . something they still do, but now they have a manager on the southern place.

'But it was good for the children,' says Rosemary of their unconventional decision to regress to a more pioneering lifestyle away from carpets and comfort. 'It was all getting too luxurious. Things were getting a bit too easy. We didn't think that was good for the kids. We hadn't had it easy, so why should they?' Down south, with heavy machinery and its inherent dangers, there wasn't a way for the children to develop a work ethic either.

'When we came here, they just had to help. The kids still remember coming out from school and weeding the bananas . . . It's been good for them,' Rosemary says. The children thrived on the adverse conditions. Although in the shed there was no separate area to do homework and even if there had been, insects around the lights drove them mad, two of the three were dux of the school and all eventually went to schools in Perth. Although they missed out on music lessons, they could go crocodile hunting, playing in waterfalls, swimming in rivers and have all become keen photographers. 'Nature is a part of their life a lot,' Gordon says.

Their eldest, Paul, is now 25, works on the farm and is getting married next year. Andrew is nearly 22, runs the newspaper and presents a weekly radio program with an Aboriginal counterpart, and Rachel, aged 18, is spending a year on the farm before starting nursing studies in Perth or Adelaide.

The dairy produces up to 2000 litres a day from about 200 cows. 'The only reason we can survive here—because we've got a high costs structure, we've got a low production per cow, the wages here are higher, and we haven't got economies of scale in the processing factory—but the reason why we can survive here is the wholesale price of milk is higher than most places in Australia because of the freight factor,' says Gordon, explaining that they compete against five other 'imported' brands.

They won't stay forever in this demanding and tough country where it doesn't rain for up to eight months of the year. The cracks in the black soil plains open so wide that when he first arrived, Gordon's foot slipped down one and he broke a toe. They also comment that relations between Aboriginals and the white community have deteriorated over the years which they blame largely on white administrators who appear to have created two separate races. 'It was all one, but they are gradually being separated by the politics and the policies of those people who work supposedly to help the Aborigines,' Gordon says. He illustrates his point by saying that his children went on a school camp to Darwin by bus and had to raise funds for it by baking cakes. The Aboriginal children were flown up at no cost, causing resentment and anger among the other children. 'If you wanted to dream up a plan to demoralise a race, we're doing a pretty good job,' says Gordon, who is president of Rotary, on the board of the Ord River District Co-operative, the board of Ord Sugar Industry and has been an elder in his church.

Gordon and Rosemary say they struggle with the heat of Kununurra for six months of the year and talk of spending time on the other farm for a few years after their son and his wife take over the dairy. They also have some land overlooking a waterfall in New Zealand where they hope to build a house, returning to Kununurra to see their family when the weather is pleasant.

In harsh late afternoon light, I watched the cows walk in, picking at cottonseed in their troughs. A truck collected cartons of flavoured milk and in the milking shed, frenzied tourists pushed against each other to watch the cups go on swollen udders, giggled at squirting manure and videoed and flashed every bovine movement. Yep, there's an opportunity for more attractions for these people who have come so far. In the meantime, Rosemary's chilled lime milkshake will do me.

Over the road from the Mocks' farm, I bought fresh fruit—rockmelon and bananas—and ate a mango ice-cream. Then I went to Ivanhoe Crossing, the original road to Wyndham where water gushes from Lake Argyle over a perilous-looking ford. People swim there despite large signs warning of crocodiles. I looked hard, couldn't see one but decided against swimming all the same. Wandering lonely as a cloud, I returned to my room and discovered it was raining at home.

Seeding a Free Spirit—
Spike Dessert

Friday, 7.00am. I am heading out to meet Spike Dessert, a Yankee-born specialist seedgrower. I am subliminally apprehensive, the hot and prickly-sounding name makes me think of cactus or a baddie in a western. Look for the row of coconut palms he had said. There they are, and on the end of a barn is written 'R.B. Dessert Seeds'. I park the car in some shade. It is already sweatingly hot.

The door of the upper-floor corrugated-iron office swings open and for a moment I think perhaps this really is the set of an American cowboy movie. Across a wide wooden verandah followed by a couple of dogs comes a bloke in denim jeans, workshirt, big broad hat and a pair of stout blue braces. I half expect to hear the jangle of rowelled spurs and see him swing into the saddle; or even do a bit of a hoe-down. So this is Spike—not the brash, loud dude I expected but rather lovable, infectiously enthusiastic and as I was to find out during the day, bubbling with plans to inject new spirit into the area. He greets me in a warm, clear voice and an accent from California softened by 12 years here. 'Come on, I'll take you for a look around,' he says, walking down the steps to the ute below. The dogs jostle to be first up on the back of the vehicle, but we have to be introduced first. 'Now, this one here is Bill Clinton,' Spike said, patting a white bull terrier-heeler cross. 'And this here's Nixon,' a blue heeler that decides to charm me by thrusting his nose into my crutch.

Regathering my dignity I climb into the ute. We race off, the dogs lean into the corners and Spike gives a robust commentary on rows upon rows of sculptured plants coming into seed, many resembling decorative topiary specimens. The unfolding picture is of a huge and colourful Amish patchwork quilt. Bright green cos lettuce in blocks, then deep red mignonettes, dark green cotton plants, rows of corn, swathes of lucerne, all interwoven with rust red soil, embroidered with

Spike Dessert

neat furrows. It has the folksy air of a Grandma Moses primitive painting, with hardly a weed to be seen.

Spike Dessert grows seed for chemical research centres and seed merchants, and produces his own varieties for domestic and export markets. It's exacting work, not one stray seed from his annual 100 or so different crops producing millions of seeds can drop into the wrong batch. His multi-skilled staff are always on their guard. 'I normally don't fire anybody for an honest mistake if they tell it to me,' but Spike says it's instant dismissal otherwise.

With an arm out the ute window Spike gives a lively running commentary about what is going on in his 360 hectare plot. Come along for the ride. First up you are looking at a row of 400 varieties of grass suitable for tropical home lawns or golf courses. From the best of them Spike will breed a new improved variety.

Next, sunflowers on the point of bloom. They are producing seeds suitable for salad sprouts and this variety is one that Spike has discovered and 'trued up', which means it has been made consistent and reliable. 'We are not genetic engineers, we are just selectors. We found something and brought this up to the forefront, so it is something new,' says Spike.

Next stop is certified bean seed, which is starting to be grown in disease-free Kununurra instead of the traditional bean seed area of Idaho. Then Asian beans with foot-long pods. 'We've brought in a selection from around the world . . . and now we will start marketing them into Asia to the farmers who have never before had disease-free beans.'

Then lettuces, some look like small Christmas trees as they come into seed. Others are like church steeples. American and Australian farmers are not allowed to plant anything but virus-free lettuce seed, so 30 000 seeds from each lot are tested to ensure a zero reading. Then there are hybrid sunflowers, sorghums and chickpeas. Many crops are interplanted with niger, an attractant for pest bugs. Spike tells me he has a good story to tell me here, so he stops the ute. Known mainly as a birdseed, the little black one you see in canary seed, niger had never been grown in Australia until Spike decided to grow the 40 to 50 tonnes used here each year. Its bug-controlling ability was discovered by accident. 'About six or eight years ago, we were growing niger next to some cotton being grown for chemical testing purposes. The chemical company came up, the cotton was at a certain size and the bugs were supposed to be bad. We had three or four patches around the farm but one patch had no bugs. So they sprayed it with something

Spike Dessert

to kill off predators, thinking this was a fluke. They came back in a week and there were still no bad bugs. So all of a sudden you start looking for a reason, and next door was the niger.' What they found was that niger, which is never sprayed, attracts destructive bugs like heliothis but is also attractive to useful bugs because of its nectar, pollen, eggs laid by the bad bugs and its good leaf cover. The Department of Agriculture started research into niger three years ago as a result of Spike's findings. It is now planted alongside commercial cotton crops and with sweetcorn, enabling a reduction in the amount of spray used on them. In Queensland, experiments are being conducted on the use of niger with tomatoes and early indications are that growers may be able to use about a quarter of the previous amount of spray. Sweetcorn previously couldn't be grown in Kununurra because of insect build-up, but with niger, it is now successful.

Spike says the organic market is not yet big in Australia but in the States, organic, unwashed, fresh, raw produce is in great demand. 'Thousands of hectares are grown with no insecticides,' he says, adding that shortly he will be involved in trials in Southern California of niger, companion-planted with lettuce and other salad vegetables.

We climb the steps back to the office where an overhead fan stirs the breeze. Spike takes his position like a boxer in a corner, not belligerent, but eager to get on with the job of telling me about himself.

'First of all my name is Raymond Bernard Dessert III, better know as Spike, and the name of the firm is R.B. Dessert Seed Company,' he intones into the microphone. He explains the R.B. is important for differentiation. In the States, where the family seed business began three generations ago, the Dessert name was used by a former family business, by two Dessert brothers and a cousin.

'I grew up in the seed business, moved here to Kununurra 20 something years ago for the previous family business, but moved back and forth and eventually we were bought out. I sold up and then moved back here on my own to this farm in 1986 at about a time when the Ord was probably at its lowest levels after the failure of cotton, the failure of rice and the failure of a few other government-sponsored projects. We bought this farm, my wife and I, and our four children. We now produce seed crops for Australia, but also for ourselves and also for seed companies in Europe, Japan, Asia and the United States. Our main thing is that we produce them off-season, disease free and very high quality. That's the only way to compete from an isolated area like Kununurra.'

While he is rattling through his credentials, I study his face, noting the smooth, glowing skin which is in quite good shape for a 54-year-old outdoor worker. His hair is still mainly dark. A pair of eccentric, pink-framed glasses keep sailing down to the tip of his handsome Roman nose. A moustache as thick as a broom head hangs like a verandah over an elastic ready-to-smile mouth.

Spike explains that the climate in the Ord Valley is almost perfect for seed production which he pioneered there 12 years ago. 'We are just now getting it going in that we are recognised as a legitimate seed production area in other parts of the world.' He also grows sugar cane to keep diversified and 'make the bank manager happy'.

Spike was born in Southern California into the business started by his grandfather in Canada. After business troubles in the Great Depression, they were attracted to Arizona and central California where there were subsidies enabling the United States after the First World War to take over from Europe as the leading seed producer. 'That family business grew and we eventually became the largest small-seed producers in the world,' Spike says. 'We had about 250 full-time employees. We had research doctors. We were growing [seed] from the Canadian border to Mexico. We controlled probably 20 000 acres of seed crops and we marketed all over the world. In 1972, the man running for president was called McGovern. He was a Kennedy person, a socialist, and one of his platform planks that he was going to do if elected was to eliminate corporate farming.' The aim was to get people back to 100 acre farms. 'We went looking for a seed production area outside the United States then.'

His father flew to Kununurra, saw it as the 'promised land' and made an application for land. He told Spike, then aged 28, that he was going. 'I was the oldest of the third generation.' Spike cleared and developed the 3000 acre farm on other side of the valley from his present farm. In 1974, when oil prices rose dizzily, a huge US oil company went into genetic engineering for tax reasons, and bought the Dessert Seed Company to market their products. Spike found his new bosses didn't understand mother nature so he left, along with 20 other top people. After some years in the United States, Spike's wife asked him if he ever missed the Ord. 'Well, that's all it took. A year and a half later, we moved back here,' says Spike, who by then was forty-one.

The beauty of Kununurra is that the climate is reliable and doesn't cause delays in supply for Spike's customers. 'Reliability is something that is very crucial, and to be proven reliable takes years,' he says. With no rain for eight months of the year, he can use irrigation when he wants it and at the right rate. 'It is a very nice area to farm and it all just adds up to be a good seed production area.'

But there is more to Spike than his seed business, absorbing though it is. As we walk outside, he is like a kid on Christmas morning and leads me into a former machinery shed. Blow me down . . . if this bloke isn't setting up a whisky and rum still. He's going into the booze business, says it's all to do with value-adding. Images swirl of sleazy blokes with machine guns, bootleggers with backyard stills and two-tone shoes. But no, this is quite legit. Spike gnawed at the Western Australian authorities for a distillery licence until all their arguments wore out. 'I kept pestering them, and they finally figured out I wouldn't go away.' Apparently the rules state only one type of alcoholic drink can be made in one place. He's planning to make a whole range, which threw the bureaucrats somewhat. 'I've got a Special Licence—Production of Alcohol,' he says triumphantly.

'We're setting our factory up so that we can actually make grain wine and beer, or distil the grain wine and beer to make spirits. We'll give the tourists different things to look at and buy, and make fruit wines and beer of different types, and a few different spirits relying on such local products such as mangoes, rockmelons, watermelons or whatever there is. A lot of our future, I think, is cellar door sales for the tourist trade.'

Well, I thought, that's the grumpy tourist syndrome solved. A few shots of Spike's Ord brew and they'll be dancing in the streets.

'Maybe it's a lot more fun to go around selling whisky and rum than it is to flog seed,' he says with a raised eyebrow and a cheeky grin. 'At least I can always sit back in my old age and drink my own product.'

Up on the shed the word HOOCHERY will be written alongside R.B. Dessert Seeds. 'Hoochery is a coined word I've trademarked,' he tells me. 'I can't call it a distillery because I've got wine and beer. I can't call it a winery because we have beer and spirits. I can't call it a brewery because we have wine and spirits. "Hooch" is an American and Canadian slang word—it's in the dictionary—for alcoholic beverage, not necessarily wine, spirits or beer, so I just put the "ery" on the end of it, so it's a hoochery. We have it trademarked and that is going to actually be our brand name.'

He calculates his first batch will be under way in just a few months. Kimberley Whisky, made from local corn will be the main line, but his Ord Rum made from local sugar, he predicts will taste like the famous Caribbean rums. In two and a half years, after mandatory ageing of two years, they'll be on the market. In the meantime, he might sell cane spirits, very young rum, in next year's tourist season.

Revealing my down south wussy ways, I foolishly ask about qualifications for whoever is going to make the spirits. I got the sermon I deserved. 'Man has been making alcohol for 5000 years, so it can't be that hard. And everybody thinks you have to be trained. But where did the first French people learn how to make wine? Where did the first Germans learn how to make beer? My attitude and philosophy is that nobody has ever made Kimberley corn whisky or Ord rum so I don't need a brewmaster who trained someplace else because this is a different climate. Everything is different here, so why start a business with these preordained rules of "you have to do it this way"?

'I have done a lot of reading. The last time I made home brew beer was over 30 something years ago when I was in university, but things are simple, things are modern and to do it the old way, I feel is wrong. So we are going to do it the Kununurra way. And if it turns out we are not making American whisky, we're making Kimberley whisky; we're not making Bundaberg Rum, we're making Ord rum, we'll just let it evolve. We'll keep our records, we'll keep our notes and we'll train our own people. Maybe my daughter or son will come into the business and become the brewmaster in a few years. They will be the expert at making Ord rum because that's the only way to make it, that's the way it evolves and that's what we're going to have.'

Spike reckons it's just as simple as bunging a whole pile of barley or corn and a bit of yeast into a vat and letting it bubble, then boiling it in his 500 litre pot still, condensing the liquor and leaving it in oak barrels for two years—all done the traditional way for full flavour.

He coached a friend with a pot still to make a batch of rum, and he tasted it after just 30 days. 'It is actually quite good,' he says with relish, telling me that it matches in quality some other well-known rums. 'If you put a line of glasses down and equal amounts of rum and ice, and took a sip of each, you would not be able to pick this 30-day-old spirit.' Most commercial rum is made in modern 'continuous stills', he says. 'This local stuff is made the old-fashioned way and really does have the old-fashioned flavour.'

I wonder aloud if being an outsider is an advantage—giving him a clearer view of things and greater freedom. 'Coming in here from the outside, not being Australian, allowed me to actually go [to the States] look at the future and bring it back. It's like a time machine . . . I still go and visit every couple of years, see how they're progressing. They're basically, in some things, 20 years ahead of us.' Then he allows himself to smile broadly. 'The other advantage, I think, is that I'm a loud-mouthed Yank and people do say, okay, we're not going to argue. They just let it go. Where if I was an Australian they'd say, that's not how you do things. It's kinda nice being a bit different. And you're not stuck in a mould,' says Australian citizen Spike, who sits on his shire council. 'This place is home. I'm not going anywhere.' It's a place he's fiercely proud of and has a vision for.

'Eventually I see the state of the Kimberley', he says, citing as reasons for a buoyant, populous future its plentiful water, good climate, ready markets for its products and the availability of farming land. Spike talks too about the frontier feeling of remote places. Being so far from Canberra and Sydney is a bonus. It encourages a spirit of independence. People with ideas can get them off the ground in the north. There are so few services, therefore huge opportunities for anyone who wants to do something. There are no preordained ways of doing things, which allows room for free spirits and creative approaches to problems.

I drove off in a world-conquering mood . . . loosening the chains of conformity, taking on the self-belief of the isolated. Now, if only some of that rum was already available, I'd have been really flying. The self-confidence and individuality of the remote citizen is precisely why, in this task of exploring the work and ideas of contemporary people on the land, I have aimed for regions as far away as possible from the dominating nature of large centres. Unaffected by inhibiting doubts or the jealousies of others, or the rules of large groups requiring submission of the individual, the people of isolated regions are some of our most creative.

The Buffalo Farm of Kakadu—
David Lindner

I flew back into Darwin dining opulently on roast turkey and three veg. This is an outpost route seemingly overlooked by airline accountants. An enjoyable pampering but I got indigestion watching the cabin staff rushing our expansive meals out and back in the one-hour trip. A hire car was waiting for me at the airport and I left almost immediately to make a trip into Kakadu, far from opulence and civilisation.

David Lindner was just finishing deliveries of buffalo meat to people in Jabiru. A few hunks were still in plastic tubs in the back of the Toyota. Those distributed, I followed him down bush tracks into his camp in the heart of the World Heritage Kakadu. David, aged 54, farms 1000 water buffalo on 100 square kilometres of non-tourist area for the Gagadju people, traditional owners of Kakadu.

This is a surprising site for a farm—pest animals being raised among the jewelled swamps of a national park. I found few outside Kakadu knew it existed. The farm's purpose is to provide 'bush tucker' to tribespeople around Jabiru who had come to regard it as traditional food.

Dave, formerly of the eastern suburbs of Adelaide, has had four Aboriginal wives: three were Kakadu bush women. He turned his back on so-called civilisation long ago, preferring to live a simple and uncluttered life devoted to nature. He is a highly regarded wildlife observer, a deep thinker about Aboriginal issues, someone sought out for his opinions by academics, researchers and the likes of Professor Manning Clark.

Dave Lindner lives in a big iron shed with cement and dirt floors, open to the weather. He has no phone or television. His only luxury is a fan rotating overhead to keep the air moving through. The living end of the shed is open but has a rainwater tank and tap close handy. Shadecloth hangs off the roof to stop rain blowing in. Wooden planks

David Lindner

David Lindner

are shelves, some blue and white material closes off the cooking implements from view. A radio and electric kettle sit on the tin-topped table. His sleeping quarters are curtained off beyond the rudimentary cooking facilities and a refrigerator.

It was dark when we arrived at the camp hidden in the bush. I could see little except a light on over the coolroom housing fresh buffalo meat. I could hear a generator thumping some distance away. In the bush, back from the track where I stood, I heard a large animal cracking through undergrowth. It was a horse, Dave told me later. Apart from Dave's dwelling and another shed covering a caravan for Aboriginal workmen, and where I parked my things, I could see nothing, so black was the night.

We had a cup of tea. He reminisced about the Adelaide he last knew in 1961 and we awaited the arrival of friends and family for a party—well, it was Saturday night after all. Lights wound through the bush and Dave's son Gary, a Kakadu ranger, his Aboriginal wife Dottie, their children, another park ranger and his family from Victoria, turned the night festive.

They brought plates, chairs, food, drink and we had an instant and delicious feast of crumbed barramundi and salmon caught in Kakadu, fried rice, potato salad and buffalo cooked with shallots by Dave. The Jabiluka protests were under way but no-one seemed terribly fussed about the mine; instead, they found amusement in the antics of protestors, laughing that the wet season would quieten them down a bit.

When everyone had left, Dave threw the scraps from the plates onto the floor. I was alarmed at his housekeeping. 'Don't worry,' he said, 'the cats will have it clean by morning.' And there they were—chestnut fur and white spots, little furtive quolls, native cats that materialised from the shadows: darting, watching, worried about the stranger in their midst. Greedy, grabbing, eating in quick sneaky attacks. They once lived in South Australia, but they have all gone now.

I heard barking. I was surprised there were dogs out there. 'Barking owls,' Dave corrected. He doesn't say a lot, Dave Lindner, unless it is really necessary. The owls kept up a racket all night. We talked more about wildlife—the quolls were still skittering around gathering up bones and scraps. 'The pythons are probably watching us,' said Dave. I drew my feet up onto the box nearby. 'But they won't come out because you're here.' Olive pythons, harmless and quite friendly, according to Dave. One lives in the kitchen cupboard and Dave pats it on the head. It doesn't recoil now that it knows him, Dave says. 'If you give them the run of the camp, they'll crawl between your legs to drink water out of a bowl on the floor and that sort of thing. They're an incredible snake to have around the place. These animals get to recognise you and their attitude to you is not of fear.'

I heard a curlew cry. I started at the sound I know so well from home, that few will ever hear. They're in plentiful supply up north, Dave thinks, but with foxes and dingoes he admits it's hard to know. He sees them at night eating the insects that gather under the lights at the coldroom. They were once plentiful in my region too.

Dave delighted in telling me of how he shoots red-tailed black cockatoos for the Aborigines. These majestic birds, so few in number down south and seriously endangered, are common up north. He reports with a wicked smile that they are delicious to eat. I would hope so. Alive, they have a black market value overseas of at least $30 000 each. Expensive tucker.

I retired to my caravan to a night of feverish dreams—of barking dogs with beaks; plates of cockatoos, their red tails dripping blood; quolls chewing up my tapes; while all around curlews screamed. I was relieved when finally I heard Dave knocking on the shed at 5.30am. After a cup of tea and a muesli bar, we set off to Duck Camp swamp to record Dave's story.

In the battle-scarred Toyota, we bumped and slid through water, sped along tree-lined tracks and finally drew up to a large swamp covered with birds. Magpie geese took off in great rising curtains of black and white. Ibis, spoonbills, egrets, cranes, waders, whistling ducks and cockatoos continued their morning tasks of feeding and grooming. Waterlilies in full bloom dotted the swamp and at a nearby lagoon with tall palms and eucaplypts fringing its banks there are plenty of barramundi and crocodiles, according to Dave.

The morning was still cool and we sat on a thick mat of dewy grass next to a waterhole flipping with silver fish. 'I basically supply buffalo meat and game meat such as magpie geese, goannas and other wild animals to people living in Kakadu who are mainly full-blood Aboriginal people,' says Dave, embarking on his word journey. 'The most basic thing about them is they speak Gunwingu language. They still speak in language at most times among themselves. This differentiates them from other people of some Aboriginal ancestry who come here to work or for other reasons and who are not what you'd call part of the traditional owner population.'

When the Kakadu park came under federal control in 1978, it was infested with feral buffalo that were ravaging the swamps, ruining vegetation and turning vast areas into mud wallows. Dave worked with the Northern Territory government until 1979, co-ordinating buffalo culling, organising helicopter shoots and issuing contracts to hunters.

'I came out here with my wife at the time [Violet]. She was a traditional owner for the area, and she just wanted to come back into her country.' When they came to Kakadu, Dave was unemployed for 18 months after he got offside with federal park authorities by insisting that buffalo killing should go on as a top priority. At that stage it had been stopped. So privately, Dave started shooting buffalo and delivering meat to the traditional owners to give himself something to do. This became paid work in 1981 when the Aborigines formed the Gagadju Association to receive royalties and up-front monies when the Ranger uranium mine came into production.

When the National Bovine Tuberculosis Eradication Campaign (BTEC) started, every one of the park's 100 000 buffalo was due to be killed. 'So provision in the management plan for the park at that time allowed for the establishment of a controlled herd of buffalo, TB free, for a continuing supply of buffalo meat killed in the tradition of Aboriginal people's use of buffalo since 50 or 60 years earlier when they first came into the country. The herd was to be made available to people if they wanted to set up a farm. So I took this on.' The last few animals left in Kakadu were handed over to the Aboriginal people and the Gagadju Association. 'In 1989, we ... started the herd which makes the present buffalo farm.' The farm is run like any other livestock enterprise with the total area divided into paddocks suitable for use in the wet and dry seasons. It includes swamps and watercourses for buffalo to wallow in. In the stressful dry period when feed is in short supply, urea blocks are put out. Dave kills 200 two to three-year-old animals a year for the Gagadju people. The herd has a 55 per cent calving rate because of the low nutrition of the pastures. He sprays herbicide along fence lines to prevent shorts in the electric fences in the wet, or fires in the dry. The farm operates with an annual budget of $150 000, and he would like to employ labour but can't. He delivers buffalo meat on a 460 kilometre round trip to about 50 households when the animals are fat from November to June, and magpie geese from July to October shot in early morning or evening. Dave calculates the value of the buffalo meat at around $8 a kilo and the geese at $10 a bird, but no money changes hands since the community owns the farm. Dave calculates the value of its produce at over $150 000 a year. 'The farm is now extended to its full projected area, fully fenced and the balance between stock and food resources for the stock is fairly good. The herd is in good condition,' said with some satisfaction.

Indeed, all was smooth and buoyant until a few months ago, when the Gagadju Association was suddenly put into receivership. It had been set up to administer and invest the traditional owners' mine royalties in such businesses as pubs and the farm. 'The meat supply was always funded, as the return from the meat supply expenditure was meat delivered to people's places . . . The administrators in Gagadju couldn't handle that . . . They kept saying this should be making a profit. Well the profit, of course, was obvious to the Aboriginal people—they were getting the meat. They were getting a return in no other area of the financial administration of the royalties. Pubs were bought but nothing ever came out of them because there were bank loans, there were buildings, expenditure and this sort of thing . . . The buffalo farm and its previous wild-shot buffalo pre-BTEC wipe-out days, has been a continuous input into the community from their payment of my wages, equipment and the farming establishment out of their royalties . . . Eventually mistakes in business administration led the association into debts it couldn't repay. They were wound up by creditors through court and the buffalo farm was a victim of this court action.'

Dave is working presently on a voluntary basis with what equipment and fuel hasn't yet been taken by the receiver. 'The herd is probably safe,' he says. 'It is disputed. The receiver wants the buffalo herd. The buffalo are worth quite a lot of money. There are very few left . . . accessible ones. These are TB free.' Any replacements would cost a fortune. Dave argues, however, that once the buffalo are removed it would be unlikely they would ever be allowed to return to the wetlands of this world heritage area, even if it is to a farm as securely electric-fenced as it is.

Dave says Aboriginal people, being easygoing and not good at planning, have only just started to fight to keep the farm. However, the loss of their fresh meat supply would be accepted just as a severe drought or flood would be accepted. 'This buffalo meat is a delicacy or a preferred meat, but it's not critical for people to remain alive and well fed. It's just something they like to pay for,' Dave says.

They certainly wouldn't be going without food: social security provides more than enough food for their needs. Also, Dave explains, that being bush people they are able to go without food for quite a time. Their bodies are adapted to cope with feast and famine. 'But if it goes, well, things have come and gone for years . . . Most people haven't got strong feelings on those things because prior to contact, it was a cop-it-sweet existence on the environment's terms and things have been very much like that for Aborigines since contact.' So, if the food from Dave stops, it won't make any difference. They just won't have it, that's all. Some will go hunting and get geese. Dave does say though, with a bit of a laugh, that if he was delivering free cigarettes instead of bush tucker, he thinks there would be a bit more of an effort to retain the service. Meat is not an addiction like tobacco—'In a sense, it is a luxury.'

He does point out though, that the people eating meat, mothers and old people, have fewer health problems in relation to bone structure and malnutrition in children, and for women 'who have continuous babies'. 'But the health problems of the people in Kakadu are related to lifestyle rather than diet. They are not walking. They are overweight people. If they ate wholemeal bread instead of white bread, if they ate waterlily instead of breads and rice, they would still, across the board, be very sick people, because they are not walking.'

'The problem with social security is what happens to it, what it buys. I said it was adequate for buying food, you can buy an excessive amount of food. The situation in Kakadu is that people are entitled to social security payments without being encumbered by school attendance by the children, that sort of thing, rules related to gambling, and so on.' There needs to be policy, not to save the government money but to get people to adopt a lifestyle which is in line with a monied community, he says. Withdrawing money if their children weren't going to school would help them to be a functioning component in wider society and cut down their dependence on medicine, and make them realise it is the responsibility of people receiving money to have recorded attendance at school by kids. 'It might pull a senior member of a family who is a total drunk, absorbing all the family's money, away from his drunken habits,' he said.

'Social security has led to a lot of people spending a lot of time sitting down . . . a lot of people who had a good bush education, those certain number of people who had a work experience in younger life, and now not doing either, not living in the bush, travelling in the bush in a Toyota and not moving more than about 10 metres from that Toyota at any time while they're in the bush. It is not to my idea of bush experience in accordance with Aboriginal culture—because they are a walking people.'

Profound sadness hangs heavily in Dave's voice and over his white-whiskered face as he talks of the people he has lived with for most of his life and whom he deeply respects and admires. He believes the scourge of diabetes among Aboriginals will diminish if they resume exercise. 'A friend of mine was diagnosed with diabetes about 30 years ago. She's in her seventies now. She's worked on 5 acre blocks . . . where she's been living, [in] good housing, mowed the lawns with virtually the smallest mower you can buy, pushing, and she's had virtually no trouble with her diabetes since it was diagnosed. Everyone else who was diagnosed with diabetes at that time and who's been in this Toyota travel culture, they're all dead.

'The diabetes population of Kakadu now is in its forties and thirties and it's correlated to vehicle travel replacing walking. Things have been brought up, like dogs in camps, that they are unhealthy and that sort of thing. The worst dogs in Kakadu are in a camp called 009, but the people there are the healthiest. They have no vehicles, they just walk everywhere. They are very healthy people.' He believes other lifestyle diseases like hypertension, heart disease and cancers would also decrease.

It is not right for the white population to be holier than thou about its apparent good health and civilised lifestyle. It has its own problems, according to Dave—writing its own death warrant: driving everywhere, destroying the atmosphere—too busy killing itself to really worry about the Aboriginal population. 'I can't see any way out for society. It's just an arrogant animal on the rampage and it will pay the penalty.'

He believes that if everybody who is currently poor and living in a tribal way in Australia, Asia or Africa started to live like the average well-off civilised person then the 'global environment would just be extinguished like a defective light bulb going out more or less in a year'.

'The average Aboriginal, even with the amount of junk material people buy with their social security cheques, has a very low environmental impact in terms of use of fuels and energy compared with the non-Aboriginal counterpart in Australian society. It is a disorganised life. They are propped up by a huge medical input . . . But even so, their environmental impact is very low.'

Dave Lindner believes wider society should be worrying about itself and its effects more than what Aboriginals do. His sociological observations were shared with Manning Clark in a meeting with famous elder stateman Bill Neidjie, Kakadu Man. Dave said Clark seemed unable to understand Aboriginal culture. Dave found him an 'unrealistic idealist' with 'naive do-gooder attitudes'.

The impact of mining royalties on Aboriginal communities is low compared with social security money which is regular and comparatively large and comes with no strings attached. Mine money is invested through their specially set up associations but some royalties are given out as cash, about $1500 each a year. It is a small amount overall, he says, but it causes fights, vehicle accidents from alcohol, allows car dealers to have a field day getting rid of 'bombs' but it is all over within a week. Some of the well-organised people buy washing machines and furniture, and pay off debts.

We touched on the stolen generation debate. His views again are unconventional, controversial. He maintains many people in the north did well out of being the stolen generation. 'Many people doing well in cities and enjoying life may be protesting strongly but if they had stayed in their communities they would be dead of diabetes or murdered or drunk themselves to death and so on . . . Seeing kids disappear is just part of life in families . . . These sorts of events are regular things in their society.'

Down south, a different group of people were victims of stolen generation—often taken to suit the needs of employers. People in southern Australia 'were traded around'. They have a right to be outraged.

The sun was getting hotter and the birds noisier. I wanted to know about Dave. He told me he spent much of his time as a youth tramping around the Adelaide Hills in what is now Cleland Wildlife Reserve. He paints a picture of a highly intelligent boy, but one who enjoyed being unconventional, even obtuse. He told me he changed from being right-handed to being left-handed just to annoy his teacher. He has had a lifetime interest in reptiles, started off with snakes 'as a spectacular, dangerous thing, ego thing, that broadened out predictably into crocodiles'. He feeds a 'friendly' crocodile called Roughnut once a week during goose-shooting season. He also entertains large goannas around his house.

Whistling ducks circle overhead. Two birds, a pied heron and an egret, begin fighting over a fish not far from our feet. Why they bothered to fight . . . the bony brim or herring were jumping up as if to dare the birds to catch them. I asked if we were being observed by crocodiles. 'I don't think so, because they would have stuck their head up and I haven't noticed any,' he said. 'There's a goanna over there, walking over the top of the hill.' His bush eyes had picked it up. I couldn't see it at all. This was the beauty and magic of the place. There were probably thousands of eyes watching us.

Dave says as an A-stream student in matriculation at Norwood High School he was doing badly, going out every night after school up to Waterfall Gully and not doing his homework. Instead, he caught snakes, patrolled sheep for dog attack, and chased girls. He asked his mother to get him a job with a family friend who had a sheep and cattle station at Wilcannia. He promised he would go back to school, but never did. He stayed there for two years, then got a job with Sandy Pye on Tod River Station out of Alice Springs for another two years. He then managed a place for Sandy Pye at Oodnadatta. 'In the process of working on these properties, I was catching snakes and lizards and sending them off to museums. The wildlife authority bloke in the territory at the time, Ken Slater, was a reptile fanatic. I got very well known as a person who was collecting rarely collected animals for research, and he offered me a job. So I left station work and went and worked for the wildlife authority in the territory and ended up staying there for 14 years. I got married to an Alice Springs girl, her father was from an Aboriginal family. They owned a property next door to Sandy Pye's place. I wasn't making much money, I had rent to pay. A ranger's job came up at Coburg Peninsula on the extreme north coast of the Northern Territory. So I said I'd take that job for one year as long as I could have a job back in Tanami, where there was a major wildlife sanctuary.' In Coburg, he became completely absorbed in his work with marine turtles. 'There was material there that was little understood scientifically and I was working with Harold Cogger at the Australian Museum and we ended up working together. He got a lot of material for the museum and his own knowledge out of that area.' Dave stayed at Coburg for five years then, in 1974, moved to Darwin, shelving ideas of returning to the Tanami. Marji, his wife of ten years, left with their four children for Alice Springs.

In Darwin, Dave Lindner was responsible for Kakadu before it came into existence as a park. 'I ended up, I suppose you could say, being married to one of the local girls here, Violet, for seven years, and she initially came to Darwin with me.' Violet's father was half Aboriginal, mother a full blood—same as Marji, but Violet 'was a language-speaking Aboriginal. She had never had education, she had lived in the bush all her life, a very good bush woman.' She had grown up in Kakadu. 'There were only about two or three families out here who opted to be bush people, and in a sense they are very different. They just get addicted to bush life. Everything else is not right to them.'

Self-government came to the Northern Territory in 1979, along with a lot of money. Dave hated seeing money being squandered on the wrong things. 'I lost my dedication. I had never been a career bureaucrat. I had been a career environmentalist in the wildlife outfit. I lost that dedication, so when Violet said, I'm going back out to Kakadu, I came with her. I was unemployed for 18 months. I just did a lot of environmental work when I was on the dole. I initiated the mimosa control which has been successful in Kakadu.' The horrific nature of mimosa can turn grassland into thorny shrubland. Dave said he used to kill every plant in a clump by hand and keep going back, burning the ground to make the seeds germinate. 'Now they use a lot of herbicide, then we did it all physically.' That work, plus providing meat kept him busy.

Violet then got a job as a fully employed ranger 'and fell in love with a young white ranger, so old bloke me, I had to step aside'. Dave then married Violet's older sister, Jessie, living for seven years in a lovely homestead built for commercial buffalo-shooting safaris, near Cooinda, on Jim Jim Creek. Jessie and Dave separated, the deciding reason was that she wanted to put in a satellite dish for TV. 'I told her I would fill it up with bullet holes if she did, so she left and went to Jabiru.'

Then the head man around Kakadu, Toby Gangele, died. He had been a very good friend of Dave's. Some three years after his death, Dave married his widow, Ruby. It only lasted three years. 'She was very ill from diabetes. She was a great bush woman, a full-blood woman . . . She died two years ago. She was a person you couldn't spend enough time with.' He is talking very softly with great sadness in his voice.

'Many people think a good bushman is someone who turns the bush into a livable place. A good bushman to me is a person who goes into the bush and when he comes out of it, you can't see any difference in the bush and he survives,' he says. 'She was at one with the bush. I just liked watching her all the time, just what she was doing and the way she did it.' He tells of her beautiful personality, strong opinions but gentle nature. He told how one day Ruby was fishing at a waterhole and continued even though a fire was burning all round her. It was so hot the waterlilies were singed, but she kept on fishing. The bush was her preferred environment but Dave says the women can't pass their traditional values on to their children. 'It's finished. Finished by law, the intrusiveness of modern society, it just doesn't happen.' For every woman who has survived from the old bush culture, 'a lot go under from drink'.

I asked Dave if there was something in particular that attracted him to Aboriginal women—was it their submissiveness to their husbands, since under Aboriginal tribal law they are regarded as the property of their husbands. He says Aboriginal women are 'better as social companions, not as glamour mates, but as real companions in life for my chosen lifestyle'.

'It may have started with an obtuseness. For example, when I was at Wilcannia, people were still being gaoled for cohabitating. I just couldn't see any reason why, if you liked one of those people, you shouldn't go with them.' In Alice Springs where cohabitation was not an offence, he found himself looking for a wife. 'Marji was a person I just found very attractive, a very quiet person. Got her own strong views and everything like that. There's no suggestion that you're getting a slave.

'But having broken from the conventions of the pastoral industry and crossed the tracks. It's a bit like catching a snake because it's dangerous and then becoming interested in the scientific research aspect of reptiles. It takes over from the thrill side of it . . . then you just find that you are living in that community.'

What sounded like gunshots at the lagoon interrupted us. We left the waterhole hastily, but could find no sign of crocodile poachers. We headed back to Dave's camp, stopping to watch partridge pigeons, buffalo cows and calves grazing. The day was now very hot. Drinking water at the table under the fan, we talked of Dave's other great loves—guns and hunting. 'Hunting is an extension of the hunter-gatherer Aboriginal existence, the highest form of man that I recognise.' I was staggered at this statement. He explained further. 'A hunter-gatherer might modify his environment with fire and other things but essentially what the seasons and the environment in terms of nutrients and climate produce, is what man has to live on. He is not storing food, he is not doing anything like that, so his population is of necessity very, very low in the wild community. The ecosystem is a component in it, he's not fighting with nature. By the time he's got a feed, he's generally not interested in going and killing things for fun, except alien groups of humans. This is really an expression of normal animal behaviour throughout the animal kingdom. Once you get into people who fight nature to grow, who destroy ecosystems to grow crops, for storage, for power, for commerce, you are talking about a very degenerate animal, in this case a human, in which the result is fairly well inevitable because enough is never enough and they just keep going, they want more. It is an interesting thing that hunter-gatherers almost always had fairly ruthless rules for controlling their own numbers so that presumably in flush seasons for reasons that they had long forgotten, when numbers go up, they are controlled by infanticide and ritual killings and that sort of thing—the sort of thing that is fairly well documented for Aranta people, but seems to be a thing worldwide in hunter-gatherers. Once you've got the capacity to store food, it seems that if the population gets too big, you go and clobber someone next door and take some of their country and enslave people and so on. All this is degenerate behaviour because it's ultimately going to bring the species to its knees.'

For Love of the Land

As for cities, Dave said, 'Cities are the ultimate expression of human degeneration. They are self-serving and they expect the rest of the world to justify itself on their terms.' I say I think his judgement is very harsh . . . He conceded they were useful for hospitals.

Dave may have broken the promise he made to his mother about going on with school, but he has never stopped learning. He reads widely and is self-taught across a wide range of topics. His huge collection of books is treasured. In a remote area, they give access to information not available from anywhere else. He houses his books in two rooms of a separate and secure transportable building, as well as an extensive and probably very valuable collection of photographs recording environmental changes over the years, Aboriginal art and tools he has discovered. He has sent many of these to researchers.

Books, boxes and albums of photographs are crammed onto shelves and into crates. He showed me happy family shots of naked black children and his wife Marji laughing on the shores of rivers, at the beach with Violet, with fish they had caught, always happy. I couldn't bear to go on looking, not because I didn't find them beautiful, but because Dave was still mourning Ruby and his sadness for all he had lost was too uncomfortable. He carefully locked the room again, and the bush buzzed loudly with the sound of a million insects. I collected my things, took one last photograph of Dave in his quarters, and left for Katherine.

I was deep in thought absorbing Dave's views on development and greed. It was well after 1.00pm and I had eaten just a few biscuits since the muesli bars and tea at 5.30am. At Mary River store I quelled my pangs and watched a massive army tank-type four-wheel-drive tourist bus full of young, confident, flirting, affluent world travellers who could never have understood Dave's concept of overcivilisation.

The next day I would talk to Bill Harney, Aboriginal elder, head of the Wardaman tribe, which owns a cattle station and is encouraging its people to go back to the land. I found a motel, had a swim to the entertainment of drinking youths nearby who thought I must be made of steel. They thought the day was cold. I slept without dreams, excessively deeply.

Part VI

Centred Around Cattle— the Northern Territory

A Swag on the Ground— Jan Hayes

Bill Harney hadn't been home. He was at the cattle station west of Katherine, documenting dreaming trails with an anthropologist. I was all for driving out there but I would never find him, said Mick Peirce, white administrator of the Wardaman Aboriginal Corporation. So we had coffee and a good chat and I returned to Darwin in the late afternoon through countless fires, lit to make way for fresh grass shoots when the rains come.

At home again—school holidays, the junior cattlehandlers' Heifer Expo, an art exhibition to organise, a perilously dry winter where the house rainwater tank ran dry. Then somehow I found myself on the train to Melbourne with 74 students on a school music tour. Why? I asked myself as they frolicked all night with excitement. By the time I had co-ordinated my plans with my interstate travelling husband, it was to be some weeks before I could take off again—this time to Alice Springs.

It is early evening and I sit on a verandah looking across a wide flat valley of grey mulga trees to an amphitheatre of radiant sunset-drenched rocks, craggy and mountainous. I am with Jan Hayes, a woman who, it seems, is so well known in Alice Springs that I thought I must surely be with the Queen of the Alice. Our passage through the airport, then the streets, mall and shops was continually impeded by friendly well-wishers and people wanting to chat. I had recognised her from the milling throngs at the airport because she looked as her voice had sounded on the phone—purposeful, strong, steady, self-assured, businesslike, open and friendly.

Jan Hayes, aged 55, needed to have all those qualities. Four years ago, she and her husband Bill, also aged 55, had faced the prospect of losing a famous property, Deep Well, that had been in the Hayes family for over a century. Bill is the fourth generation of Hayes in the district, their son and grandson make it six generations. The Hayes are indeed well known in Alice Springs—as early settlers, as top-class

Jan Hayes

cattlemen, for their large landholdings and for the care they take of their land. Over the years they have bought and sold depending on their fortunes, an ebb and flow with the rains or droughts. In the mid-1980s when a former Hayes property called Maryvale came on the market, Jan and Bill bought it, through sentiment as much as anything, plus it was next door to Deep Well. In hindsight, Jan says it wasn't the right time to make the move to expand, even if they were keen to set up their sons with land. Interest rates rose to suicide levels and a bad drought hit them.

So, being a woman of action, Jan Hayes moved herself and Bill out of the Deep Well homestead, a fine and well-established home with every comfort, to set up camp in a remote corner of Deep Well. There they started Ooraminna Bush Camp, which gives tourists an authentic taste of outback living. Their speciality is the Pioneer Suite, a swag on the ground. Jan cooks hearty tucker for small groups, busloads of young or elderly, and huge and elaborate corporate functions. Business, four years on, is going well with strong forward bookings. Jan Hayes will tell her story, while I watch the sun ignite those ancient ranges beyond the mulga with orange and red.

'We were having some pretty tough times. We had gone through the droughts and the high interest rates and the problems that a lot of people faced. I couldn't see how else I could help the family or help Bill survive or keep going in the way that they wanted to. If I went and got a job in town, then the home fires had to be kept burning. Someone still had to be there or cook his feed or whatever, and whatever I earnt I would be away all day and I couldn't see any other way.'

The decision to leave the old homestead and put their son and his wife in charge of Deep Well was not easy. Jan and Bill were in their early fifties, had no cash flow, no money, no home and cattle prices were pathetic. Things were bleak.

They slept for quite some time on the corner of the verandah of the shed they were building for quite some time. 'We didn't mind, it was a challenge and we were building the place up. Eventually, we built a little room around the back here, so that's where we actually live now.' They also built an office, kitchen, indoor eating area and coolroom under the big, high shed roof. They did all the building themselves as they could afford it. It seemed an extraordinary sacrifice. 'Yes, and having had all the comforts that we had, it was a bit of a culture shock to say the least. But I just had to get on with it. I just had to keep going, knowing that down the track things had to improve.'

Considering the extraordinary natural beauty of Ooraminna,

tourism was the obvious way to go. 'Apart from that . . . nobody seemed to be able to get access on to a central Australian property. This is just the top north-west corner of the property and although it is pretty to you, in the eyes of a pastoralist it's a pretty worthless piece of land as far as grazing; otherwise I would never have been allowed to do this here. He wouldn't have let me.

'We started off just cooking under a tree and we built this little slab hut down here. It was built by an old mate of ours, Stick Beamish, from the High Country in Victoria, and he can literally make a chainsaw sit up and talk. So we decided I'd have a Christmas party and I put the word out around the traps.'

Bill and Jan turned on a real bush experience for the jewellery firm that jumped at the idea of trying something different. All her station cooking skills were brought to the fore. Jan made individual steamed Christmas puddings for each of the 50 guests and roasted some good station beef.

'At that stage we didn't have any real toilets so we had two shovels, one with a big pink bow and one with a big blue bow and we had one of those porta-potty things.' The party was a great success and on the strength of that, Ooraminna was launched a few months later. 'It's been a long hard road in a way, because I haven't got any marketing experience as such and . . . I had no idea of the learning curve that was ahead of me.'

By the letters Jan has been sent by delighted clients, she seems to have coped. People tell her in glowing terms that the Ooraminna experience is unforgettable, particularly for city-born people who constitute much of the clientele. Group after group, and many individuals wrote that it was the best experience they had ever had. One man checking out the place for an insurance group had recoiled when Jan told him that the accommodation was a swag on the ground. 'Oh no,' he said, 'my people are used to being around the world four or five times and used to five-star stuff.'

'I was really worried after we'd talked him round, but anyway they came. And, oh my goodness, there's something about this area that makes people let their plaits down and relax. These people that came in quite stuffy, at the end of the night they were literally, well, they were trying to linedance. They slept out under the stars and they just had the most wonderful time.

'A lot of people have never slept in a swag.' She makes them up with sheets like a bed and with a foam mattress. People are surprised at how comfortable they are. 'Our central Australian beef is second to none, it's chemical free and it's just beautiful beef, and being a cattle station, we like to let them know that,' says Jan, ever the promoter. 'What we are giving them is what they would have if they came to visit us at home. Genuine bushies do the barbecue cooking in their RMs and bandy legs. People from cities like seeing the genuine article.'

They stand around outside, enjoying those beautiful warm outback nights and the fantastic view of the inflamed ranges as the sun sets. 'It's like an iridescent paint has been put over them . . . and sometimes we have a didgeridoo player in the rocks down there.' They finish off their meal with bread and butter pudding, apple crumble or sticky date pudding. 'You'd be surprised today how many people don't have those down-to-earth things . . . I think it brings them back to their roots.' They're allowed extra helpings; go wild about Anzac biscuits and some people even request stew.

There's been too much fast food and people want to go back to home cooking, she thinks. Many ask how to cook basic things like roasts and puddings. 'It's surprising really,' says Jan, who like station women everywhere can probably cook with her eyes shut. 'And the way they hoe into it! They absolutely love it and it's really so ordinary, such ordinary food.' Jan says bookings were so heavy at one stage that she thought she'd treat herself and employ a cook. He was a trained chef but didn't know how to produce a straightforward meal. He lasted one day.

The first group to book when Ooraminna got under way was Henry Buck's menswear. 'They came in from all over the world,' Jan says. 'There was a couple having an argument and I thought, oh, they don't like it. The guide later told me they'd come to Australia and . . . all they'd seen was glass and cement. But in her mind, this is what she pictured as Australia. She wanted to stay the night and they had booked her into a flash hotel in town. She'd put her foot down and no way was she going back.' Jan says this seems to be too often the experience for the international traveller. They often don't meet anyone apart from the people behind hotel counters.

'Another thing that is funny, people have never heard silence . . . at night the stars here are just unbelievable so they love sleeping out there and listening to the birds, looking at the stars, and not having any noise.' We forget that is a luxury for many people, Jan says. 'I couldn't believe it when a lady said it to me. She said, you don't realise that where I live there are cars going past 24 hours a day. Even when I shut all my windows, I can still hear them.'

Jan and Bill also offer nature walks with bird and plant experts and horserides. Bill is a well-known horseman in the area and takes even the most nervous person. 'He takes them over there into those red sandhills, and white ghost gums and the craggy outcrops, desert oaks and there's birds and kangaroos going past and there's cattle. We're not a dude ranch. What you see is what you get—warts and all, I might add.'

Since those early, tentative days with no toilets, there are now septic systems and showers, albeit with water heated in a 44 gallon drum with a fire under it. They have a bough shed, a rustic bar by the slab hut. Groups that have had seminars, launched products there or filmed advertisements include Toyota, Massey Ferguson, RM Williams, the West Indian Cricket Team, and in the week before I visited, Jan and her small team of helpers had cooked for 350 Cemeteries and Crematoria people. All up, they had fed a thousand people that week. Everyone was exhausted. You could hear it in Jan's voice; as well as a certain wistfulness, sadness—the legacy of years of battling.

We talk of the Maryvale experience again. 'Those high interest rates . . . we were paying exorbitant rates to the agents and no matter what we did down there, we just worked seven days a week, but we didn't seem to be able to get anywhere. And then Bill had a nasty accident. Our son was taking off in the plane and he was watching him, I think. He must have been looking up and a stone must have hit him right in the eye, and it split his eye open. We took him in for surgery in town here. He had problems later and we ended up having to fly him to Adelaide and . . . they ended up replacing his eye. He really wasn't very well for a long time. I just didn't know what to do really.' Jan says it was a very hard time, and hard to see a man down with such problems. 'And then we had those drought years and you know, when the men come in at night, and they've been pulling dead cattle out of bogs in dams and that sort of thing, you can't take it away. There's nothing you can say when they walk in that's going to make them feel happy . . . It affected me because it affected him. You'd know when he got out of the car by his walk what he'd been through. Eventually Bill picked up, but it took a long time. He could see his empire, so to speak, slipping away from him and he had worked his insides out . . . and then this accident. It was just too much.'

They sold Maryvale four years ago, and Billy junior and his wife who had been at Maryvale moved to Deep Well; and Jan and Bill, who have been married for 32 years, moved out to give them a go. The emotional and physical toll on them both has been great. After Maryvale was sold, they were left with debt of around a million dollars. The prices for cattle at that time were poor.

On Deep Well there are now 5500 head of cattle but numbers vary depending on the season, 'but we are having a beaut season at the moment'. Deep Well is just under 700 square miles. Maryvale was about 1236 square miles. Undoolya, next door, Bill's brother Jim's place, is about 600 square miles.

We are still on the verandah, but now sipping cold wine, and it is dark with pinprick stars starting to shine through. Bill Hayes is still out working. He had started that morning at 3.00. It was now 7.30pm. While we have been talking, there have been frequent breaks for the crackling two-way radio with messages from the men who were spending that week mustering and yarding a total of 1300 heifers for a feedlot buyer from New South Wales.

'You rarely see him in daylight,' says Jan, as if Bill is some strange, shy, nocturnal creature, then adds, 'If he's got cattle in hand, they're his prime focus . . . he's a cattle man to the back teeth, that's his love and that's what he is interested in.'

He called again on the two-way to say he had just left a bore on Undoolya where he had yarded cattle. He was going back into town to get hay at the trucking yards, then would go back and feed the cattle. He wouldn't be home for an hour or two.

It seems to be the lifestyle from hell. Since Jan is the licensee at Ooraminna, she has to be last to bed when guests are there, frequently entertaining tourists who want to stay up till midnight. Bill is usually up at 3.00am, kindly bringing Jan a cup of tea which she feels compelled to drink to keep him company while he gets ready to start his day's work. Station life, she says, is 'a lot of work, and not a lot of money—but it's a lifestyle that we love. It's just the realness of it. I don't like anything plastic, whether it's people or synthetic materials. I feel you can be yourself, and I'm not much good at putting on any acts.'

Headlights of a Toyota ute then threaded their way up to the verandah. Out jumped a heap of handsome blokes wanting a few slabs of beer, and we now turn the page to another interesting chapter on Ooraminna. On my way in with Jan this morning down the track past craggy outcrops, I had noticed some very beautiful early Australian buildings—a pub, corrugated-iron houses and a big shady thatched roof shed. There were just struts at the back of some of the buildings and I realised it was a film set. It is the 'township' of Newcastle Waters as it was in 1910 and put there for Ted Egan's film *The Drover's Boy*. The boys looking for the slabs were set-builders.

'The hotel has been built to last which we really appreciate because we'll be able to use that as a tourist attraction,' says Jan, who admires Egan greatly for his efforts to put the story of the Aboriginal girls who accompanied white drovers on to the screen. Egan is a long-standing friend from their campdrafting days. Bill Hayes has a role as a stockman with some mates, droving 1000 head of cattle.

Jan, when filming is finished, is planning to have the old Ghan train come right to the door of the film's 'hotel'. The original Ghan railway lines were left in place in the section from Ooraminna to Alice Springs, and Jan hopes to run four kilometres of train line to the film 'town'. They have surveyed a route and are sure they will get funding for it. Jan will licence and operate the pub. 'It will be wonderful,' says Jan, Queen of the Alice, entrepreneur and bush survivor. 'It will save the old Ghan.' People will travel in old open-top carriages for a dinner under the stars and either stay the night in old sleeper carriages or travel back.

Jan's capacity for starting new ventures and making them successful is not new. When her first child started boarding school, she bought a saddlery in Alice Springs and doubled the turnover for five years to help with cash flow. And she couldn't even ride a horse!

Not every venture succeeds, though. Last year, she decided to bring in the Darwin Symphony Orchestra. A large stage was erected in the open and dinner prepared for 250 guests in formal dress, dining in style. 'And on the night, it rained. It rained—I couldn't believe it. And of course one side of me was saying, you don't knock rain, being on the land all your life, you'd be divorced. Anyway, it cost me dearly.' The event was cancelled—it was meant to help take out a lot of debt. 'It made it worse.' She laughs. 'I couldn't win.'

Her advice for people who are in survival mode is to keep busy. 'Just get up and do something. Start, and it rolls from there.'

I comment that she seems to simply brush away the small fleabites of annoyance in her life, that she seems to have enormous strength. 'It might be a big bluff though,' she says.

Next day, we were out on the verandah early because Jan had to get into town and was dropping me in too. Bill had eventually arrived home at about 10.00pm, had his meal on the verandah, and was still as chirpy as a cricket. He'd sold a lot of cattle at a good price into New South Wales. He told me between mouthfuls that the buyer had said it was the best line of heifers he had ever seen.

'Ooraminna is now making a contribution to Deep Well, the prime business,' says Jan. 'But even if it was only just keeping us, it is still helping. If we didn't have it, we would be relying on the place as well. And now that we have sort of gotten over the worst part of the set-up . . .

I mean, it's only in the last week that I've really felt that we are getting somewhere . . . and I've got money coming in that up until now we hadn't. It's just like we've been slogging up this hill and now we're just . . . we're not over it . . . but we can see the light at the end of the tunnel.' With a good season as well, and better cattle prices . . . 'hopefully everthing is going to be okay'.

Anguish of the Pastoralists— David and Penny Bayly

Next day, I drove two and a half hours north of Alice to Stirling Station, home of David and Penny Bayly. I should talk to David, people said, because he is the president of the influential and powerful Northern Territory Cattleman's Association, and when he arrived at Stirling in 1979, he introduced some controversial southern management techniques to the station. Penny came from England, married David and runs a station store for the Anmudjera and Kaytetye tribes of Aborigines who also live at Stirling.

It's strange how things evolve. On top of the comments by Dave Lindner about mismanagement of Aboriginal issues, David Bayly continued the theme, piling scorn on government policy and blazing with passion for the people who in his opinion deserve far better than the treatment they have had ... an opinion surprising in its intensity. To be juxtaposing his observations with a talk a day later with Aboriginal elder Bill Harney was interesting, considering I, like most of us down south or in cities, have little contact with these issues.

Penny Bayly is tall and cool, slim and elegant. With her regal bearing and upper crust accent, she would not be out of place at a royal wedding. 'She would be one of the most capable women in the territory. Nothing fazes her. She can do everything, from running an Aboriginal store to organising the bores to exercising and training horses to a very high standard. Nothing is too much trouble and she is very well thought of.' That was the unsolicited tribute from David Bayly when we sat down to talk. Her story, he said, was the remarkable one, because of the massive adjustments she had to make from a genteel upbringing in Herefordshire and a glamorous existence in London to a cattle station in the centre of Australia.

The Northern Territory outback is a hot, dusty, challenging leap from cocktail parties at the Savoy, receptions at the English Derby and

For Love of the Land

David and Penny Bayly

cruises down the Thames. Penny worked for the London manager of Dalgety's and her job was to welcome international rural clients to Britain and entertain them in style. That's how she met David. He was in the United Kingdom working on a variety of farms, having some fun after jackarooing on sheep and cattle places in South Australia and the Northern Territory. When Penny decided in 1976 to go to Australia for a six-month holiday, she never envisaged the life in a hot, remote place that would be hers when she married David. He had returned to work on a cattle property for some years, then taken a job managing Stirling Station for his uncles who had bought it at the end of the beef slump in 1979. She remembers a place that was terribly run-down, with litter and mess, rusting iron and scrap lying around everywhere. 'It was like walking back into the last century and I remember thinking, this is pioneer stuff—but it wasn't, this was the twentieth century.'

The purchase of Stirling had come after seven extraordinarily wet years during which no mustering was possible. Cattle numbers had increased wildly; male calves had not been castrated; the herd had become wild and inbred; brumby numbers were out of control. Then cattle prices suddenly bounced back, the country dried out and they could destock thousands of cattle and wild horses and put the money back into building tanks, yards, troughs, fences and new roads. 'I think we were living with contractors for the first four or five years—it seemed for years.' It must have been a very tough baptism into marriage, I suggested. Penny, upright and reserved in that British stiff-upper-lip sort of way, agreed. 'I think the hardest thing was suddenly finding I was cooking for probably a minimum of 12 people at a time . . . and just trying to keep meals up to them. It was a seven day a week job. One of the things I'll always remember was cooking up a lasagne, which I prided myself on then. I dished it up to one of these cement tank contractors, and he said, erhgh, what's that? And I said, it's a lasagne. Erhgh, what's that? I couldn't believe there were people who didn't know what a lasagne was.'

These fussy working men who only wanted steak, peas, spuds and carrots found they were contending with very much a stand-your-ground person. Penny says she continued cooking what she wanted to eat and they had to put up with it. 'I must admit I wouldn't recommend it to anyone starting off their married life, having your staff virtually live with you seven days a week. It was only when the children were born that I said, that's it! I can't do all the cooking now. I've got to get a cook . . . but she lived in the house as well!' It was one of the few times that Penny's stoic exterior relaxed. She admitted with a wry laugh that 12 for meals, people constantly in the house, young babies and the demands of station life had been just a trifle testing.

As well, she ran the station store for the Aboriginal community that had always lived on Stirling. Twenty years ago there were only about six families and the store was simply a small inside room. 'I always found them to be very polite, very good-natured, very happy and very willing,' Penny says. Over the years more families came to live at Stirling and today there are 150 people, so the store has been expanded, air-conditioned and carries a bigger range of stock.

'In the old days when people used all Aboriginal labour on stations, each station would have a small store. The Aboriginal stockmen would be paid with their ration—some tucker, clothing, whatever their needs would be, possibly a bit of cash, but not a great deal. In those days, the whole of the community would be looked after because the women and the children would all have jobs as well. They would be helping with the housework, helping with the washing, tending the sheep or the goats, collecting firewood, or whatever—they would all have a bit of a job to do.

'When the government brought in the minimum wage and consequently the dole in the mid-1970s, many stations found they couldn't afford to employ all these people. They just had to send them away. Whereas this station, it only had a small community here, just a few families, and I guess they were able to keep them on the payroll.'

When the recession hit and cattle were practically worthless, and during drought years, it was the stations with stores that managed to survive. The Aboriginals spent their cheques on tucker, clothing, footwear and whatever else they needed.

Penny's has expanded to be a mini department store. 'It's not just clothing and vegetables and frozen foods, it also includes all manchester, sheets, blankets, towels, beds, mattresses, doonas, footwear, household things like saucepans, plates, mugs, cutlery as well as hardware, electrical good, toasters, electric kettles, microwaves, fridges, freezers, washing machines, televisions and videos of course.' She laughs. 'Televisions and videos are the biggest sellers . . . And anything extra that they need, I will get it for them, and they know that. We run a complete service.'

Three major wholesalers deliver to her door. I worried that there might be room for exploitation by store owners through overcharging. 'Any shop can charge higher and put a far heftier mark-up, but they are cutting their own throats in the end because there are plenty of other stores in the area that they will go to,' Penny says in that very upright, but pleasant manner of hers. 'I mean, they are not stupid. They know how much you charge and how much Ti Tree or Barrow Creek or the next station store will charge, and they are quite capable of working it out for themselves.'

The profits from the shop go into running the station, the house and to making improvements. They also pay for casual wages. 'And at the moment, the shop is paying the fuel bills and the larger bills the station can't cope with,' Penny says of the current beef slump, which is making life particularly stringent. Her store opens on three mornings a week and Penny says she spends another 12 or more hours a week tidying it up, doing orders and unloading trucks.

'Definitely not restful, peaceful or uneventful—there's always something going on', is how Penny describes life at Stirling. 'Even after the boys were born I have always been on call for horse work, or drafting in the yards, loading cattle, fencing, whatever's on. I was always that extra pair of hands, but because I was able to ride a horse, I was always needed when we were helicopter mustering or just mustering the house paddocks.'

Her background in England had included classical riding and competition at eventing and shows. At Stirling she uses her dressage skills on the stockhorses. She handles the foals, breaks in, schools and trains all the youngsters. 'It was certainly a huge asset being able to ride when I came here. Over the years, we have gone from having a lot of staff and a lot of horses to becoming a lot more finetuned and improving the quality of the horses, so we could cut down on the number of staff we needed to have. By improving the quality of the horses and their training, we've been able to do a lot more economical and effective job with the cattle.' Penny says a good stockhorse works the same way as a good sheepdog, watching and anticipating the stock, turning on its haunches, moving fluidly.

The Baylys' typical station homestead, large and sprawling, with boots at the back door and coats and hats on hooks, is set in a civilised green lawn studded with trees. Beyond the white rail fence is a superbly productive, well-managed vegetable garden, then flat dry brown paddocks, and mulga, spinifex and gidgee. Horses nearby wear winter rugs, although to a southerner the day is hot; clearly for locals, it was not. Enormous steel cattleyards stand further over towards the main road.

David—ruddy faced, dark-haired, focused—had been loading trucks with cattle. We sat down outside at a table under sweet-smelling cedar trees where Port Lincoln parrots were chattering and squabbling over the blossoms. David retraced his history for me. Born and raised in Broken Hill, then the family moved to Adelaide for his schooling. His vast experience on the land in South Australia, Northern Territory, New South Wales and the United Kingdom combined to give him, at age 28, the intellectual and technical skills to cope with Stirling's uncontrolled wild cattle and horses on two million acres or 3000 square miles of country where fences had been washed away or broken. Even if mustering had been possible in those wet years, prices had been so low it wasn't worth it. He said the previous owners had sent five rail vans of cattle to Adelaide, and they got a bill for $27 for freight after the selling charges and commission had been taken out.

So the station had been virtually shut down except for its store, which had kept the homestead afloat. Neglected and run-down, Stirling had 25 000 cattle on it instead of the 10 000 estimated at sale, as well as 4500 brumbies. He trapped and mustered every animal between the distant boundaries—one was 150 kilometres from the homestead, the other was 90 kilometres in the other direction. The station is now a model of efficiency, running 8000 Hereford cows.

I get the impression it is the welfare of the 150 Aboriginal people who live on Stirling that now occupies a large chunk of his mind. They can hunt, fish and gather where they like, and there is a mutually happy and co-operative relationship with the Baylys. David says, however, that poor understanding of issues by government has created some appalling anomalies which strain relations.

'We have got a magnificent tribe of Aboriginals here. In the early days, we had some very sensible older people who wanted the drunks out of the community. We had 24-hour drinking at the local pub, so we had a lot of grog problems, but only a minority of the Aboriginals were involved in it, and they have left now. Actually, most of them are dead . . . and we have got a very quiet peaceable community and we have no problems.' No alcohol is allowed in their community, but the Barrow Creek hotel is 30 kilometres away and they have two hours a day drinking there.

In 1979, David employed about 25 Aboriginals. 'When the equal pay situation came about, I couldn't afford to. We were having four o'clock starts in the morning and going through till eight o'clock at night, drafting at night, and then starting at four again the next morning. The Aboriginals were fine and they would work for two or three weeks, but then all of a sudden when payday came on the last Friday of the month, they'd all go to the pub and that would be the end of them for three weeks, especially if you had mustering again on the following Monday morning. So I made a conscious decision that I'd just use them casually when I needed them but I only use two or three of them now. They've got to a stage of sit-down.'

In the past month a new government policy swept in, making a further massive attack on the equilibrium of the Stirling community and others through the district. They stopped receiving unemployment benefits in cheque form. 'Some bright, white fellow has just decided . . . that they [should] get paid for cleaning up their rubbish at the camp,' David says. 'They're paying them cash now, instead of paying them something that they can bank. They're paying them cash,' he repeats in exasperation, 'and that money is dissolved within two hours of them getting it. And, they have to collect their cash at the local pub. And this is a white fella's idea,' he says, shaking his head in frustration. 'I've got so much disdain for the white people that have been involved with Aboriginals. It really makes my blood boil, it really does.' His voice crackles with despair. 'Instead of sitting down and talking to the local pastoralists and local Aboriginals before they start these schemes, they bring them in, and then cause that many problems. To try to resurrect that problem now is going to be a huge job.'

For 18 years, he said Penny had worked with the women and arranged to have their cheques split, so the husband could take half and do what he liked with it. The women would still have money for food and clothing for their children. 'It's worked happily, but overnight that's all changed.' Now that they get cash from Barrow Creek, the women can't keep a share because their husbands who have driven them there, claim the lot. 'Ludicrous decisions, made without sitting down and consulting with the people that have been here . . . It's just very disappointing when outside forces come in and change everything.'

David has not sat silently over these changes. As president of the powerful and influential Cattleman's Association, which represents 91 per cent of cattlemen in the Northern Territory holding 96 per cent of the cattle and with members including Kerry Packer, Standbroke Pastoral and the Kidman family, he has called on the ATSIC chairman in Tennant Creek, the Aboriginal Affairs Minister in the Northern Territory, and his senior advisers to review the policy. ATSIC was currently discussing it. The Aboriginals want to go back to the old system, David said. 'They don't mind working for the dole, but they don't want to get paid with cash at the local township. They want to get paid in the mailbag or at the store where they can buy some goods.

'The Aboriginal industry and the politicians of the world have got a lot to answer for with Aboriginal matters, in my opinion. It's very easy to throw money at a problem, when money is not the solution.'

He says it is also important that Aboriginal people be made responsible for their actions so that when a young drunk smashes something, he should be charged and made to pay for the damage. Once the old people would also have given him a hiding. David says the old people no longer command respect because they are trying to work between white fellas' law and Aboriginal law.

He has seen fine, once proud people disintegrating before his eyes. 'As an example, when I came here I had one Aboriginal stockman who had been one of the stolen generation. He had been taken away from his family at the community and brought up in the Stirling homestead by the manager's wife. He was sent off to boarding college in Darwin and came back an absolute credit to his race and to himself. I took him on as my right-hand man. He could drive a bulldozer, drive a grader, ride a horse . . . After two or three years, he had a bank account in town with a lot of money in it. He used to eat in the house with Penny and me at lunchtime and he'd go back to the community on Friday night and come back Monday morning. One weekend, he'd taken his street car down to Ti Tree, the local township, to watch the football. I had a phone call from Alice Springs to say his car was there. The Aboriginal drunks had hijacked it and taken it. I got some stock agents to find the car and get him on the road to home. Everything was all right for another month. They [the drunks] realised he was here at the [Stirling] community. They took both his cars to town [Alice Springs] with him and got him on the grog. He rang me three nights later from Woolworths, outside the bottle depot, wanting me to find him. I went to town but couldn't find him. Two days later he was dead, stabbed by a woman in a drunken brawl.' This incident continues to haunt and anger David Bayly.

'It's been a huge clash of cultures', which has not been helped by Canberra bureaucrats being so far from where Aboriginal people live. David, who is frequently in Canberra for cattlemen's meetings, said most bureaucrats have only vague ideas about how Aboriginal people behave and do not understand the problems pastoralists have when they drive cars, shoot with high-powered rifles, use spotlights and light fires on leased land with livestock on it. He said pastoralists sometimes walk out of meetings with frustration, amazed at the naive views of decision-makers.

One of the great difficulties in dealing with Aboriginal issues, he says, is that the needs of town-based Aboriginal people are different;

they want a cash society and his local community doesn't. 'They've come back to me time and time again and said why can't we go back to the coupon system? The cash is the ruination of their society.' The people on Stirling are 'the very quiet old-time Aboriginals, but unfortunately they're losing their voice. It's been taken over by the very powerful young Aboriginal bodies, the militant bodies, and that's where I feel sorry for these fellows down here, I really do.' He tells how the old men are afraid of the young people in their community who have no respect for (traditional) laws and literally thumb their noses at them. 'To see a very proud race and a very great race of people gradually disintegrating is probably the most disappointing thing about being at Stirling or being in the Northern Territory. The proud old people have lost their ways . . . The old fellows are losing their influence.' The young no longer want to hunt, instead they'll buy frozen kangaroo tails; and they all want to make big money by playing football. He points out the same difficulties could be said to exist in a lot of areas of white society too.

David, as a young southern outsider to Alice Springs, was under intense scrutiny from the locals when he overhauled watering systems, put in laneways, introduced solar pumps and solar-powered electric fences and sold young cattle instead of holding on to them until they were two or three-year-old bullocks as had been traditionally done. It was management by brain power instead of brawn . . . the end of the outback wild west show where cattle were thrown down and panicked. Buyers wanted quiet, well-handled cattle to put into feedlots. He found a market also for the brumbies, instead of just shooting them and letting them rot. Eight hundred mares were sold to the veterinary laboratories at Werribee and others went to Peterborough meatworks, which with such a big and reliable throughput was able to initiate its successful export horsemeat works. 'If I'd been a local I think I might have listened to the advice and said, oh it's useless, we'll go on the way we were. But because I came from outside, I couldn't see why it couldn't be done,' he said. Now, most people sell weaners; solar technology for fences and pumps is widely adopted; and Landcare issues connected to flooding and washaways are being addressed through the study of ponding banks and controlled flood irrigation.

One of the biggest problems the pastoral regions face now is the finding of labour. Once outback phones would ring with people wanting to come up and get experience. 'We've had huge problems in the last five years getting staff. We're not getting the quality of the kids out of the cities that we were ten years ago.' David said last year he advertised and got eight replies. Ten years ago, an advertisement for the same position drew 72 replies. The perception that there is no future in the bush is keeping people away. When the boom times return, however, which he believes they surely will, people with the right experience will be able to name their price.

David and Penny themselves admit life in the outback comes at a heavy personal cost. It's physically demanding, they are far from friends and family, and even neighbours. As Penny says, 'It's a complete social desert.' She reflects, 'I don't think David or I can physically keep going on at the pace that we have been. It always seems to be a race against time. I'd love to be able to slow down, be able to look at the birds and the trees, and listen to other people, rather than just race against time, all the time.' They don't see themselves staying at Stirling more than another five years. Someone younger should take over, David says. His flow of bright ideas is slowing, but he'll stay with beef cattle—perhaps in feedlotting.

UPDATE: August. Severe drought has hit the Alice Springs area. For more than three months the station has been urgently destocking. To date, 9000 cattle have been trucked out to Queensland, New South Wales and South Australia.

Aboriginal people now have their payments made directly into their bank accounts which they access by Eftpos. They no longer have to drive to collect cash from alongside the pub.

The Dream of a Self-sufficient Man—Bill Harney

Before flying out to Katherine, I spent three hours hiking around the Desert Park on the edge of the town. Birds of prey swooped out of the MacDonnell Ranges to the calls of the rangers, and the three types of desert country in the region had been brilliantly re-created and populated with their appropriate fauna and flora.

On Air North's stylish Brassilia, dining on gourmet sandwiches served on china plates and tea from proper cups, I realised then where all the decent airline crockery had gone before the plastic invasion. From the window, the country outside Alice looked like a red-skinned tiger, black stripes of mulga and gidgee in creases where the skin of the earth crumpled into creek beds. Bouncing and jiggling on the hot breath rising from the beast below, the plane fidgeted like an animal in fear. At our Tennant Creek stop, bucking and rearing and fighting, the craft seemed unwilling to touch the beast that by now was a dot-pointed spinifex leopard.

In the air again, the earth became a marbled slab, swirling with red, yellow and grey: veins of dark creek beds, flakes and fissures overlaid with cloud shadows. The plane continued to fight like a horse saddled for the first time. Outside it looked as if the wool stockpile had been set free to float in wild chunks past the windows. By the time we landed in Katherine, the sun was insulated by a thick layer of cloud. To meet me again was Mick Peirce, of the Wardaman Aboriginal Corporation. He directed me to a working-man's club which provides bed and breakfast for $25, and a three-course evening meal for $10. It was a hungry, single girl's dream palace . . . buildings full of fit, strong outdoor men and huge meals. As a non-single girl, I still had a good time. Electricians working at Tindal airforce base, told hair-raising stories about security and machine guns when they forgot their identity passes one morning.

Next morning at 7.00 I was collected by Dwayne, a shy but charming Wardaman Aboriginal, who told me much later when he found out I knew of the Crows, that Andrew McLeod was his cousin. I was very impressed.

We were heading out west of Katherine on the road to Timber Creek and Kununurra to visit Bill Harney at the Wardaman tribe's own cattle station, currently called Innesvale, but being renamed in Wardaman language as Jalijbang. I stocked up on water, a sandwich and locally grown bananas. Mick Peirce had told me to be self-sufficient. After an hour spent collecting passengers, we set off at great speed in the Toyota troop-carrier, covering the 250 kilometres in two hours, which included 37 kilometres of dirt and two stops for gates. In this, the land of no speed limits there was no point in worrying. On board was the station's head stockman, Billy Harney jnr, and three young lads of 14 or so, whom we picked up from the Wardaman settlement outside Katherine. They were being taken to the station on old Bill's orders to work, as well as to get them away from the undesirable influences of the town.

The settlement was built in the bush and people slept on outdoor beds. It reminded me of our family camping trips in the Flinders Ranges. People were cooking breakfast over open fires. Blue tarp shelters gave protection from the sun, which even at that hour was starting to bite. Billies were boiling and people were cooking toast. It was a pleasant, leisurely, relaxed scene. A tall, beautiful slender young woman walked down the road with two naked five or six year olds. The children were meltingly lovely. As we stopped for the last boy, his round and shining mum called out, 'You coming to take my boy?' When the neat and polished lad was aboard, she told Dwayne, 'Now you look after my boy.' We mothers are so embarrassing . . . the poor bloke cringed and rolled his eyes, and I had to smile to myself. The trip out was fairly silent; the white stranger's presence ruined the boys' fun. At one stage I asked what a particularly eye-catching tree was called. When Dwayne said the word incorrectly, 'Wunyarri', with a wrong syllable emphasised, there were hoots of laughter from the back. It had meant something rude.

We arrived at the station compound of red gravel and dirt, tired houses spread around, sparse trees and thin, long yellow grass. We drove past the schoolhouse where the manager's wife teaches her children and any Aboriginal children that turn up. Beyond was Bill Harney's almost brand-new house, built of smart red Colour-bond with dark green railings around the verandah.

Bill Harney

Bill came down the steps to meet us, a short man with a proud, kind face, grinning from under a battered hat. 'Shall we go and talk in the bush?' he said. We sat under a 'snubby gum' on a small hill where we could catch a cool breeze from across the valley floor in front of us. In the distance was a low range. Around us were coolibah, ghost gums, ironwood, bloodwood, black wattle, cajeput and desert gum. We started the tape rolling. Burning rays already stung my bare shoulders.

Bill attacks the task of recording his life story with gusto. He's no stranger to broadcasting. A few weeks earlier, a Swiss film crew had camped with him to document his life in the bush. Bill is also a seasoned international traveller, having given speeches about tourism and demonstrations of didgeridoo playing. He has his own tour company. He also harvests one of the more unusual crops I've ever heard of—hollow sticks for didgeridoos. His current batch of 5000 is destined for Holland.

Above all, Bill Harney has a vision for the thousand people of the Wardaman tribe. Chairman of the Wardaman Corporation and tribal elder, Bill has never drawn the dole and wants his people also to be self-sufficient. All his life, Bill has lived off the land. He started work on cattle stations in the territory at the age of nine, and over the years has acquired a huge range of outback skills. Now aged about 67, he has set up companies and trading opportunities so young Aboriginal people can go back to the land. There are 3000 Brahman cattle on Jalijbang's 282 000 hectares and groups of young people are brought out regularly to work with the resident station manager, as well as learn traditional bush skills from Bill. The Wardaman have a firm goal of expanding their landholding.

Bill recalls some years ago learning that a welfare person once reported he would only ever be a good stockman. He bridles slightly at this. 'I was raised in the bush and I started my business. I started the fencing contract. I started the tourism. Now on artefacts and here I am. But I was the only one. The other people have been taken away down to the schooling and that, and they still down the gutter. It hasn't started anything.' He draws himself up, tilts his chin . . . 'And here I am, one of the bushmen, started a business in the bush.' He chuckles, savouring his achievements. Proud. But so wanting more for his people.

Bill was born in the bush not far from Jalijbang and raised by his full-blood mother, Ludi. His father was a white man called Bill Harney, a road maker, who took Bill's grandfather, grandmother and their young daughter with him on the roads to help with his job. 'My mother mated up with old Bill, and that's when I came on,' Bill says.

'Later on old Bill left, went back and I think he joined the army.' Ludi then married a Wardaman Aboriginal, called Joe, who raised Bill and taught him Aboriginal history and his culture.

The government, in the meantime, made a rule that white people weren't allowed 'to interfere with the Aborigine. Old Bill was very frightened ... He told my mother to take me out in the bush and hide me. And I was raised that way.' His father insisted that young Bill was taught Aboriginal ways so he couldn't be differentiated from other tribal children, and possibly be taken away. Bill senior, by this time, was involved in welfare and knew the dangers facing his young son as the idea of relocating children started to take hold.

So Bill junior grew up in the bush. 'We explored on foot all our life with the traditional gear with all old people ... and know pretty well every piece of rock in this country. From the hills to the waterholes.' The accepted step for young Aboriginal children who had grown up in the bush, was for them to be involved in work on the station property. 'That was part of our schooling.' So Bill, at the age of nine, started learning about horses and cattle under the guidance of people he remembers as very caring and knowledgeable.

'They took great care of us, make sure we didn't get hurt, show us how to do everything the right way.' Bill was taught how to shoe horses, first quiet ones, then wild and rough ones. He learnt how to break in horses, to muster cattle. 'Out on the field with a branding yard, we used to be enjoying it, lassooing calves, branding ... and we'd have probably 1200 to 1500 bullocks in the night camp and we'd be watching them. We had to night-watch wild cattle all night, galloping all night. Other places we went out to brand cows. There was no yard at all, just what we call an open bronco ... Of course some of them were very large big bull when we brought them up to brand, and of course you had no other trees to climb on. You ought to have seen the fun then,' and his face puckers up into a merry grin. 'When they'd let the old bull go, he'd go berserk and the people tried to climb in this one tree. There's about half a dozen of them trying to climb into it. God, we used to have some fun with them.' He's laughing infectiously. 'I reckon it was great fun, yeah.'

When cattle work ended and the wet season began, the Aboriginal stockmen would drop their boots, shirts, trousers and hats at the station store and go bush again. 'We'd be back in our traditional gear and out in the field again, putting on our naga, having a big ceremony, and gathering up all our traditional outfit like the spears and boomerangs and all this, so we can live off the land.' Bill's voice is getting a brrrr up, not unlike the sound of a didgeridoo. It has a lovely, earthy musicality to it.

Bill worked his way up to being 'a boss man' of a stock camp in 1954 and spent 20 years working on the huge landholdings of the Vestey empire and also for the Durack family. He pays credit to the many people, black, white and part Aboriginal, who taught him skills like whip and belt plaiting, how to make ropes, spurs, saddles and harness, coming up with names like George Manfong, Harry Huddleston, Jack Little, Alec Pott and Fred Gutte. 'Before then, my mum showed me how to weave all the grass fur and pound them up to make it like a cottonwool, and we used to spin it, make it like a cotton, then we would put four fork stick and run it up and down and make a cloth out of it.'

In 1975, when the Duracks sold their Kildirk Station to the Ngaringman Aboriginal tribe, Bill was employed to drive tractors on an Ord River farm, seeding and harvesting sunflower, peanuts, sorghum, and also as a fencer. He returned to the Territory, helping the Kildirk Aborigines for a while. 'When I left, everything was in good order. Then when I went back, the saddles was all buggered and wrecked and hardly was any surcingle or a girth strap or anything left. I ended up redoing all this up for them.'

In 1984, Bill discovered Yubulyawun land from his clan dreaming was being made available for claims. 'Some of the land was just on the inside of my country. We went over and put a land claim over it . . . When we went through the court, I got it straightaway . . . because we have the knowledge to know our heritage in the country.'

Bill indicates the successful claim gave him confidence to set about bringing his Wardaman tribe back to their country. In 1994, the lease of Innesvale was purchased for them by ATSIC, and in 1995 they lodged a claim which was accepted in late 1996. 'I don't want to get any money from the government. I just go by myself. I make my own money and that's what I say to the people. You can do artefacts, get money and make money for yourself. You don't have to go to the government to get dole and all this . . . We'll build up from our own herd. We don't want to look back to any government.' The station would make money to build houses for people who would live and work there, but there would be 'no handouts'.

Not all of us are layabouts, Bill emphasises. I understand the heartbreak he must feel when he sees his people sitting on the streets with nothing to do and drinking too many beers and getting into trouble. 'I don't want to be on the dole, I don't like dole.' He said he once collected empty beer cans for about $10 a bag, instead of relying on the government.

In 1984, Bill first discovered his bush skills had commercial appeal to an international market. He had been asked to look after some young overseas exchangees who were involved in building stockyards in a national park. 'We took them young fella walking, canoeing, camping on the bank of the river. We ran out of white man food. I said to them we got to live on *Aboriginal* food.' This was said with great flourish, emphasised with a hand in the air and a look of triumph. 'They were catching fish, a lot of honey from the bush, a goanna or two now and again. We couldn't catch any kangaroo, but we lived on a turtle and a lot of bush yam. Oh, they enjoyed it. A lot of those people, they came from New York, California, everywhere.'

He set himself up as a full-time fencing contractor, working at Tindal base, employing up to 18 people, but when Film Australia featured Bill in a documentary on Aboriginal art in Wardaman country, his future in tourism was set. When the film was launched in Sydney, Bill's phone rang constantly with people wanting to see the works. 'I went back and talked to all my people about taking [tourists] to see art. My mob said okay.' After discussion with the Tourist Commission in Alice Springs, he set up his own tour company.

'I went over and built all my tour camp. Set it up proper way—bough shelter, all the swinging beds, toilet, shower.' Swinging beds are made with chain mesh and a piece of pipe through fork sticks and raised off the ground. 'We call them a chloroform bed,' and he grins. 'They put you to sleep.'

The first lot of people he hosted were Austrian. Then a Dutch tour operator came and looked around. 'He said, I've been everywhere. I haven't seen any camp as good as this.' Tours for Dutch travellers then came twice a week, and many others have followed. He charges $150 a day per person and supplies everything. The camp is upstream along the river I could see in the distance on the far side of the valley.

Overseas visitors no doubt watch in fascination as he catches wild food for the campfire, particularly birds like kites. Being curious birds, Bill says they will fly down if you have a few feathers in your hand that look like a captured bird. 'Then you just reach up and catch one,' he said, 'chuck it in the fire and eat it.' He also catches pigeons in snares.

He teaches tourists how to cut didgeridoo sticks, which they take home. Orders started coming in for more—10, then 20, 50 at a time. 'Gradually my didgeridoo market was getting bigger. I said, jeez, I can't keep up to the people. Anyway, I ended up going big way now on the didgeridoo.' Indeed, he is. His current order of 5000 is large by anyone's standards. It is slowly being met with the help of some of his own people as well as a young American. Bill harvests all the sticks off Wardaman land from sand bloodwood trees and woolly butt. 'When I first started off making didgeridoo, it was traditional way, with a rasp and tommy hawk. When the market was getting bigger, I ended up getting a grinder, chainsaw and proper electrical equipment to make it.' Bill runs a virtual factory at his homes in Katherine and Jalijbang for a thriving business grown from one man's enthusiasm, promoted only by word of mouth.

Bill's dream is to leave several viable businesses that his people can take over and live on. 'When it gets bigger, it will swing across to Wardaman and they can pick up the money. Many young people can be working in artefacts on the cattle station. At the same time we are going to get them organised on the tour side—some of them can be tour operators.' He also hopes to develop an agate fossicking tour on the richly endowed Jalijbang country.

'This is where I am going with the young ones today. They all have a good feeling . . . I am encouraging them on the artefacts side. They are taking a great interest in that. I think they will get there in the end.'

With royalties accruing from mining, Telstra lines and an RAAF bombing range, the Wardaman people intend to purchase nearby 300 000 hectare Delemere Station, which runs 20 000 cattle; but Bill says the owner, Peter Sherwin, at present is asking too much money. They will raise the money eventually he says, and then they'll be better placed to be truly self-sufficient. To this end, Bill encourages the young people to access training funding instead of the dole, and to learn skills. His own son Billy is being trained in livestock skills under the Jalijbang manager.

By now, it was stinking hot on that hill. Flies were buzzing around us. I was light-headed with dehydration, since my water had also been popular with Bill. Across his knee Bill holds a large didgeridoo, newly made and painted. While we have been talking, he has been softening some native bee honeycomb in the sun, then rolling it between his fingers until it was pliable. He now presses it around the top of the instrument. 'This one here is a stringy-bark.' Bill describes how termites eat the wood out of the middle and seal the insides with their spit. He then takes off the bark, sands them smooth, paints them.

He sets himself in a comfortable position, breaks off a stick from a tree and starts to blow, beating the side of the didgeridoo in four/four time. Despite the heat, the flies and my parched state, those primal, repetitive sounds had me floating beyond myself. On the mesmerising rhythm from within that simple stick, I saw naked dancing dark-skinned bodies and heard the cries of animals and birds. Bill made the sound of the indigenous long-tailed pheasant coucal on the didgeridoo—woop, woop, woop. Bill said this sound on the didgeridoo goes up to the heavens where the spirits help keep happiness all over the land. His people play the instrument during marriage and initiation ceremonies, to protect them in floodwater, for burials and for healing. 'This ritual sound of the didgeridoo sort of fixes everything up . . . it is a wonderful sound.'

Bill thinks one of the secrets to building black and white cohesion is through sharing culture. He likes to teach white people about his ways, to play the didgeridoo. 'Everyone of us here is quite happy to share our cultural ways to the white people. Whatever we got, they can have it too.' He says he likes seeing Aboriginal artefacts in people's homes.

It is this wonderful open, sharing attitude of Bill's that has made him a great overseas ambassador for Australian bush tourism, which he has promoted at trade fairs in England, Germany, America and Spain. 'Those people in Spain had never seen an Aborigine, and never heard a didgeridoo,' he said. 'I blew one in Seville. These thousands of people came to see what happened.' International names roll off his lips like a seasoned businessman. 'I seen the whole world,' he says with pride. 'In Washington, I gave a very big talk to America, about the cultural way and the tourism side. And all over America they heard it, and everyone was chasing me.' As a result, many American tourists came and he is also noticing an influx of Japanese people, who also love playing the didgeridoo. Bill chuckles about how great it is that Aboriginal music is catching on around the world. 'When everything will go ahead, I think the Wardaman will never look back,' he says. Bill wants so much to fire up his people, 'so they can continue on what I have left behind for them when I be dead and gone. They can be up and running themselves without falling down.'

Although getting Wardaman land has been vitally important to his people, Bill wants to make it clear that Aboriginal people don't necessarily want to take over land from pastoralists; they just want access for their children to learn their heritage. Bill believes Aboriginal people and the white population are at last coming together and understanding each other better. Because of his long working life on the land alongside white landholders, he believes he can see clearly where the relationship went wrong. In the past, he says, when Aboriginal people lived on cattle stations, there was true coexistence.

White people took care of the Aboriginals. 'Even station managers who had children by Aboriginal women, they took care of the people. They did everything for them. Couldn't do enough for them.'

Then after the Wave Hill walk-out in 1966, led by author Frank Hardy and Aboriginal Vincent Lingiari, the move to stop 'exploitation' of Aboriginal stockmen began. 'Award wages killed the Aborigine off the land,' Bill says with feeling. 'When the government decided that everybody had to be equal, get paid equal pay—well, $100 a week for 300 Aborigine in a cattle farm, well that's a lot. And the property owner said, it's too many for me. We'll have to take them all into town, and we can pick up anybody from there and bring them in for work . . . Anyway, they left them there in town and of course they set up some sort of funding for them to keep them going with the food and all this. Well in the past the Aborigine didn't know how to buy the stuff, they didn't know what change is, how much [money] is, they didn't have a clue of anything . . . The landholder had been giving them food because they were free. Cheap labour, see? Well they didn't worry about the money in the past . . . They said it belonged to the white man, that money. They didn't touch that at all.' Once they had been moved into towns, the tribespeople realised they had lost contact with their ceremonies and stories about their land. And over the years landholders themselves lost contact with Aborigines, becoming suspicious and even fearful. They stopped access to the land. 'They thought they were going to run amok and make a mess of the country . . . and that's when they stopped them. And [once] they had stopped them [Aboriginal people] didn't know how to go about to teach the young kids because we can't teach them in town, we got to take them out bush because all the knowledge and the heritage [is] in the bush . . . Anyway when they done that, most of the Aboriginals were based in town . . . One race in town speak half English and half languages and some other kids, no languages at all, just speak English. And they are losing their culture very fast.'

Bill maintains it was only in 1984 when the film on Aboriginal art was made, that the government realised why Aboriginal people again wanted access to the cattle stations. 'But it was too late then because they had already stopped all the young ones growing up [on the land]. [They were] getting on the booze. Now purchasing all this property, that makes us feel better again.' Bill says his people work in with neighbouring stations on an equal footing and liaise with pastoralists on heritage agreements in sacred areas. They are coexisting very well. 'The pastoralists are really working in well with the Aborigines in this country. But I think it is the government getting confused there somewhere, I don't know what they are talking about.'

Governments mystify him, he says, as does the voting process. Bill says he and most Aborigines he knows just share their votes around and only vote to avoid a fine. He seems to think our method of choosing our tribal 'elders' is a very odd process indeed.

Reconciliation makes no sense to him either. In his view, we are already friends together in a partnership of sharing, where Aboriginals work with conservation departments to identify sacred sites, and whites record and preserve Aboriginal history. We are already brothers he says, so what's the fuss? I was fascinated by this bushman's observation that 'reconciliation' might simply be an excuse for another government department. It was enlightening to hear also that he has never encountered racism. If people choose not to employ Aboriginals because they are lazy and unreliable, that's not racism he says.

It was time to go. The 38° heat and 85 per cent humidity had finished me off. Bill, perfectly adapted to the country, was in fine spirits. I had wilted. Back at Bill's house, the Toyota was loaded with three adults and five children, bed-rolls, a television set, boxes and blankets for the trip back to Katherine. The children had been at the station school for a few days at Bill's insistence. The small brown man farewelled us and returned to work on the pile of didgeridoos stacked on the verandah of his neat red house.

Back in my working man's quarters, as I rehydrated myself, I feared for Bill and his noble dreams. His fervent hope that the young will want to better themselves and learn skills like he did may be shattered by a generation now too far removed from the bush. Dwayne, his mother a Wardaman elder, was more interested in his prestigious town-based job. He also wants to earn money as a rugby player.

UPDATE: Delemere Station was sold to another buyer. The Wardaman people are disappointed because the sale puts their dreams of self-sufficiency on hold.

Part VII

**To Paddocks East—
New South Wales and
Victoria**

Sensitive, New-Age Glamour—
Peter Glennie

I stepped from the long-haul interstate bus in Moree, upper New South Wales, to be whisked off to a farm so vastly different from Bill Harney's that I might have been in different continents. I was on my way back from seeing the babe newly born to the Queensland daughter with whom I had travelled previously. Travel by bus, I had decided, would be fine: cheap, flexible and a door-to-door service—albeit to doors 44 hours apart. For those of you who have never travelled by bus, you are missing some of life's essential experiences: dictatorial 'captains' who decree there is to be no eating, drinking or moving for four-hour stretches between stops; malodorous toilets; changes of bus at alarming hours in the night; and, lucky us, for extra entertainment we had a drug bust somewhere between Renmark and Mildura when sniffer dogs checked the luggage hold following suspicious behaviour from one of the more colourful passengers who kept falling out of his seat. Best, though, was the glorious moment when Brian, behind the wheel at four in the morning, in all seriousness softly announced to his sleeping load of captives that we were approaching the last meal stop before breakfast—it was a final opportunity to obtain refreshments. Several of the weightiest passengers then unwedged themselves from their seats and waddled into the roadhouse to stock up on tucker for those arduous hours to breakfast. Really, I do quite enjoy bus travel. I like seeing the changing landscape, having time to read and think, as well as observe the others in the hurtling tin can.

Having boarded the bus at 2.50am, I was really pleased to be breaking the journey in Moree for 24 hours and rehumanising myself. I would need all my wits about me—I was at a high-tech farm where soil, water and plants were totally programmed for maximum production. While Bill Harney was harvesting sticks for ancient musical instruments to call on the spirits, a cotton farm plugs into satellites.

Peter Glennie

The cotton industry strikes me as a very front-foot, pushing forward sort of industry. It seizes on new technology, is highly geared to innovative research, manages its public image professionally and markets its product enthusiastically. Its participants seem to enjoy affluence and prestige. In many respects, it has much in common with the wine industry. A friend recommended that I meet Peter Glennie who is just outside Moree. Peter had won the 1997 Australian Cotton Grower of the Year award and is also a very successful four-wheel-drive rally driver. It seemed an interesting mix, and I didn't know too many people on the land who had that much time or energy to indulge themselves in such a passion.

Moree was blooming with jacarandas on that warm November day. Its ornate colonial buildings seemed to have a look of India about them and my bus-weary brain imagined people appearing in pith helmets and safari suits. But another grain truck thundered through town from the wheatfields to the north and woke me up. Peter had a few jobs to do and then we sprinted out to Norwood in his Landcruiser—not the rally one of course, that's far too hot.

Norwood, of 10 800 acres, is bounded by the Gwydir River on one side, and although I saw cotton fields stretching into the distance wherever I looked, Peter said half of the place was covered with native vegetation, and another 10 per cent, which was once grazed is now left for birds and kangaroos. Peter, his wife Barbara and three daughters live on the block that was first taken up by the Glennie family in 1868 and used for sheep and cattle. On another property, his forebears bred horses for the Indian army. They started irrigating their first crops in 1955, then when Peter came home in 1963 from boarding school, and after work experience in Queensland, he launched the family into cotton growing. He had worked with one of the cotton pioneers in the Darling Downs, and was sufficiently revved up to be the first to grow cotton in the Moree area in 1976. They now have the capacity to put in about 3800 acres of irrigated cotton.

Not having seen a cotton farm before, I was unprepared for the massive system of canals, drains, channels, crossovers, dams, reservoirs, flood run-off and ponding areas. It was a design engineer's delight. Peter said he had strategies in place to cope with heavy rain storms, to keep soil in the paddocks and to prevent pesticides running off into sensitive areas.

'Cotton growing is probably one of the most multifaceted businesses you can become involved in,' Peter said as we negotiated our way along a high-mounded levee bank. To stop water taking off soil and plant debris, the whole farm was surveyed and fields levelled to a grade that was not going to wash. With a 10 metre fall from one end of the farm to the other, they could build banks to stop water surge. In 1996, five inches of rain in one hour tested his systems to the limit. Peter says it was a one in a 100 year event, but everything worked well and no crops were flooded.

Everywhere I looked there seemed to be young staff hard at work—driving huge cultivators delicately over crops, ploughing and spraying, modifying machinery in sheds, checking pumps and channels, and in the upstairs office, handling the books and phone calls. He employs ten people full-time and more at harvest.

Sitting comfortably in the stylish, large upstairs office with light streaming in through big windows overlooking cotton fields on several sides, we got down to the business of taping. Having heard how responsible Peter and the rest of the industry was about chemicals, I was keen to talk about reports of residue from cotton sprays being found in beef. Peter wouldn't have a bar of it. The bad practices are all in the past. The research arm of the industry has now put it well ahead of the image that is projected. 'The cotton industry is very unfairly targeted,' he said, 'probably because it is easy to focus on, I think. It hasn't always been totally innocent, but that's not specifically cotton either, it's agriculture.' Cotton growers have adopted world best practice with aerial spraying which is now very high tech and accurate because of the use of satellite navigation. They also use Global Positioning Systems minimise compaction of soils by keeping machinery to within two centimetres of track-lines down rows.

Growers are sponsoring research into breeding disease-resistant cotton with better yield, for less water use, and with genes to help kill predator insects so less spray can be used. They are starting to use 'trap crops', which attract harmful insects away from the cotton. Peter is passionate about defending his industry from unfair criticism. He has a full-time agronomist who guards against overspraying and oversees crop health.

Another development is Envirofeast, a food spray which attracts good bugs into the crop which then attack the damaging bugs. Peter has worked closely with researchers on this project. 'We are really developing a very efficient system that is using less and less chemicals and more and more predators,' Peter says.

In short, he feels wounded, and probably annoyed but he doesn't say so, by the misconceptions and inaccuracies. 'I think agriculture has been under seige for a while,' he says. 'There's been a sociological change recently. Urban dwellers' only contact [with farming] in this day and age is through the media. In the past, everyone in the city had a relative in the country. They used to communicate and there was a much better understanding. Today, very few people go out into the bush . . . I know that a lot of city friends that come up here are absolutely amazed at the way agriculture conducts itself compared with the way it's depicted.'

With his farm being in such an environmentally sensitive area—next to the river, native vegetation, wetlands and close to neighbours' operations—Peter says he can't afford to have slack systems in place. He says there is absolutely no reason why cotton could not be grown in spectacular and precious areas like Cooper Creek or the Kimberley. He says the great thing about the crop is that a lot happens in a small area. For instance, in the Gwydir Valley cotton takes up just 1.7 per cent of the area, yet yields 50 per cent of the area's wealth. 'And it has a great domino effect, because it is an expensive crop to grow and it requires a lot of people.' He implies that it is a good industry for isolated areas, bringing in wealth and people, mainly young. Overall, cotton is now the nation's fourth biggest rural export earner, although crops are clustered tightly around the river systems of the east coast.

Peter says cotton is a young industry, a fun industry and he, at age 54, is regarded as one of the old men, despite being younger than the average age of people working on the land. Other rural enterprises with fewer prospects are shunned by the young. 'I think the cotton industry enjoys itself and that's what we do on this farm,' Peter says.

The youth of its participants is one of the factors in the industry's strength. Their fresh ideas drive the marketing, and they'll prevent cotton going the same way as wool. Oversupply is unlikely because of the high entry costs for new growers, but also they'll ensure its image stays young and vital and environmentally acceptable. Cotton, which is processed and graded in a similar way to wool at a gin has, unlike wool, many uses for its by-products—the seeds, the husks and the lint—which are used for oil, stockfeed, paper-making and lacquer.

By now it was almost dark. There was one more thing Peter had to show me . . . his 'fun' machine downstairs in the shed under the office complex. By the way he approached this imposing Landcruiser which he has modified for speed, strength and endurance, I could tell this was a serious long-term relationship. Peter has won a round of the Australian Rally Championship, been fifth outright in the Round Australia in 1995 and fourth in the four-wheel-drive event, the Australian Safari in 1995. He led in 1996 before having to retire because he said he had pushed the vehicle to the limit with his secret tinkerings.

He says he loves the sport because it takes him to extraordinary places in Australia, meeting people from all over the world. 'Never lose the boy or girl in you,' Peter said as parting wisdom. That gave me something to ponder while I soaked myself in the natural artesian spa at my motel where water bubbled out of the ground at 41°C. The girl in me was strangely unexcited about the prospect of a further 29 hours on the bus before I reached home.

There the curlew hen was sitting on eggs in the fox-proofed front paddock. We could go off bore water and back on rainwater in the house as there had been a few decent falls.

From Liability to Asset—
Elisabeth Cuming

It's February. Two baby curlews hatched last month. Joy turned to sorrow when parents and young completely and mysteriously vanished from their safe haven.

I head to Hamilton, on cattle matters. As you enter this elegant and gracious town there are large signs proclaiming it to be the Wool Capital of Australia. They probably should be taken down. Being part of the wool industry once implied success and affluence. With the failure in recent years to sell wool to the world, prices have hardly covered the costs of production and woolgrowers have had to lose their landed gentry status, instead in many cases adopting a peasant-like subsistence.

Victoria's Western Districts were once 'silver spoon' territory. In its heyday, the Hamilton area was fun and fashionable, rather like Moree. With the crash of wool, many women on large ancestral properties found themselves looking for outside work; men were shattered by the unaccustomed drop in income.

On the other side of Hamilton where the Grampians start rearing up at you, I went to speak to a woman who took matters into her own hands when wool went bust. Hers was a last-ditch desperate grab at staying on the farm. She milked their sheep.

Elisabeth Cuming

Elisabeth Cuming

A row of brooding cypress trees ushers me down the driveway of Stirling towards a pretty gabled shed painted turquoise. From inside, the tick-tick-tick-tick of a small pump. In the soft light coming off aged wood and iron, a row of sheep place their heads into bails, and milking cups are put on their teats. It was the morning's final group to go through the dairy. Once finished, they walked out in an orderly fashion, turned right and put themselves back in their paddock. They reminded me of Babe's sheep. A door away, I found Elisabeth Cuming, slightly frantic from having made yoghurt until three that morning and trying to get the containers washed and labelled in time for collection by truck. I wiped, she labelled and packed. Then we walked to the rambling 1850s homestead set among roses and English trees where she and husband Bruce have raised seven children. We had a proper cup of tea at the huge kitchen table slightly buried under the papers and important items that farm kitchens attract. A clock on the wall chimed eleven.

Elisabeth, open-faced and smooth-skinned, is a lively, easy and entertaining conversationalist. She is also a bouncy, bright and energetic 54, but looks much younger. Desperate for a way to make the farm pay, she hit on the idea of milking their prime lamb mothers, the New Zealand breed Coopworth. 'I knew that sheep had been milked in Australia during the Depression and I thought, why not? We haven't any money to diversify and reinvest. We've got to use what we've got.' Her accent is that of a well-educated Melbourne girl. 'We were shooting sheep at the time, everything was so bad.'

She and Bruce set off around Victoria visiting sheep dairies. They decided the idea would work, so Bruce ripped off the corrugated iron from the side of the shearing shed, extended the raised floor, put in bails and herded in the first victims.

One of the people they had visited was Jim Konas whose family had been milking sheep near Melbourne for 25 years. Jim agreed to buy whatever milk they could produce.

Elisabeth bravely makes their early days of milking sheep sound hilarious. With primitive equipment, they could manage to milk just four sheep at a time. They had a weird system of coloured pegs to indicate which sheep were waiting to let down their milk. 'When the machine is put on the sheep they will let the first lot of milk down, then like all mammals they get another rush of oxytocin and they have a second let-down . . . So we had sort of a strange system of blue and red coloured clothes pegs, and sheep that had blue pegs had been milked once and sheep that had red pegs had been milked twice, and you can imagine what a muddle we got into with the pegs,' she says, laughing heartily. 'There was almost divorce on several occasions, and we are still picking up pegs from underneath the shed.' She is still laughing at the memory. 'And strange as it might seem, we did end up with a bit of milk in a bucket.'

But this was a deadly serious venture, their only hope of salvation. 'We would have had to have sold,' Elisabeth says firmly. 'We had three children at boarding school at the same time and we were unprepared to sacrifice that. To rob them of that would be worse than us trying to do something else. It was either that or go.'

They were also locked into a lease on land for woolgrowing that wasn't giving a decent return and were also buying their home farm. 'We were in the very first wool sale after the floor price went and I think we ended up with $10 000 or something to run a farm and ourselves for a year . . . and very high interest rates at the time. I think they were 25 per cent.' So the Coopworths were brought to the rescue. They had only about 200 'and they were pretty old, but fortunately we discovered that the older the sheep, the better they were at being milked'.

Sheep milk sells for $1 a litre so to get the $700 a week they needed to stay afloat, they set out to achieve 100 litres of milk a day, which often took them all day. 'We then realised we'd have to bring in more sheep other than the Coopworths and we had every sort of sheep you can imagine. We had Corriedales, we had Border Leicesters, we had first cross ewes, we had merinos. We tried everything we could get cheaply and easily.' And, interestingly, the very best milker turned out to be the meat breed of Dorset. They had a longer lactation period, yielded better and coped well with dairy life.

'We'd finish milking and it was often very late at night. It was a very wet winter, I remember . . . and somehow or other we got the children to and from school. And then Bruce would get up at about two o'clock in the morning and drive the milk to Melbourne. There was no other way of getting it down there in the cool. We just had a big plastic drum which we insulated with paint and all sorts of things on the outside. He would come back terribly tired and have to start milking again. It was tough.' Her voice trails off and she smiles grimly.

She remembers in that first year, about 1991, mainly feeling sorry for the ewes. 'You sort of felt you were exploiting them and it was a terrible feeling. We had taken away their lambs and we felt really miserable about it.' Meanwhile, Bruce was angry with the sheep. 'He felt furious that he was reduced to this, I suppose, and annoyed that it was him and all those sorts of things.' One cold night, two ewes dropped dead in the bails and Elisabeth felt 'this terrible well of sorrow for the sheep'.

'But we had to press on,' she said with almost a military jut of the jaw. 'Because it was the only way. And I have to say that I wouldn't have been able to do it [alone]. Bruce's anger was a much better reaction than my sorrow, because he had a sort of grittiness that he was going to do this, whether or not it succeeded. I would at various times feel much less positive about it than that, and so sorry that we were forced into doing this,' spoken softly and reflectively. 'But mercifully, the sheep yielded and you'd look at them and feel . . . very grateful.'

Elisabeth says over the years it has been rewarding to have the sheep respond to better management, feed and handling. 'They are very quiet. You ring a bell and they come in. The gates are always open, and they know when they hear the bell to come.' The dairy is only a small part of the Cumings' overall enterprise. They run a total of 2500 adult sheep, of which 600 go into the dairy. The rest rear prime lambs and grow wool. They also grow crops.

Elisabeth says the difficulties of the past decade were particularly hard on Bruce. 'I think he imagined that he'd collected his bride from Melbourne and he was bringing her back to something that in his mind was romantic and beautiful. I did see what he saw in those very early years of being married, and I too fell in love with what I knew he was really in love with . . . other than me. He feels for the country more than I think he reveals . . . and I think he did feel a sort of guilt and disappointment in himself, none of which was very realistic. But the bar was pretty high.' Bruce's parents had bought western districts land in the 1930s and had enjoyed the lifestyle that the wool boom years had made possible.

When Elisabeth, second of a family of five girls and a nurse at the Alfred Hospital, met Bruce, she knew little about the country. Her willingness to tackle adversity, change direction and continue living in a traditional and conservative district where stalwarts kept the lid on money matters and frowned on those who didn't, comes not only from strong character and having clear goals, but also a solid Christian faith. On every carton of yoghurt she sends out she writes 'AMDG', which in Latin stands for 'To the Glory of God'. 'I write it on there as a sort of reminder to myself that I do believe that in the end all will be well.'

'It was fairly difficult from a social point of view,' she says. 'Dairying isn't a glamorous activity and somehow milking sheep seems the absolute bottom of the barrel. But when you are able to stay on your farm because of it, I am very proud of it. It looks sort of quirky and a bit folksy and somehow a bit socially unacceptable, but we weren't terribly worried about that.' The critics, in some cases, have since been forced to sell up.

'We have been blessed with the most wonderful friends and they were so supportive. I remember once, it was Christmas time, and we had just shorn the milkers. Bruce and I were going off to do some shopping in Ballarat and we left two or three children at home. They were going to do the milking for us. A dreadful storm blew up, a really terrible storm in which limbs were torn from trees. When we got to Ballarat, we realised that these freshly shorn milkers could have died. We quickly rang home only to find that the children were very aware of [the problem].

'Well, when we got home there was a most touching scene. I'll always remember it. I wondered what had happened because there were all these trailers and cars and stock crates and horse floats in the drive and around the shed. When we got closer, it was all our neighbours that were helping save the sheep, and we felt the most wonderful well of . . . I remember us crying because it was so moving to think that we mattered so much. There they all were, these very people whom we'd thought might think we were rather infra dig, and they were all helping us. I don't think anyone realised what that actually meant to us. It was far more than just saving the sheep. It was an acceptance of something that we almost could hardly accept ourselves.'

Elisabeth and Bruce stopped selling raw milk to Jim Konas after a few years. For the past seven years they have been able to milk fewer sheep for better returns through value-adding. Elisabeth makes 50 dozen containers of yoghurt each week under the Lesna label for sale in Brisbane, Canberra, Tasmania and Sydney. Her own label of Grampians Pure is dispatched direct to Melbourne, Sydney and Hobart and sold on the farm to tourists who regularly visit the dairy. The flavours of lemon, coconut and vanilla for her label were developed with the help of young French food technology students they have had on exchange over the years.

She also had some help in the early days of making yoghurt from George, a Greek 'mentor' from Mount Gambier. 'You had to make your own mother cultures,' Elisabeth says. 'I've found out since that brides in Greece and Macedonia are often given a tiny little piece of the family culture when they are married. And it can be hundreds of years old.'

Freeze-dried cultures, which she uses now, give consistent acidity and flavour. George taught her how to make fetta cheese and she is considering one day getting into making hard cheeses for farm-gate sales. I tasted a delicious parmesan cheese which had been made by their son Marius, who learnt cheese-making at the Victorian agriculture college in Geelong and then travelled overseas on a Queen Elizabeth Trust award to study sheep dairies.

The extra milk that comes with the feed flush in spring would be used for the cheeses. Last year, Bruce and Elisabeth visited Roquefort in France, a large centre for sheep milk dairies where cheese of the same name is made. 'Roquefort, they say, is the king of cheeses,' says Elisabeth. It cannot be produced in Australia since it relies on the use of unpasteurised milk sourced only from the French Leconne sheep. Some of the Cumings' milk had previously been taken back to Roquefort for testing by one of the milk controllers. 'They couldn't get over the content of Australian sheep milk. It is very superior to the French sheep milk,' Elisabeth says with some delight, noting that French sheep have to be housed and cannot eat natural pasture.

Now that the Cuming offspring are almost all independent, financial pressures are lighter. They range in ages from 28 down to fifteen. The youngest is at boarding school, two are in tertiary study and the other four are occupied in interesting professions—two are teachers, one a nurse and Marius is an ABC broadcaster.

Although Bruce, aged 56, has had some recent ill health, they want to continue on with the farm. Two of their sons are interested in running it one day. 'I think the thing is that none of them wants it sold. They all know how hard we've tried to keep it and they all know that we have expended a lot of life's emotional energies on it.'

I returned to my world of beef cattle at the showgrounds in Hamilton. Misery and complaint have been on the lips of beef producers for many years now. Elisabeth and her gutsy story of pulling her sleeves up and doing whatever had to be done with the assets they had, kept resonating.

A Life on the Track—
Ron and Hilda Cherry

I'm nearing the end of this odyssey, so I decide to treat myself to meeting a couple whose lives fascinated me when I met them through their stories about working dogs and horses published in the eponymous books. They are Hilda and Ron Cherry, who have been drovers in the back blocks of New South Wales for more than 40 years. They are among the last of the full-time professionals of the stock routes. Today, few young people are interested in the job and government boards have changed the rules, making returns to drovers less attractive than they once were.

Nevertheless, romantic notions of a life free of care on the road drew me towards their settlers' cottage and farm in the hills outside Armidale. Hilda and Ron dispelled any ideas about romance during our day together, but my view that drovers have well earnt the 'legend' tag was left intact.

The Cherrys were taking an unusual day off droving to cut up a steer for the freezer. They had a mob of 900 cattle in their care, grazing in a roadside stop a half hour away. They'd be on the track again the next day but in the meantime they still needed checking and the horses fed, so Hilda, Ron and I squeezed into the truck with a couple of dogs on the back. While Joe, the Appaloosa, and Trump, a bay clumper, tucked into their breakfast nosebags, we sat down under some blue gums to talk.

Ron has the calmness and wisdom of the long-time stockman at ease in the bush, with watchful eyes that see into the core of man and beast, preferring to listen rather than speak. He leaves that chore mostly to Hilda. He does tell me, however, that he started full-time droving as a nine year old, assisting his father, a veteran of 52 years on the stock routes. Ron, at age 58, is not far behind. He has spent nearly 50 years in the saddle, moving livestock from one end of the state to the other. He reckons he would know where he was if he was taken blindfold to any stock route.

Ron and Hilda Cherry

Ron and Hilda Cherry

Hilda, aged 56, is one of very few women boss drovers. She's been in charge of mobs of well over a thousand head for about 14 years, a job brought on because the Cherrys frequently have more work landed on them than just one team could handle. Instantly likeable, with a dependable, down to earth, no-nonsense quality, it's clear why she's never had any problem with hard-nosed cattlemen trusting her with around $500 000 of their livestock. I might have expected her to be leathery and rough of speech after a lifetime outdoors spent mainly among men. She is certainly not either of these things—rather round and motherly and gentle instead.

The second youngest of a family of 11, Ron got his own droving plant at 18 and teamed up with Hilda, who at 16 had run away from home, fallen in love and produced Ron a daughter, Tracy, their only child. Hilda says she had gone through a rebellious stage—not without just cause, I thought. Second eldest, also from a family of 11 children, Hilda said she remembers nothing but a childhood of heavy responsibility and hard work. Her parents were real battlers, with a little farm where they grew vegetables. 'As kids, we didn't know what it was to play. We had to go to work with Dad at weekends. We had to come home after school, so that the tea would be on the table, the cows would be milked, the wood would be got in by the time Mum and Dad got home from work,' she says. 'I have followed draughthorses, dropping carrot seeds behind the furrow of the plough. I have washed carrots, I have pulled corn, and all as a little kid. We had to, we would not have survived if we didn't.' She was resentful when she couldn't go to friends' places or play weekend sport for the school. 'I left school and went fencing with my father to get money to help support the family. We had it tough as kids.'

But she picked a hard life to escape to, and a bloke who himself had suffered dreadful hardships. Ron was born with chorea, or St Vitas dance, a disease that causes involuntary spasms to face and limbs. Few signs remain now of this disability. When Ron went to saddle up, Hilda told how it had affected him. 'He couldn't hold anything in his hands. He had no control of the movements of his legs, or his arms, or his head. Because of that, he missed out on a lot of schooling. He was teased and ridiculed, and made fun of at school all the time. He couldn't hold a knife and fork to feed himself until he was probably about 12 or 13, and because he couldn't hold a pencil, he didn't learn to read or write.' So his parents gave up on school and took him droving. They gave him a pony and then a bicycle to help get use of his hands and strengthen his legs. Hilda says when they first started droving together, and up until only the last 10 or 15 years, people used to think Ron was drunk. 'We've had many people apologise to us in later years,' she says.

Hilda accordingly runs the business, does the accounts, handles administration and organises the labour, but she lets him always take the spotlight. When I was trying to track Ron and Hilda down, I spoke to a number of agents and landholders. They all knew Ron. 'An A1 bloke,' said one. 'Totally reliable,' said another.

We left the cattle and spent a few hours bagging up steaks, roasts and stewing meat at a neighbours' coolroom. We returned to the cottage to sample a scotch fillet sandwich, and sit and talk on the verandah.

Hilda and Ron say they've seen many changes over the years. When they first started out in 1958, they recall there were 36 drovers living on the outskirts of Moree waiting for jobs. Now there are just a few. The jobs are drying up and the government's Pastoral Protection Boards oversee the feed supply on the stock routes, issue permits, restrict mob sizes, impose rules on distances to be covered each day, check on the stock and keep an eye on the drovers—check that they are doing the right thing. 'Many years ago a drover was an irresponsible thief, a stock thief, and a lot of people still have that concept that drovers are like that,' Hilda says.

Horses and dogs have been the constants in their life . . . also the open skies and far horizons . . . and the 4.30am starts to have the cattle on the road by 5.00am. Always moving on, always catching and feeding horses, collecting dogs, packing up the camp, saddling up and getting away by first light, day after day. It's not the romantic life that people imagine it is, says Hilda. 'People reckon it's a real lazy, bludging life,' says Ron with a snort.

People often stop and talk. Best are the overseas tourists who are amazed at the lifestyle and 'want to know everything'. Ron and Hilda enjoy those visitors. They are not so sure about the people who pull up when they are having a snooze against a tree while their horses are at their nosebags, and say, 'Gee, you got it easy'.

'They don't realise we're up in the dark and looking after stock seven days a week,' says Ron. 'One night we were camped there at the Washpool Reserve on the Inverell side of Moree. Everything was peaceful, then bang, the cattle rushed. They flattened the fences. We were going till 12 o'clock that night by the time we got them back in and strained up all the fences in the dark.'

Changed, too, is people's stock sense. They call them idiots, the people who toot and roar their cars through the cattle. 'The worst thing you can do in a mob of cattle is blow the horn,' says Hilda. 'Older cattle will stop on the road and look at the vehicle. Skittish cattle will rush away, kick out and do damage to the vehicle.'

They were battling once to get cattle across a road into some rail yards. Traffic was banked up, but then around the outside, at quite a speed came a vehicle which hit her favourite dog, badly injuring it. Other times they have had horses killed, and 'heaps of stock killed' by vehicles ignoring the need to slow down. Hilda says it has always been found to be the drivers' fault because the animals have been under control.

Cotton growers are a new headache too. Many of their paddocks are unfenced and then there are all those channels of water. Keeping cattle out is a major exercise. 'The cotton trucks are ruthless. They don't care about stock; they complain about them all the time,' says Hilda.

Hilda and Ron say living on the road is not much different from living at home these days—especially having mobile phones. They've made a major difference to life on the road. In their caravan, they have television, a washing machine, and 'a new garden every day'. They do worry, however, about the bashings and murders they hear of in areas they travel through. 'You are camped on the edge of the road all of the time. You don't know who's coming or going,' Hilda says.

The truck that tows the van has boxes for 25 dogs underneath the tray and room for eight to ten specially bred tough, smallish horses on top. Hilda says they take more dogs than anyone else. 'We are probably known to be the people with the dogs.' Having plenty means they have dogs for all needs—ones for heading the mob and holding the lead, heelers to hurry them along, paddock dogs to retrieve strays that have separated and back-up dogs to give others a rest from the heat, the burrs and the work. 'The stock routes are wide. They are vast. Dogs have to travel long distances. They get tired, knocked up, so we find it is easier to carry more dogs and have no worries,' says Hilda, who breeds her own team of dogs, as does Ron.

'It's not a fast life—time-consuming, but it's not fast. Everything is steady. That's probably one of the things that we like about it the most,' she says. 'Life seems to be ten times slower than it is anywhere else, when you're droving.' It is little wonder that she says she finds cities claustrophobic.

Hilda's traditional 'clumper' much beloved by drovers is a Clydesdale/Arab cross, bred to be tough, gentle and placid. 'You can't afford to get hurt in this job,' she says. Nevertheless, after 40 of her 56 years spent in the saddle, Hilda has had her fair share of bumps and falls from being bucked off or knocked around. 'Probably being in the weather so much for so many hours a day every day, you tend to get things like arthritis, sore knees and hips and back. You probably get those a lot quicker than a lot of people would.

'We work in all weathers. If it starts to rain, you can't go to the shed . . . The cattle still need to be controlled. If it starts to snow, which it has done many times on us, you've got to be out in it all the time.'

In the old days before everyone had trucks, Ron used to ride and lead the horses his father needed, to the start of the droving jobs, covering distances of up to 80 kilometres in a day. Ron loves his horses and treats them well, feeding them on grain and high energy mix and keeping them clean, wormed and healthy. They are always rugged when they are working. Hilda says she rugged 16 each night last winter.

'We once got a job from a fellow because we'd been droving on his boundary for about three weeks and he asked us to take a mob of sheep for him. Ronnie asked who recommended him and he said, 'I got your recommendation off yourself.' He said, 'I've been driving past your camp for three weeks and I've made the decision that a man who cares for his own animals that well, will care for mine.'

Years of close teamwork with the horses paid off for Hilda. She owes her life to a sensible chestnut horse called Biscuit. It is a story she wrote for the *Great Working Horse Stories* book but we savoured it again that day. She and Ron had been been droving 7000 weak, drought-affected lambs alongside a river. They kept getting stuck in the sand and mud when they went for a drink. Hilda jumped off Biscuit and climbed down over a 1.5 metre bank into the riverbed. When she walked over some sand to rescue a lamb, she was sucked down, sinking quickly to her waist. No-one else was around. Luckily, she had dropped the reins over Biscuit's head onto the ground. Her only hope was to get the horse to move closer to the edge of the bank. She called him and he kept shaking his head and neighing. 'Every time he would do that, the reins would flick out and I was able to get hold of the reins.' She then told the horse to 'back up' and being very obedient, he did while Hilda kept talking to him. 'He backed up until he had me pulled out of the sand and on to the bank where I could get my feet under me again,' she said. She believes she would have been sucked right under and killed. 'I didn't really think of a horse as having brains until then,' she said.

Droughts always test man and beast the hardest. 'There's nothing worse than a thirsty mob of stock, particularly cattle. Cattle are quite ruthless when they are thirsty. They will look for anything that smells like water. It doesn't matter if it's just a little puddle on the side of the road, or if there's a dam inside the fence, ten metres away.

'There's nothing harder to watch than a water trough that will cater for probably 20 head, and you've got 1400 trying to get a drink at one time. They can smash down water troughs, break off floats, they'll knock you down too if they're thirsty enough. Water is something that you've got to look for days ahead of yourself all the time.' Another time, their mob of one thousand got hot when they were trying to force them unsuccessfully to cross a bridge over the Gwydir River. Thirst drove them to divert into the river but then they were unable to get out. Townsfolk came down with boats to help, but Ron and Hilda were left with the thousand head scattered far and wide.

Their work has taken them from Echuca in the south up to Roma and Injune in Queensland, to Lightning Ridge, Walgett, Holbrook, Grafton, Bourke. 'We always took big mobs of stock,' says Hilda. 'We've had as many as 3600 cattle in one mob. And we always had at least 1500. But now they have stopped that.' Pasture Protection Boards limit drovers to one thousand cattle now, some as few as 600 head. 'We don't understand that,' says Hilda, 'because their argument is that you can't water them on their troughs but when we used to take big mobs, we watered them on exactly the same troughs as they've still got. So now if you can get a mob of a thousand head, that is the best money you can make today. It is a good living, but it does depend on how good a run you have. There can be years when you might wait for work for three or four months. And another time, we went away for three years and four days before we came home. We do all right.' That job was in the Riverina in 1980: Ron had expected to be away for just six weeks.

They had started in Braidwood and then hit drought conditions. They kept the cattle in the south around Leeton and Hay where there was more feed. 'To have 3600 head of cattle on those narrow roads was unreal.' Hilda remembers how difficult it was trying to prevent cattle getting into ripe rice fields. 'A lot of hard work, a lot of hard work,' says Hilda, trailing off at the memory. 'It was 119 degrees in the shade in summertime.' Being away from their home so long saw the garden she loves become a jungle, and cobwebs draping themselves through the rooms. They got robbed of tools and saddles from their sheds.

Bountiful seasons bring their problems too. Cattle get bloat from too much rich feed. Their rumens puff up and they can die. Ron and Hilda use blades mounted on the end of long poles and ride among the cattle like knights on chargers, stabbing the ones that are puffy. 'Gas flies out, they make a tremendous noise and it frightens the horses and the other cattle all run. The beast that got the gas released gallops off, but we haven't ever lost any that we've stabbed,' says Hilda.

To treat sick or injured cattle individually, they have to rope them and tie them down to a tree. It's tough work, especially for people in their late fifties. Hilda makes light of it, saying they've had plenty of practice.

Hilda became a solo drover about 14 years ago when a big landholder in the Armidale district gave them two jobs at once. Ron and Hilda would catch up with each other when they were within 40 kilometres of each other. 'It costs us $300 a month for Ronnie's phone bill,' says Hilda. 'He rings me up every night checking me out.' She laughs fondly.

Not long ago Hilda took 1800 head from Walcha to Armidale, drafted off the weaners, then walked the cows out to Boggabilla, Inverell, North Star and back to Boggabilla, where the cows calved at a creditable 85 per cent calving rate. 'That was the last job I did,' she says, then adds, 'I think it will probably be the last job I do too. I'm tired.' Then the ribbing starts. First, a workmate who had dropped in razzes her for being too old. Ron laughs heartily. They think she is joking. Hilda repeats more firmly she is not doing any more riding. She just wants to do 'nothing'. Ron finds this even more amusing. Hilda persists. She wants to travel around Australia, go somewhere other than the places they've been. 'There are other things that you can do,' she insists. 'There are not very many people that stay in one job that long, and we don't have the glory of long service and superannuation and holiday pay and holidays every year, like other people.' It is certainly not as if Hilda has sat around relaxing between droving jobs. She has been a cook in hotels and at a university college with 400 students, been a seamstress making nurses' uniforms and shrouds at the large hospital in Armidale, worked in laundries, picked fruit, cleaned rooms and cared for children. She reports she had her first holiday in her whole life just five years ago when she went to New Zealand. Her second holiday was for three weeks this year with her sister. Now she has had a taste of a different life, she wants more. She wants a change from working always among men. 'I am a home person. I just like being at home,' she says. She wants to hang up her stockwhip and saddle and get on with sewing and gardening. Ron sees no need for holidays, nor does he want to retire. 'I think I'll keep working till I can't work any more, that's what I want to do,' he says.

'But the problem is he wants me to do the same,' mutters Hilda, and Ron laughs heartily again.

Hilda Cherry has become a magnet for young people when they

are out on the road, particularly girls unhappy with their lives and wanting to escape—much as she at 16 had done. It seems going droving has some of the same allure as joining the circus. 'They'll come into the camp for a yarn at night and you'll find out that they're kids that are not getting on well at home or they've had it very rough,' Hilda says of a brood of young people she and Ron have taken under their wing and been able to give a new start in life. They have run a virtual rescue and welfare program for lost and damaged souls.

One girl at Moree came to them when she was 14 years old. She had been living with the Aborigines, 'running wild', Hilda says. 'She made out to us, because she really wanted to come, that she was a great horsewoman. Anyway, we took her along.' Eighteen years later, she still helps them out. She now has her own horse and competes at rodeos, and has a job on a cotton farm. 'She says we saved her life. She calls us Mum and Dad, and she says that if we hadn't said she could come along with us, she wouldn't be here today. She knew she was on the wrong track.'

'Another little girl was very badly treated by her mother.' By the time she was 18, 'she had had four names in her lifetime and didn't really know which one was hers'. Her only friend was her horse, which she had ridden since she was three. She visited the Cherrys daily. When they were packing up to move, they saw her approaching. 'And here she comes. It was raining and she's got this mattress all wrapped up in plastic and her blankets and a bag hung over her shoulder and her dog, and everything, all loaded up on the horse,' Hilda recalls. 'She said, I'm coming to live with you. You don't mind?' She stayed with Hilda and Ron for five years. 'She became a terrific little drover, really good, and a really good horseperson. She really could ride, but she'd had no teaching, it was all self-taught. So we got her into the pony club and she won heaps of ribbons and improved her riding. Then I got her into the Tech to do the Horse Management Course, which she graduated from and she was really pleased with that, because she hadn't been all that well-educated.'

This girl and Hilda went off droving together. 'Then she went to the show and met a young cocky fellow from up at Ben Lomond and he married her. She's just had a little baby girl, actually.' Hilda is delighted about this happy outcome for a girl who previously had no prospects and an uncertain identity.

There is something about droving that has given these young people the focus they need, says Hilda. The appeal is fading for young employees on a full-time, long term basis, however. 'You can't expect any young person to come with you for a couple of hundred dollars a week and his keep, if he can go and work on the cotton for a $1000 a week,' says Hilda. 'We're getting $1000 a week, so we can't pay them any more. There's no social life on the road for young people. It's too tied down. And if I was a young kid today, there's no way in the world I'd take it on either.'

UPDATE: True to her word, Hilda had stayed home while Ron went off on the next droving job. She was waiting to have surgery on an elbow which a horse fall had damaged some time before. About four months had passed before their current job came along. The good season meant cattle had plenty of feed in their paddocks. Higher cattle prices prevented people buying stock to put on the roads.

With Ron was their 15-year-old grandson, out droving for the first time. He had got into trouble at school and dropped out, but was relishing the experience of life on the road. Hilda said it was a bit early to say whether he might one day carry on the family tradition.

In Harmony with the Earth—
Tim Peel

On my travels I have talked to highly progressive farmers, innovators and risk-takers. My next stop, near Wagga Wagga, was with someone who is proud to be none of these. Tim Peel, living on a picturesque 4000 acre holding with creeks and hills, doggedly continues to foster the heritage skills of our ancestors. He looks to be completely out of step with a world raging forward technologically. Tim Peel is so keen to hold to his line that headlong rushing is not necessary and not justifiable in lifestyle and financial terms, that he won't even go into a supermarket—the corner store is his choice. When grazing enterprises are generally finding the going rough, who would dare suggest Tim is out of step? Particularly since he and wife Julie are getting by. Retro-fashion is all the rage in some quarters. Retro-style in architecture and interiors much enjoyed. A huge nostalgia market is hungry for the ways of the past. But retro-farming—using draughthorses for real work, making harness and horse collars and keeping alive the skills and trades of our pioneering past—many might call quaint. But it works for Tim Peel.

Tim Peel is a particularly unstressed person. He is calm, gentle, dignified and without worry lines or wrinkles. For him, the joy of living is to be found in ploughing a perfectly straight and even furrow with a single-furrow plough pulled by a pair of well-matched Clydesdales. Every year he ploughs two acres of ground, then discs it, harrows it and sows cereal rye seed with a two-horse drill. The resulting tall-standing straw, which is cut with a reaper and binder pulled by three horses, is used to stuff his renowned horse collars and saddles. Tim sees symmetry and sense in using horses to grow what he needs for collars. 'I get great enjoyment out of it,' he says. 'I find that if I have a pair of horses that are going well and I put them in the plough, there are no diesel fumes, there's no noise and it's just such a lovely feeling to be out there on a nice sunny morning.'

For Love of the Land

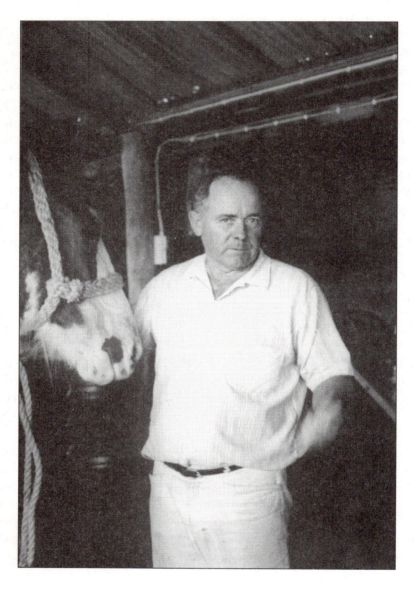

Tim Peel

Tim, who lives alongside the Sturt Highway, perpetuates the tradition of always ensuring the last furrow of the day is perfectly straight. 'A farmer would never ever knock off at the end of the day if he had a crooked furrow. It was a thing of pride.' His fastidiousness is possibly quite lost on this generation of motorists whizzing by.

Most people are familiar with the spectacular Carlton and United Brewery promotional show wagon. Tim Peel built it. Every bit of it, every hook, every bolt, all the wheel rims, the beautifully shaped wooden sides, all of it, except for the spokes. Nearly all the timber came from trees growing on his farm. He also made collars and the harness for the majestic four-horse team; and he bred and trained the horses too. Where once six different tradesmen would have worked on a huge project like this, Tim is master of all six trades—blacksmith, coachbuilder, wheelwright, harness maker, collar maker and saddler. He respects the skills of the past, so much so that he'll frequently choose a traditional method over power tools and speed any time.

Yet, before you dismiss him as an eccentric crank, let me hastily say that Tim Peel is very much tuned into the agricultural demands of the real world. He runs 800 head of mainly Angus cattle, producing steers for the demanding Japanese beef market. You will find very little modern technology on his place, however. Tim Peel, aged 53, says he sees everyone chasing the latest gadgets and devices yet he doesn't believe they are any happier for it. 'To me, if you ask most people today, they say all the stresses of modern life weigh down heavy on them, yet they've all got their computers and their mobile telephones, but I don't think people are any happier today.'

Tim Peel was another whom I had met fleetingly through stories about working horses. I had spoken to him briefly during editing of an uplifting story about a stallion he rescued from a knackery that went on to be Grand Champion of the Sydney Show. He told me then a little of his life. I was fascinated to hear that his family had a dairy which stabled 14 horses in Diamond Bay Road, Vaucluse, until 1963, in the exclusive heart of Sydney. 'The stables would have only been 100 yards from the ocean,' he says. The business had been started at Gladesville in 1915 by his grandfather but although it was cheaper to deliver milk with horses, they had to change over to vans because neither drivers with knowledge, nor horses able to do the job, were available.

Sitting in the early morning sun on the verandah, we talked about his life in the then isolated backwater of Kellyville, where he was surrounded by great horsemen born in the last century. He remembered 150 cows being milked by hand until about 1952, delivery horses that knew far more than their drivers and one that was so strong 'he would pull the bend out of a river'. Tim's job as a lad was to look after the horses resting from their hard city runs.

His life reads like something out of a boy's own annual, or Huck Finn. It was an upbringing where riding to school and the local dance was the norm, and where resourcefulness in children was much encouraged. It was a perfectly natural progression, therefore, when he left school, to set off on an adventure that today would be unthinkable for two 16-year-old boys. Where city boys of the same age today are often driven to school to protect them from the perceived dangers of the roads and streets, Tim and a friend set off by horse-drawn cart on a 1100 kilometre journey north to find work, staying away for 18 months. They wanted to do some station work out west.

'We put a pair of old trotters in one of the milk wagons. I refurbished it, and we headed off from Kellyville to Bourke,' Tim says. 'I thought it would be a great experience to drive a distance of 500 miles. It took us six weeks to get there.' They took swags, cooking gear, shot kangaroos, ducks and rabbits along the way and stocked up on flour, tea, sugar, fruit, rice and horse feed when they went through towns. 'In those days there was no fear of anything untoward happening,' he says of his getting of wisdom and independence. They had to put new shoes on the horses every ten days, cope with a week of constant rain when all their bedding got soaked, then drought and a shortage of feed north of Dubbo. They took jobs along the way and people invited them in for meals. Once they were in Bourke, they went droving, fencing, contract mustering and processed meat at the roo works. The boys lived in the wagonette parked on the town common where numerous other outback workers had tents, caravans and tin humpies. They got to know old drovers and one of the original Afghan cameleers, Morbein Peerez, who showed him photos of his 80 camels carrying a bale of wool on each side out of the back country—an amazing 160 bales, which is more than a semitrailer could carry today.

He also worked with Aboriginals in shearing teams and was appalled at the injustice of their being paid equal wages but being charged double for alcohol. So he helped them out, spent weekends at their camps and joined in their fun. 'They'd do anything for you whenever they had money or food. To me they are true communists,' as in the full sense of the word. Tim is yet another who laments the ending of station employment for Aboriginals where families of 20 or more were kept by station owners. Their culture was able to be retained and they could go on walkabout if they wanted to, because of what they called 'slow time' wages.

When he returned to Kellyville, Tim revived his passion for the Clydesdale horses he had so admired at work on the hilly dairy rounds through Sydney. He had a registered mare and that's when he chased up the stallion from the knackery, that previously had worked underground in the Muswellbrook coalmines. Tim thought he would breed a few foals to keep the threatened breed going and with a group of friends, the Clydesdale classes were revived at the Sydney Royal Show.

Married in 1969 to Julie, a former show-jump competitor, they became very serious about showing and since 1970, 'I think we've won every class that there is to win at Sydney or Melbourne Royal at some stage over the years, either at led-ins or in harness,' he says.

Today, he has between 25 and 30 Clydesdales and sells them to breweries and hobbyists for showing and fun, but also a few alternative farmers who are pursuing self-sufficiency. He laments the headlong modernisation of agricultural colleges in the 1960s, many of which had bred magnificent lines of heavy horses. He had begged Hawkesbury College at Richmond to sell him a Scottish stallion imported at great expense, but the principal insisted he be dispatched to the knackery. 'I couldn't help thinking, as his blood ran across the floor and washed down the drain, that with it went decades of illustrious ancestors and the hopes and aspirations of countless studmasters and breeders; and how the government had spent all this money bringing such a well-bred horse out from Scotland to improve the breed here.' His dismay that the college had no allegiance to these horses and the role they had played in the development of this nation, I suspect, still eats at him. His horror at the time at the prevailing philosophy for 'getting modern' and throwing away old-fashioned things sees him now going out of his way to re-create the past. The Peel pigsty is built of handmade posts, sunk into the ground with sleepers slotted into them as sides and a recycled spray dip tank used for shelter.

'I was reared on a traditional type of old farm where all the buildings were slab,' he explains. 'Slab stables, hollow logs for troughs, post and rail fences—and I've always had a great admiration for the pioneers, the way they did things. They used natural materials to build and used whatever was at hand.' The hitching rails for his heavy horses are made of huge ironbark tree trunks sunk deep into the ground. A thick rail is wedged into the tops of the posts. It was made recently but is in perfect harmony with the old weatherboard stables, foundry and coach rooms of his historic property.

Tim makes all the iron tools in the forge that he needs for his work—tongs, hammers, pritchels, punches. There's no element of throwaway society here. 'A lot of the stuff that I make, whether it is tools or wagons, they'll be around in another hundred years,' he says. The CUB wagon, commissioned in 1988, took him 18 months and, interestingly, was built without patterns or plans, no drawings or diagrams. 'I built the whole thing completely out of my head,' says this quiet, thoughtful, unassuming man who drew on his long first-hand experience with lorries and wagons. 'I said I didn't want to do it to a deadline, because when you are doing a really good job, you want the luxury of being able to put the saw through or the knife through something if you're not happy with it.'

From 1980 to 1994, after the family dairy closed, Tim worked full-time on collar-making, wagon-building and wheel-wrighting. He sold 25 acres of near-city land, raised enough to buy 4000 acres at Wagga Wagga, but finds with the large farm he has less time for his trades.

We moved over to the former jackaroo's quarters, which now house his collar shop and harness room. Inside, the pine-lined walls have aged to a glowing golden red. The air hangs with the ambrosial scents of leather and straw. Paned windows filter soft light onto his workbench, patterns and tools hang on the walls and ancient leatherworking machinery, intricate and rare, stands on the pine floor.

Tim says there is enough work in these old crafts to still employ him full-time, but it is tough making a good living out of such slowly produced handmade things. He was taught by Fred Whitticase, an English harness tradesman who had been employed on the dairy by his grandfather. Fred died at age 103 and Tim bought all his original tools and sewing machines that had come from England. Tim passed his skills on to an apprentice and is teaching one of his sons. He believes there are probably just five collar makers in the whole of Australia. Inevitably, these old trades will disappear. 'You can't earn enough money today from stuff you make by hand.' As an example, he says a current commission for Coopers Brewery of a set of single cart harness for which he charges $8000, will take between eight and ten weeks to make. Out of that comes about $2000 in costs for materials.

Outside the quarters, tied securely to a large tree, is a very handsome but very angry mare. She had been brought in from the paddock a few days before and was to be shod that afternoon so she could appear at Sydney Royal Show a few days later. She had been shown a year previously, but in the meantime had decided to revert to brumby behaviour. While she did mad dances at the end of her rope and lashed out in fury, Tim, calmly and with a smile on his face and giving off an aura of complete relaxation, dominated this 700 kilogram beast without one cross word or unkind movement. Using guile and a lifetime of experience all based on gentleness, but consistency, the mare stood subdued and sensible one hour later while hot, hand-forged shoes were pressed to her feet. It was evident, from watching Tim dealing in turn with the mare's sulks and tantrums, just how many horsemanship skills we've lost. Many people today are first-generation horse owners and have lost contact with the way things were done by the old-timers. Tim quotes the old horseman who lamented, 'There's so much to tell and no-one to listen.' He worries that in time, people in cities who are far removed from livestock will pass laws preventing the use of safe, practical and effective methods of handling them—thinking of farm animals more as domestic pets, rather than untamed and often dangerous creatures. 'As civilisation becomes more divorced from reality, people are liable through ignorance to interfere and enact animal handling laws,' he says.

UPDATE: The mare was placed second in her class at the Sydney Royal.

A Personal Battle Creates a Boom— Hedley and Irena Earl

A thought occurs to me as my travels come to a close: despite perpetual hopes of future wool boom times, this, perhaps, is as good as it gets. Never again will soldiers in woollen greatcoats fight in muddy trenches; never again will mountains of woollen uniforms and grey woollen blankets be made for the battlefields. Wars, involving masses of people out in the weather powered the wool booms of the past. I can't see columns of soldiers in the future trudging over freezing steppes and through mountain passes. Computer weapons operated from offices do the job now.

This story begins with a pair of black knickers—woollen knickers that I was given for Mother's Day when I was in Queensland. I must say, woollen undies in a hot climate seemed incongruous and particularly unappealing, but I was suitably gracious. They have, however, become my favourites ... I was later to meet the people behind these knickers when I innocently asked an ebullient beef-producing friend what had happened to the breeder of a particular champion bull. 'He's making undies,' was Bob's reply.

So I followed up the people I had previously known as stud cattle breeders and found them fresh from their own personal war zone, where they had been bombarded by bureaucracy, pummelled by financial institutions and savaged by sceptics. They have become industry pioneers who have engineered, against mighty odds, their personal wool boom that is spreading to international markets ... and certainly not just knickers.

Hedley and Irena Earl

Hedley and Irena Earl encountered more than their fair quota of disasters during their quest to regain the rural lifestyle Hedley had loved in his youth. They had a high-profile and successful Hereford stud near Geelong but it fell victim to soil contamination by dieldrin from the land's earlier use by a potato farmer. Wool was lucrative then, so in response to a dare by the very same ebullient beef-producing Bob to 'do with sheep' what they did with cattle, the Earls switched to producing superfine wool. Three years later, they set a new seasonal Victorian record of 13 000 cents a kilogram for a bale.

They bought a large block of land for expansion but then were left with massive debts when their backer, the Pyramid Building Society, collapsed and the fine wool price went the same way. They were to suffer three years of extreme hardship; they were on the brink of financial ruin. Yet only eight years before, the Earls had been on top of the world. They owned Earl Gallery, an art gallery based in Geelong which rapidly made a name for itself when Hedley and Irena paid the highest price ever recorded, one million dollars, for an Australian work of art—the very famous and beautiful 'Golden Summer' by Sir Arthur Streeton.

It is extraordinary, even ironic, that the very fibre that is currently the ruin of many on the land was eventually to be their saviour. Standing among brightly coloured woollen garments of the softest, finest texture imaginable, Hedley and Irena Earl revealed what sort of personal battle they had fought. They were locked into a $2 million land purchase, locked into running sheep and had no income, just incessant interest payments; for nine months they had no money for food for themselves and their two young sons. They were forced to sell off furniture in order to get by. It was something only a few of their closest friends knew. The shame of such penury cut deeply. They had been mixing with the glittering high spenders of the art world, playing golf with high-flyers, travelling widely and bidding on famous art works at august auction rooms. Their gallery sent out glossy brochures full of works by highly prized artists sought by wealthy collectors. Irena and Hedley sipped champagne at gallery openings with socialites and dealers, among silk and diamonds and pearls.

When it all ended, Irena and Hedley's sister Beverley found themselves at work on sewing machines in the former gallery building, making knickers from a brand-new silky wool fabric which they had developed in association with the CSIRO. The sheep were worthless, their staff had to go. Hedley ran the farm as well as ticketed, packed, dispatched and sold the garments they produced. 'We had a dream and an idea. We knew what was possible. It would just take time,' Irena says.

That someone used to the fine things of life, to wealth and comfort, could push notions of haughty grandeur aside to become a humble seamstress is astounding. Irena, aged 51, however, is not the sort of person who caves in. Her genes alone would have powered her through. She is the daughter of Polish refugees who fled their home, were taken to camps in Germany and arrived in Geelong in 1951, penniless and with no possessions. She studied business administration, but when they had their cattle stud, rolled up her sleeves and learnt artificial insemination, although she had never before had anything to do with cattle. 'Necessity makes you do things,' says Irena. 'Most things are possible.' Link that attitude to Hedley's 'I will never be beaten' and 'believe in yourself' approach to life and suddenly there is no mystery about how people with absolutely no experience with sheep or the wool industry have succeeded in not only producing a revolutionary fine wool fabric that can be machine washed and thrown into a tumble-dryer, but in wiping their debt and once again making a solid profit.

It really is an astonishing achievement—rookies to the wool establishment, browbeating mills and wool technologists into pursuing their goal with them, then marketing the resulting fabric and garments around the world. Now, only six years after their blackest days, Hedley and Irena Earl have their own Juswool/Hedrena retail shops operating in Geelong, Camberwell and Adelaide. Within the next three years they expect to have shops in all major cities and in New Zealand and South Africa.

Their company, Hedrena Textiles, exports to Taiwan and Hong Kong. The Hedrena range of fine wool knickers and bras is stocked at the high class department store Barney's, in New York and Chicago.

Their fairytale began when Hedley, aged 53, started as an accountant at Alcoa, where he met Irena. They were transferred to Western Australia, just south of Perth. Irena took up painting landscapes. They advertised them for sale in the local paper, and started investigating the prospects of the wider art world. Adopting a commercial Perth dealer as a mentor, they learnt fast, bought good paintings, continued selling from home and established a reputation. When the business grew, they moved back to Geelong. Hedley became an accredited art valuer and bought fine works sourced through an increasing number of high-profile contacts. When Pyramid Building Society commissioned the Earl Gallery to buy $6 million worth of paintings for their collection, life was at its rosiest. 'For once in our life we had some spare money,' Hedley says. His gentle exterior gives little indication of the bold determination and burning self-belief that is at the core of his being. They bought land for the farm he had long cherished. It was just a small holding outside Geelong, but perfect for their young sons to grow up on. They entered stud cattle breeding by using the same tactics that took them to the heights in the art world. They targeted the most expensive sires and dams in Australia. Suddenly all eyes were upon them and they started taking out championships at shows around the country. They sold a half share of the first calf they bred for $30 000, and eventually sold out of the art business as the stud grew wings.

When dieldrin ended the cattle dream, they repeated the formula of buying the best animals available to establish a 15-micron sheep flock. Almost immediately, Hedley and Irena approached the business of breeding consistently fine wool as few others before them had. The wool of each of the 100 ewes bought from a well-known fine-wool breeder was tested. They discovered with alarm that only 30 per cent were actually under 19 micron. Most people producing wool assessed the diameter of their wool visually, something Hedley, as a deep-thinking outsider, found illogical and impossible to do. In time, they put together a flock of 3000 sheep and knew each one's micron, so at shearing they could simply direct fleeces to appropriate bales. When fine wool prices slumped in 1993, the Earls moved lines of fine micron-tested fleeces to their empty art gallery and invited agents of the prestigious fabric mills of Italy to inspect them. Two bales of 16 and 17 micron wool were shipped to Germany for preliminary processing. The narrow micron range gave the wool a new silky softness that had fabric makers raving. The Earls used their fleeces to have fabric made in Adelaide by Onkaparinga, and Irena and Beverley set about making baby blankets that were bought by London's Harrod's. Dressing gowns followed and then sports clothing, which Hedley took to Armani in Milan with the help of Austrade. His aim was to develop a global business. In a taxi in Paris, the development officer from Austrade suggested they make underwear. They took up the challenge almost immediately. Irena made samples, the Myer group jumped at the range of spencers, singlets and briefs, and the girls sewed furiously to fill the order. Quickly, the business moved from being a cottage industry to a full-scale factory and they moved to larger premises where they employ 22 people.

In the Juswool shops, the silky fabric, finely knitted like cotton on a $60 000 circular 90-spool machine, has been brightly dyed and made into T-shirts and long-sleeve tops. A range of pure wool garments by other manufacturers is also sold. Hedrena garments are supplied to 300 retail outlets around Australia, but Hedley says in his quiet and modest way the number grows daily.

'You've got to have enormous tenacity,' says Hedley of his vision during their battling days of selling fine wool products around the world. Especially since all around them other people also raising sheep were distressed and complaining, but waiting for someone else to fix their industry. 'It is almost impossible to make money on the land today unless you have a niche market for something, are very big, or have a lucrative sideline.'

Now debt free, Hedrena for the past three years has paid dividends to four loyal associates of the Earls who came into the sheep-breeding business as partners but have stuck with them through the rocky years. 'They never lost their belief in us,' says Hedley. 'They knew we could do it.' It is a rich testament to Hedley and Irena that they could inspire and keep the faith of city professionals through such an ordeal, especially when they had each parted with considerable sums of money.

The initial, seemingly far-fetched dream of creating a brand that would be recognised internationally is now being achieved. Although they still live on their original small holding, they have sold the larger block and no longer own sheep. Instead, they buy low-micron Australian yarn which has been spun overseas into a fine, specially designed two-fold thread. They tried to buy locally spun yarn but manufacturers could not supply to the required standard.

I wonder aloud if the renaissance of wool is imminent. Hedley responds that he believes people genuinely want to get away from synthetics. He says he emphasises in their marketing and promotion that wool is a 'pure, natural fibre' to overcome years of ingrained prejudice that wool shrinks and itches. He has little regard for the years of glitzy corporate spending by wool institutions which missed their consumer targets.

'We are standing at the beginning of a very exciting decade where we are going to make quite an impact on people's understanding of wool,' says Hedley. He believes wool is on the way to becoming an everyday product, and that one day Hedrena's wool knickers that don't itch, don't ride up and are soft and light, will be the company's 'bread and butter' product.

Part VIII

Full Circle—South Australia

Fight Hard to Win—John Wamsley

I wonder whether a 'traditional agriculture' exists any more. Out there, a tribe of people is questing and pushing the boundaries to find something that is a 'goer'—a breed of sheep or cattle, a crop, some endeavour, an untried species such as alpacas or ostriches, to be the farm saviour. Under our noses, however, is 'livestock' waiting for exploitation. Our very own native animals, having moved out to make way for traditional agriculture, are craving survival. Curiosity about what once lived on our land is growing. Animals, birds and plants that are rare or endangered have become a big business for a fearless, much reviled, often scorned and criticised pioneer.

Living at Mylor in the hills outside Adelaide, John Wamsley 'farms' wildlife. He charges people to see animals he has brought back from the brink of extinction, and has changed community attitudes about wildlife and conservation. He has managed to put a value on wildlife.

I meet John Wamsley, a towering hunk of a man, outside Warrawong Sanctuary's restaurant overlooking land sloping steeply into a gully smothered in trees and effervescent with bird calls. Braces hold up his work pants, a white frizzy beard spills over his T-shirt. He is not someone who would pass unnoticed in the street. His is a handsome face—also wise, gentle, charming, and at times, intimidating, calculating and mischievous. His restless, thinking eyes are like cursors on a computer screen—moving and busy in tune with the mighty colossus of a brain that thrives on complex problems, stores myriad numbers and equations and made him a PhD by the time he was 30, his thesis spawning a whole new branch of mathematics.

Despite, but probably because of, his powerful physical presence and acute mind, John Wamsley speaks softly, carefully, almost hesitatingly, always putting building blocks of logical argument one upon the other. He has won his way into the stiff boardrooms of major industrial companies and the heart of a once sceptical public, which more often than not viewed him as a red-necked crazy.

John Wamsley is probably best known as the man in the cat hat.

John Wamsley

The picture of him in 1989 wearing the skin of a feral cat, with the head still intact and jaws wide open, made front pages of newspapers all around the nation. It was a stunt he pulled when he was presented with a tourism award in Adelaide at a time when it was illegal to kill any cat, feral or otherwise. It succeeded in getting the law changed quick smart.

'People always accuse me of hating cats. I actually love cats,' he says in suitably hurt tones. 'But I can't eat a whole one.' That carefully composed statement, delivered with the skill of an actor, is often the starting point for his many public speaking engagements, and it always raises a good laugh.

John is a man driven by a fierce passion to replicate an environment he knew in childhood. He has persevered with unswerving zeal in face of numerous furious protests about his activities. 'When I was seven, my father bought 166 acres of land on the central coast of New South Wales and cleared 35 acres of it for a citrus orchard. That land when he bought it was virgin bushland and it was in the middle of literally millions of acres of virgin bushland.'

He was fascinated that under the giant blackbutts there was no undergrowth: there were plentiful small native animals to graze it. He watched pademelons, a small species of kangaroo, eating the debris from the eucalypts, and poteroos, bandicoots and lyrebirds turning over the forest floor. He saw gliders, platypus in the creek and echidnas. 'I had six sisters, which meant that I couldn't spend much time at home,' he says, and I laugh. 'So I found myself spending a lot of time out in the bush.

'Then when I was 12, the first of the foxes and cats appeared. It was a very quick transition from the bushland being full of these wonderful animals to there being none. I saw it happen. And also there was a change in the bushland—when I was seven to 12 I could walk through it anywhere. By the time I was 14, the undergrowth was coming, by the time I was 16, you couldn't walk anywhere.' The grazers had gone. 'Then the big fires came. That land had never burnt. When I was 16, the first big fire came, I might have been 17, but it was a massive fire and everything was burnt.' Everything that follows in the story of this man's mission to farm the Australian bush with native wildlife stems from that childhood forest experience—and the need to escape from that horrendous house full of females!

At 11, John went to Hurston Agricultural Boarding School, having won a scholarship. He spent fourth and fifth year at Gosford High School then, at 16, left home intent on making his fortune, a goal he achieved a few years later. Even at that early stage he had ambition and knew he needed money to fuel it, so he headed for BHP in Newcastle. 'I started as a trainee metallurgist, but then I found you could earn more money working on the furnaces. So it wasn't long before I transferred to furnaceman.' He shovelled dolomite into the open-hearth furnaces to make steel. 'I thought it was such an incredibly hard job that I couldn't believe people could do it, so I had a go at it . . . it made me grow up,' says this man who even then didn't mind seemingly impossible challenges. 'I was a tiny boy when I left school. I think I was about five foot and weighed about eight stone. I grew up not frightened of a day's work.'

By night he fed the furnaces; but by day, he bought old houses and did them up. 'I think I bought my first house at 19, and by the time I was 24, I owned 13 houses and had done very well out of making money.' This extraordinary feat is told in a slightly crackly voice that is almost a whisper. John restored them, painted them and repaired them himself. 'Because I came from a farm, I found I could do all the work myself. I could do plumbing and electrical work, painting, bricklaying—anything that had to be done, I could do.' He could have retired then and there on the rental income from all these houses. 'At 24, I just went fishing for six months. I was pretty exhausted.' This man who claims he has never had any trouble making money contemplated with his young wife what his future would be. 'I didn't need to work again if I didn't want to, but I had this driving ambition to do something, I didn't know what exactly. I had the vision about wildlife, but I didn't have the vision to know how to do it. All I had was my memory of what used to be.'

At age 25, John Wamsley started looking for places to buy to pursue his dream. He was, however, working on the assumption that wildlife couldn't generate an income. 'It had been drummed into me, I suppose, that conservation was some sort of socialistic thing that you did for charity or something,' he says in that whispery voice. 'So I looked around and I thought, well, what's the easiest job that takes the least amount of work and you get paid the most amount of money for? So I decided to be an academic.' And there you have an insight into John Wamsley at his cheeky best—poking, provoking, fearlessly irritating a normally protected species.

He went to university at age 25, determined to become a university lecturer in mathematics, the subject he had always found supremely easy. He applied to Newcastle University but was rejected. Finally, after much perseverance, he was told he could enrol as an adult. 'I said I wanted to start in second year Honours mathematics and they told me not to be bloody stupid. I wouldn't be able to do first year ordinary mathematics because, since I had left school, mathematics had gone a long way.' His first lecture was a third year algebra class. 'I really and honestly did not know whether I was in a French lesson or a maths lesson,' he says. 'I didn't understand one word said in the whole lecture.' But where most would give up, not Wamsley with his vision. After the lecture he went up and admitted he had 'a bit of catching up to do'. He asked what books he could read. The lecturer told him if he was sensible, he would go back to first year. 'I said no, I haven't got time to do that.' So, he was given a pile of books to read and decided to give himself one term to catch up. By the end of first term, after putting everything he had into study, he came top of every maths subject. 'And four years later, I had a PhD in mathematics,' he says, and with his voice trailing off dreamily, 'It was pretty easy.' Easy! What did he take me for? I said. He continued, 'Many a time, well, every night, it got light before I went to bed. That was the hard bit.' By that stage, he and his wife had three young children.

'I did all my university in a room, with a television down one end and three kids playing in the middle and my bench in the corner.' By the end of it, he had shaken the maths fraternity with his accomplishments; his PhD thesis revolutionised mathematical thinking. The following words might read like a boast, but they weren't said like that. 'My supervisor described me when I finished as, if not the best, then the second best mathematician of my generation . . .' I ask if he meant in Australia . . . 'In the world.' And I reel back, humbled.

'I could have got a job anywhere,' says this humble-sounding genius. Just for the record, his thesis was on group theory and abstract algebra: he invented the Nil Potent Quotient Algorithm. He starts explaining what it is: 'I really invented these things so I could outdo a computer.' He was using a functional representation of things, so instead of having, say, a whole computer page, he produced a formula saying where all the dots would be. This was neater and quicker than previous methods of actually spelling out in detail where the dots would be. This discovery meant literally millions of times as much could be done with a computer than previously, and in those early days of computer science, enabled greater storage of information. 'So I did very well and I was thought of very highly and I published quite a few good research papers.' He had the pick of the maths faculties of the world, but he elected to work at Flinders University, all because of that cherished wildlife goal.

'South Australia was the only state where it wasn't illegal to do a Warrawong Sanctuary, so I had to come to South Australia,' he says. Thus starts the next chapter of a dogged pursuit of a dream.

'For the private sector, to do conservation today in Australia, is [mostly] illegal. If you put a fence around a place and eradicate the ferals, then any animals that are inside are considered captive, and when you have captive animals, they have to be kept in pens as prescribed by the zoological society.' He pauses, then adds, facetiously, 'Every good zookeeper knows that animals can't live in the wild.' He is, just in case you missed it, no supporter of zoos. 'There has not been one successful release of anything put back into the wild by any zoo, anywhere in the world ever, and yet there is $50 billion a year spent throughout the world in the name of just doing that,' he says. 'The whole thing is the biggest scam in the world and nobody's game to take it on.' He cites an example of the San Diego Zoo breeding 28 mountain gorillas in captivity but says the money spent could have by now 'bought the whole of the mountain gorilla habitat . . . Now surely, that's the direction we should be going.'

In New South Wales, Victoria, Queensland, the Northern Territory and Tasmania, it is still illegal to put a fence around wildlife to protect them from feral animals. Only in South Australia and Western Australia is it legal. 'That's why the world is in trouble, because we have stupid laws, stupid politicians,' he says, warming to a favourite subject.

Warrawong, the sanctuary that blazed a conservation path through numerous bureaucratic obstructions, and has gone on to be a model for the rest of his multi-million dollar conservation company, was in 1969 a degraded 35 acre dairy farm milking 30 cows. On its bare hills folding around a little gully at the top of a catchment where no-one else's pollution would run onto the land, he planted many thousands of trees. 'The aim was to put back all the habitats that would allow the animals that once lived here to live here again.'

It is salutary to see how far we as a society have come since those days in 1974, when there was massive opposition from green groups and the community over his council-approved removal of 600 pine trees on the farm's boundary. Few people then valued native trees over introduced pines. Because of heated protests and opposition, John subsequently found himself arrested and condemned as a troublemaker by the South Australian government. Conservation in those days was just not sexy and certainly not something done by private enterprise. Nine years later, John Wamsley received a Civic Trust award from the hands of Labor premier Don Dunstan. He took great delight in reminding the red-faced premier that he had locked him up 'for doing exactly what he had just given me the award for'. John finally erected the first of his novel cat and fox-proof fences and a sceptical public sat back and watched. Six foot high, of wire netting which is folded over at top and bottom, and with offset electric wires, the Wamsley fences are destined to surround sanctuaries in all states if John has his way. But he needs every bit of his prodigious fighting and intellectual power. He says if the fences were erected to enclose deer, no-one would object, but he still has 'horrific problems' mainly from green groups, for wanting to enclose native animals—even if the enclosure is hundreds of square kilometres. The company now employs lobbyists to help negotiate through community and political opposition.

John says green groups seem to believe conservation is not a private sector job and explains his theory for this. 'I like to compare how we went with conservation with how we went with agriculture, because agriculture was probably one of the first businesses in the world. Probably the first thing anybody ever did was sell or swap something to eat. So when we set up our Departments of Agriculture there was no question that they should be a socialist sort of thing. They show farmers how to grow things and the farmers do it. Whereas when we set up the Departments of Environment, it was at a time when socialism was at its height in the world. The Departments of Wildlife we set up were socialist organisations which actually did it, and didn't show others how to do it. That was our basic flaw in conservation, I think, all over the world. If our Departments of Wildlife had been set up under the agricultural system, rather than the socialist system, I think we would be a lot better off today.'

We are losing so much habitat and wildlife because it's not under the free enterprise system, he says. Farmers should be rewarded for conservation work. If they produce environmental assets, they should be paid accordingly—or fined for losing them.

Because of his intense and drawn-out battles over the pine trees, John Wamsley's first marriage broke up. 'My kids were getting belted up at school because they had a nutty father.' And his wife objected to all his money going into Warrawong, which at that time was valued at only $104 000 despite his having spent $2 million on building it up. After the break-up, he was left with nothing, just a dream and his 35 acres of revegetation and its swamp, the building of which convinced most in his circle he was truly mad. At that time everyone was draining swamps.

Embattled, broke and alone, John hit the bottle. 'I was on the way out. I was on a flagon of sherry a day there at one stage.' But then he met Proo Geddes, a teacher, living nearby. 'Proo saved me from dying pissed and broke.' He laughs softly to himself. A year later, Proo's house burnt down in the first of the Ash Wednesday fires. She also lost everything, but teamed up with John and together they got on with the job of building Warrawong. John said that although the neighbours were burnt out, Warrawong was not touched. 'We were able to demonstrate then the concept of what grazing animals were all about.

'In 1985, I made the bravest decision of my life, I think. I left a well-paid job at Flinders University to make conservation a business,' John says. 'It was something that I decided would be my life's work. I believed that the only way we could save anything of value, was to give it value.' Warrawong was opened to the public in January 1985. 'For the first time, many people started seeing their wildlife. The reaction from the Adelaide public was unbelievable, because they saw potoroos and bettongs and it just blew their minds.' It was the beginning of tourism at odd hours; dawn and dusk walks to accommodate the animals' nocturnal habits. He and Proo even located the same species of pademelon he had known as a boy in New South Wales. They are the only ones with white hip stripes and they found them at a backyard zoo in South Australia. 'We now believe they are the last of that subspecies in the world,' John says, a claim which has been accepted recently by the Australian Museum. He started breeding platypus by providing the right muddy environment they need. 'They are creatures of the mud. They live in mud, they eat mud,' he says. He rejects suggestions that he has particular expertise with wildife, instead saying, 'I have a great faith in wildlife. If you give them a bit of Australia back where they lived as it was, they will thrive, and that's all. You don't have to understand why they thrive.'

Warrawong doubled numbers of visitors every year and brought in a good income. By 1988, business was booming and they formed a company, Earth Sanctuaries Pty Ltd, so they could bring in shareholders and raise capital for further expansion. The shares at that time were 2.5 cents. They are now about $2 each. 'Warrawong was first of all a revolution in wildlife management,' he says. 'Up until Warrawong was completed in 1982, nobody in Australia believed that the problem with Australian wildlife was feral animals. They were blaming farmers, they were blaming miners, they were blaming everyone except their cat on their lounge, and really that was the problem.'

The company bought 3000 acres of relatively uncleared mallee land for $60 000. The eventual insurance payout on Proo's burnt house paid for its fence and their second project, Yookamurra, was up and away. They cleared every feral fox, rabbit, cat and dog out—a massive undertaking—something John says had never been achieved on such a large scale anywhere in the world. Then they hit a snag. They were told by the national parks department they weren't allowed to put wildlife on to the place.

So they bought 4000 acres of the Flinders Ranges which already had wildlife—yellow footed rock wallabies. It was where national parks officers often had field trips. So John and Proo struck a deal which allowed the trips to continue, so long as they were allowed to put wildlife back on Yookamurra. Immediately, they moved in dangerously rare numbats which eat termites and live in the hollows of mallee trees. 'It takes 400 years for a mallee tree to grow a hollow in it big enough for a numbat to live in,' John says.

'In 1983, David Attenborough was on television with a numbat and named them as the next species to become extinct in the world. He said because of their diet of termites they couldn't be kept in captivity. He said there were only a hundred left in the world. Well, there are now 200 numbats at Yookamurra Sanctuary,' which is now open full-time, accommodates 40 overnight visitors and employs five staff.

John says they will move numbats to Scotia sanctuary in far-western New South Wales, where despite the law, they are erecting a fence, and where there are vast numbers of termites. He expects numbat numbers to grow to the thousands on the 650 square kilometre former sheep property, and feels satisfied that this species now appears to be safe. 'We've [already] brought five species of endangered mammals back into New South Wales, the woylie, the sticknest rat, the bilby, the bridled nailtail wallaby and the hopping mouse . . . and at no cost to the government or the public whatsoever.'

The company has now bought Tippera, an ocean frontage block of 2000 hectares on Yorke Peninsula, in South Australia. An overnight experience on an island beach where there were no feral animals made John realise how denuded of wildlife our mainland beaches have become. 'The whole beach was moving with wildlife, and I suddenly realised what Australia's beaches were like 200 years ago.' Getting permission to fence the coastal area was another major battle, but his conservation track record and business credibility now result in a government that is enthusiastic and a national parks department which is on side. John has plans to put cabins over the water so people can view marine wildlife like the endangered leafy sea dragon, as well as luminous seaslugs and giant crabs. To the sand dunes, he will introduce hopping mice which have become rare, also bilbies, woylies and wombats. Regrowth of native trees in the past five years is transforming Tippera's former cropping paddocks.

In New South Wales' Blue Mountains, once the law has been changed about fencing in wildlife, the company plans to transform a former coalmine and its surrounding land near Katoomba into a sanctuary accessible by train from Sydney to cater for the vast number of tourists who come to Australia wanting to see wildlife, but who frequently leave disappointed. He has similar plans for a sanctuary between Melbourne and Geelong. There is no doubting that ecotourism and wildlife 'farming' is big business. 'We have made a profit every year for the past five years,' John says. Between 30 000 and 40 000 people visit Warrawong alone every year. 'Warrawong will crack a million dollars income this year for the first time.' Not bad for 84 acres, which it now is. Yookamurra has brought in $150 000, compared with what John reckons would have been about $3000 from sheep previously.

I gasp about the amounts of money being spent—$4 million at Scotia so far, just on fencing and installing solar power units to run the electric fence. 'Solar energy!' We digress briefly while John lambasts that sacred cow. 'Solar energy is one of the biggest scams in the world today. It absolutely fails . . . To set up a solar unit to run one energiser that is equivalent to a 60 watt light globe running, costs $8000. In its lifetime of ten years, it produces $300 worth of electricity. If you bring that back to what it means, we have put $8000 worth of energy into producing $300 worth of energy. It is an absolute scam.' I enjoy his mathematical analysis of everything, even if he overlooks the usual crippling remote area costs of bringing mains power out to the bush, if it were available, or the alternative cost of running a diesel generator. But we come back to the basic motivating factor for all this expenditure.

'I can't say this too often,' he says, sounding rather like a university professor. 'Half the world's endangered mammals are Australian. Half of them used to live at Scotia, which is one of the reasons we bought it. That one project at Scotia Sanctuary will increase over a quarter of the world's endangered mammal species over tenfold in number in the first instance. If it grows to what we think it will, over a hundredfold in number. It will save a quarter of the world's endangered mammal species in one hit. And the world today spends $50 billion a year in the name of endangered mammals.'

In Australia, according to a recent analysis wildlife tourism earned $8 billion. 'That's three times as much as sheep,' says John, ever and always the mathematician. Yet wildlife officially has no value. Extrapolating from the $8 billion figure, John Wamsley calculates that bilbies, for instance, could be said to be worth to tourism about $300 000 each.

John Wamsley's aim for the future is for Earth Sanctuaries to own or manage 1 per cent of Australia within 25 years. 'If we achieve that, we'll employ 6000 people and there'll be one hundred species of mammal that live only on our land. If we don't do that, we'll lose that hundred species. It's as simple as that.

'One of the things I have done all my life is I have decided what direction I should go in and I've stuck on that direction no matter what, and I've used every attack on me to my advantage . . . You need faith in yourself,' he says. 'The secret to winning is to be right and to fight hard enough, and you'll always win.'

UPDATE: Earth Sanctuaries plans to publicly list its shares on the stock exchange.

The project in the Blue Mountains, near Katoomba, was stymied by government and green protesters. An alternative site, Murrawoollan, north of Goulburn, has been bought and is now under development.

The sanctuary near the You Yangs, not far from Melbourne, has received permission to go ahead.

The company has recently bought Mount Gibson Station, of 133 000 hectares, four hours north of Perth, where another numbat colony will be established once the entire boundary is feral proofed.

It was fitting that after my day with Dr John Wamsley, still infected by his passion for restoring wildlife, I should come home to find the curlew pair had returned. Plus one baby curlew all bright and fresh in its new plumage. I was so excited—this was the first time 'my' curlews had successfully bred. This was the first reversal, albeit small, of the trend towards extinction in our area. All I had to do was keep the ferals out of their nesting site.

At Journey's End

This wonderful country, spreading like a rumpled doona between the seas, had me romping through its folds and over its plains for more than a year. Far away from the bright lights and centres of power and decision-making, I have spent my days with people who give city life only a passing thought. The focus of their lives is the land and their industry. Theirs is a lifestyle many envy but few know. And as city life continues to be ever more enveloping, ever more demanding, the distant life of farmers will become even less relevant to future generations. Once, we all had relatives and friends who tilled the soil and cared for animals. That's changed. We shock children now by revealing that chops can be found inside sheep hanging in the meathouse. We mystify businessmen by talking of putting 'super' on the paddocks. Even the need for rain is no longer fully understood by populations who know nothing else but turning on a tap. So when farmers talk of droughts and floods in material terms, too often they are dismissed as mere whingers, who perhaps should be grateful they live in a peaceful and beautiful setting. Their losses of livestock and crops are not able to be understood for their lasting impact on a family's livelihood, for the massive drop in income suffered. My two worlds are growing apart ever faster. I was born in the city and I love city life—in small doses. My friends live in cities and in the country, but it is in the country that I choose to live, not only is it where my work is, but it is also a place of enormous opportunity. Certainly there are drawbacks—distance from other places is one, but planes, cars, email and the internet soon fix that.

The journey once started never ends. My travels into the agricultural spirit of Australia have changed me and opened my eyes to brilliant new challenges in agriculture. Through exploring the lives of some of our current pioneers, I am infected by their bright ideas and energy. The challenges today are as intense as those of the pioneering days, but fresh approaches reap new potential. With a hunger for success and plenty of determination, farm people today have the opportunity to drive their businesses into new markets. The land is always changing. The seasons are never predictable. Nothing, especially income, is set or predetermined. The people of the land have to be as flexible as the wind, but as sharp as a diving hawk. They need the intellect of a philosopher and the acuteness of an accountant; and the sensitivity of a lover to cope with the fragile moods of nature, the partner with whom they live. The land demands their respect, for they are only passing custodians. Treat it badly and they too can be struck down like a rabbit on the road. On the land there is space and freedom to run, to shout and be yourself. Conformity is for herds.

My hope is that young people will come back to the land and give its industries new vigour. An energetic, gifted breed of new farmers is desperately needed to take over when the current team bow out. The wine industry has brought masses of young people to the country. Similarly, livestock breeding and grazing, cropping, tourism and the environment will be enlivened by the sometimes radical, positive and new approaches as taken by many people in this book.

Finally, don't think those within these pages are the only smart, innovative, fascinating, courageous, diligent farmers around. They are just a small taste of who lives on this nation's 165 000 or so farms. To all those who also should be included, I can only say, be thankful that you too didn't have your work schedule wrecked for a day or more! And now, I must get to work on my neglected garden.